Lots of love to Harry f[rom]

Grandpa & G[randma]

x x x

Have a lovely Christmas!

and

Loads o' Love
for 2004

Love
xx A Geoff
xx

Field Archery

FIELD ARCHERY

A Complete Guide

MICHAEL HAMLETT-WOOD

ROBERT HALE · LONDON

ISBN 0 7090 6991 X

Robert Hale Limited
Clerkenwell House
Clerkenwell Green
London EC1R 0HT

A catalogue record for this book is available from the British Library

2 4 6 8 10 9 7 5 3 1

Typeset in 10/12pt Baskerville by
Derek Doyle & Associates, Liverpool.
Printed in Great Britain by
St Edmundsbury Press Limited, Bury St Edmunds, Suffolk.
Bound by Woolnough Bookbinding Limited.

Contents

Preface

When, full of eager anticipation, I first went along to the local archery club, I had no idea what to expect, but I hoped that I would be allowed to shoot a proper bow for the first time, with proper arrows, and that someone would take time out to teach me how to do it properly. I had no idea that I was getting into something that would take over my life.

I had only ever seen one book on archery, long ago in my school library, a slim volume, Frank Bilsons' *Modern Archery*, published in 1949. I devoured every word of that book over and over, but it was a long time before I was able to do something about it, and the enthusiasm has never left me. The act of drawing a bow, feeling the power of it flow into the body, and then watching the arrow curve through the air to plop – somewhere in the target – is something that has always been a huge pleasure.

On my second or third visit to the local target club, I was told about field archery, since several of the members had tried it and enjoyed it. I thought that this sounded more like my style, plodding round woodland rather than gently shooting at the same target all day on a flat field. Not far away was the local field course, the only bit of woodland for many miles, since east Yorkshire is remarkably deficient in trees – something I ascribed to the attitude of the local inhabitants, who regarded trees as enemies to be vanquished rather than an adornment to the landscape, something to do with man's eternal struggle against nature. However, this bit of woodland was enough to accommodate fourteen targets with a bit of a squeeze, and my devotion to field archery was born there. From that time on, I have been a passionate supporter of a wonderful sport.

After a while, it became obvious that there was no single repository of knowledge for this sport. There was Don Stamp's excellent book, *Field Archery*, published some years ago, but knowledge was still growing, particularly about compound bows, so that it seemed to me that it was time to put it all into one place. This should be a place where rules could be referred to, where arcane methods of tuning bows could be found, and where I might be able to gather together all the bits of information that had accumulated over the years. I realized that this would be somewhat difficult, since I could not claim to know all there was to know about the sport. And all the time the book was being put together, new bits of knowledge were being discovered, and even when I thought it was finished, new chapters had to be added. So anyone who expects to find everything in here may be disappointed – I hope not, but. . . . It is still not complete, nor ever will be, but no body of knowledge ever is. Several times I rejoiced when I thought it was finished, but then another idea occurred and another chapter had to be added, then there was a suggestion for another area to be dealt with. Eventually I had to call a halt to it. My apologies to anyone who thinks their particular aspect has been omitted. But I hope it will encourage new enthusiasts to the sport, and give useful information to those already involved.

My heartfelt thanks go the many people who have helped, particularly the members of my home club, South Cheshire Field Archers, many of whom were very patient when I wanted to photograph them shooting, and to all the others who contributed valuable information.

Where possible, I have tried to ensure that the information provided is accurate, but inevitably parts of the book are my personal opinion based on experience over many years; if anyone disagrees with them, they are free to say so. New knowledge is constantly emerging and while in the process of writing this, more came to light, so that it became a constant learning process and it is possible that, through ignorance of some points, they have been omitted. For this, of course, I can only apologise.

I hope this book will be a valuable source of reference on all aspects of field archery, but information in today's world soon becomes outdated and although the sport changes only very slowly – one of the aspects which always gave me pleasure – change does take place.

I dedicate this book to Pearl, who gave new life, and Jean, who knows nothing of field archery, but who, metaphorically, shot the first arrow.

Mike Hamlett-Wood, February 2002

List of Illustrations

Between pages 192 and 193

Plates

1 The author's equipment:
   - (i) Martin Sceptre compound bow
   - (ii) Arrows – Easton ACC carbon aluminium
   - (iii) Arrows – Easton X7 2114 aluminium alloy
   - (iv) Quiver – Neet leather, with useful pouches and raccoon-tail decoration
   - (v) Two release aids: a Skorten forefinger release with wrist strap and a Fletchmatic TR thumb-operated release
2 Shooting uphill in a pine plantation wood
3 The car parking/assembly area at an open shoot
4 A proud archer standing by the bigfoot target at an open shoot
5 Shooting with a 'Classic Hunter' oriental-style bow
6 Demonstrating the use of the take-down hunting bow with wooden arrows
7 Showing the use of the compound bow shot unlimited
8 A typical freestyle technique and equipment but using a two-finger draw
9 Shooting compound unlimited
10 Taking aim at one deer in a group at 55 yards
11 English longbow men shooting in a 'herce' at Agincourt, 1988
12 A hand-tooled leather back quiver
13 A typical homemade big-game target face, hand-painted

Introduction

Field archery is not done in fields. Target archery is shot in fields, usually neatly manicured sports fields, but field archery is shot in woodland wherever possible. Sometimes, but not often, there may be a couple of targets in fields if there is insufficient space in the woodland for all of them. In this case the targets out in the open will usually be long shots, where the distance is difficult to judge through lack of reference points.

So target archery takes place in fields, and indoors, but field archery is done in woods, forests, rough land, sand dunes, scrub, bush – or anywhere that cannot be used for any other purpose. In Britain, it is mainly woodland.

The sport is often referred to as a form of simulated hunting, but the similarities are few, especially when non-animal targets are used. The basic idea is that a number of targets are spread round an area of rough land, marker stakes are placed at a variety of distances to show the archers where to shoot from, and each target is shot in turn, usually by groups of four. There are no tactics or strategy involved and success relies entirely on skill in shooting a bow. In the USA field archery is sometimes used as a form of practice for hunting, but in England hunting with a bow is illegal and the field archery organizations, as a matter of policy, disown and refuse to support hunting live animals. There is little similarity with target archery, which is rigidly disciplined and controlled, and where archers shoot the same targets all day, apart from changing the size of the target face in some rounds and changing the distances at prescribed intervals. Target archery tends to be more controlled and perhaps more orderly, and the sport demands little in the way of exercise apart from walking to and from the targets. Field archery sometimes requires the abilities of a mountain goat and a willingness to endure the most vile physical conditions of rain, snow, hail, mud, difficult terrain, nettles, brambles, spiky conifers, floods, streams, lakes, swamps, marshes, hills and banks, and even hostile animal life. A day's shooting on some grounds will test one's physical endurance, even though movement is slow and often cumbersome with the quantity of equipment carried. Target archers are able to sit down when they are not actually shooting or walking but field archers may be on their feet for many hours, often a whole day, from arrival at the shoot to departure.

No particular level of fitness is needed, but of course being fit does help, especially as some courses are often hilly, muddy and difficult to walk round. A shoot, especially if it is a competition shoot, will last all day, and two-day shoots are quite common. Eight-day shoots have taken place at times, but even these do not require great athletic ability, so the sport is entirely suitable for a wide range of ages and both sexes. It is not uncommon to see whole families involved, from children of seven and eight to grandfathers in their sixties. There are totally dedicated field archers who have been in the sport almost since its introduction into the country in the early 1960s, and are still shooting regularly. It is a sport enjoyed by those who prefer to be out in the open air and love the countryside. It can be done all year round, in all weathers; shooting a field course in snow is a rare experience, but immensely enjoyable and memorable.

Many field archers do not take part in competitions but simply enjoy shooting their own club ground. There is no compulsion to compete; the pleasure of shooting the bow can be sufficient. Constantly honing the skill of shooting, feeling the power of the bow in the body, watching a well-shot arrow speed to a distant target, hearing its thud, walking the woodland with fellow archers, all these can be very pleasurable.

There is also the fascination of the bow and the arrows. This is another of the major differences between field and target archery. Target archery is performed with perhaps only two types of bow – the long recurve bow equipped with sights and all the other gadgets used in the freestyle class, and the similarly equipped compound bow. Field archery, on the other hand, enables its adherents to use a far wider range of equipment, from the traditional English longbow, through various types of recurve bow and different types of arrow, to the modern compound bow in various forms. So the budding field archer has a far wider choice of equipment than the target archer.

The modes of dress, too, are different. Target archery requires competitors at certain levels of competition to wear white or an approved shade of green, which some approve of for the smart uniformity it creates. A line of target archers in dazzling whites is perhaps an arresting sight. Field archers have no dress rules beyond the request of one organization that they wear brightly coloured clothing in order to be seen easily while in the woodland. Otherwise, it allows full rein to archers to dress in the most eccentric manner, with elaborate pocketed shooting jackets, camouflaged combat gear, buckskin jackets, fringed leather jackets, wide-brimmed hats, woolly hats, leather hats, baseball caps, big sheath knives, home-made quivers, posh quivers, tatty quivers, all sorts of boots and wet weather gear. My first visit to a field shoot was a shock when I saw all the modes of dress arrayed in the assembly area. It appears that many field archers take full advantage of the freedom to dress as they please, and perhaps this too is one of the reasons why so many love this sport, minor though it may be.

There are many types of bow, far more than the uninitiated realize, and the bows themselves can become fascinating in the intricacy or simplicity of their construction. The traditional English longbow is still popular in field archery, difficult and challenging as it is to shoot, but essentially simple, while the ever-increasing complexity of the compound bow appeals to those who love gadgetry and the precision of shooting it gives. The discussion of the relative merits of different bows and arrows is a constant delight to archers.

The wide choice of targets available in field archery is another pleasure. There is a considerable range of animal targets, while people who do not wish to shoot those can choose to join an organization that uses target faces consisting of black and white rings and therefore do not offend the sensitivities of animal lovers.

A field course consists of targets at a wide variety of distances, positioned uphill, downhill, over – or even in – streams, across ponds and lakes, through, under or over trees, hidden in undergrowth or shadowed under low branches, so that every target is different and presents a different challenge. Targets are often placed so that there is 'dead ground' in between the archer and the target. This is ground that cannot be seen, in a hollow or depression. It makes the distance very difficult to judge and will often fool people into dropping their arrows short.

Each shot is different, since very often each is taken from a different position, and the degree of difficulty of each target may be highly variable. Field archery requires the ability to adapt to constantly changing conditions and circumstances, rather than the application of pure shooting skill at one target: changing weather, terrain, light, targets, conditions underfoot and many other factors. One of the most appealing aspects of field archery is that every target comes as a surprise. Until the archer actually reaches the shooting pegs he may not be able to see what or where the target is. Sometimes the surprise is pleasurable – like finding an open shot at an easy distance – but often it is challenging, a tricky shot across a slope perhaps, or through branches or twigs. At other times it is unpleasant – a difficult target, small for the distance perhaps, and at an awkward angle into dark undergrowth. Each target has its own characteristics, and each can be different from all the others on the course, as it is when shooting an animal round, where it is possible to lay a forty-target course with a different face for every target.

There have been many moments of pure delight in my own experience of the sport, many shared with others. One of the pleasures has been the friendship and humour, sympathy and support of fellow archers. These people form a common bond, from shared experiences and knowledge, and meeting old friends at a shoot is one of the great pleasures of the sport. Part of this evolves from the feeling of being a small, perhaps slightly beleaguered minority who struggle against the odds to continue. I have often wondered whether, if it were a hugely popular sport – which is unlikely ever to be the case – field archers would still be so friendly, or whether they would be divided by rivalry or politics.

Politics certainly plays a part now, to the regret of many, since it seems to rear its head in almost any group, but it rarely seems to achieve any good and lasting results. It has to be admitted that, in the opinion of many of the people involved, field archery would be improved if it were run by one national organization rather than the three now in control. It seems unlikely that this will come about in the near future since the three organizations have different views and philosophies on how the sport should be run and what its aims should be. Meetings have taken place to try to resolve the differences, but they have come to nothing. These differences not only exist among the councils who run the organizations but extend deep into the memberships. Many of the ordinary members are aware of the clash of opinions, and perhaps regret them, but they are unlikely to agree to any erosion of their positions in order to bring about the compromises that might unite the sport. So the situation is, at present, one of peaceful co-existence.

It is possible, although expensive, to belong to all three field archery societies and shoot according to the rules of each in their competitions, but there are very few who choose, or who are able, to do this. Some belong to two, and are able to shoot in both, but belonging to one would normally be sufficient if the number and quality of its competitions were satisfactory. The number of field shoots held by one organization is now so few that it seems to be slowly declining towards extinction, prevented from doing so only by a small hardy remnant and its support of a national team for international competitions. The biggest organization has many clubs shooting to its rules and these clubs put on open shoots – shoots that anyone can attend provided they are members of that organization. It is not uncommon to find at least six shoots being held on one day over various parts of the country.

One major advantage of field archery is that it is cheap. It may not appear so at first, looking at some of the equipment carried by enthusiasts, but it is possible to begin by using a club's equipment, while learning to shoot, and to go on to second-hand bows, then later aim for something better and perhaps – but not necessarily – more expensive. Thus the initial cost of equipment may not be high. Club membership is usually not much of a burden either, since few field clubs have facilities that are costly to keep up. Few, in fact, even possess any buildings. The rent for woodland is usually not high and in some cases it is even free. It is not necessary to move on to competitive shooting, although it is my belief that those who ignore it are missing a very pleasurable part of the sport, and the entry fee for a day's competition shoot is usually far less than anything comparable for the same length of time. In fact beginners are often amazed at how cheap the sport is.

The cheapness of the sport, of course, has a downside: there is little money in the sport for development or expansion. For example, it would be highly advantageous if the national societies were able to purchase areas of woodland for permanent use, rather than having to rent or borrow it, often on a short-term basis, as is the case now. None has sufficient funds for this, nor is likely to have in the near future. The reasons for this lie in the desire to keep membership fees as low as possible while, in the case of one society, struggling to give financial support to a national team. There is little or no sponsorship from large commercial organizations, and no income from spectators. There is little chance of the sport being taken up for regular television viewing, because of factors which are difficult to overcome, such as the problem, simply, of seeing arrows in the targets and understanding by whom they have been shot. Many years ago, one field archer – rather naïvely, I thought – asked me why the prizes at competition shoots were so poor. The answer, in a word, is spectators – or the lack of them. Income comes entirely from competitors, and if a club puts on regular open shoots that are well attended, it can rely on a regular income just large enough to keep things ticking over, but never enough to make any big developments. The purchase of imported 3D targets, for example, is a major step forward for many clubs, and few have been able to acquire many thus far. This means that the development of 3D shooting in this country has been very slow compared to the USA. The cost of the targets is greater in Britain, since they have to be imported from America.

A club that finds that its ground is put up for sale can have real problems, since it may well be in difficult financial circumstances if someone determined to make as much money as possible from the situation buys the ground. This is an oft-occurring problem, and many clubs have found themselves looking for a new wood because of a rapacious new owner. There is no huge income from spectators to fall back on, or TV sponsorship; they are on their own. The situation is not all black, though. There are some landowners who are willing to permit clubs to use a piece of woodland regularly for a small fee or even for no charge at all, so do not be too despondent. But somewhere in the future, there must be the possibility of purchasing enough woodland to stage national championships. This would give security to the sport, as well as a national centre. The National Lottery has, of course, raised the hopes of many clubs and there are other funds available. Unfortunately, at the time of writing, National Lottery money will not be available until the sport is able to persuade those in control that it is not a dangerous sport. It appears to have been labelled as such without anyone investigating the real situation. Field archery is inherently dangerous, obviously, but that is precisely why organizers go to great lengths in order to reduce the risks to zero. Safety precautions are such that injuries are very rare and when they do occur they are usually very minor. Yes, people have sometimes been struck by arrows bouncing off trees, but they have never, to my knowledge, caused anything more than very minor injuries – bruises, mainly, and often not even those. In many years of field archery I have only seen one incident in which someone actually had an arrow stuck in them, and that was entirely the fault of the victim, a small boy who was foolish enough to conceal himself in long grass in front of a practice target and who put his hand up in front of the target when it was being shot by a girl who was unable to see him. He got an arrow in the hand for his foolishness.

There are many far more dangerous sports in which the dangers are accepted. For example, in one sport, cross-country riding, there have been several deaths in the last two years, whereas in field archery, no one has ever been killed. Injuries are an accepted part of many sports, but the safety record of field archery must be outstanding.

The variety of grounds gives the sport a major advantage in the view of many regular competitors at open shoots. There are many members of at least one national organization who travel to shoots every weekend for several months of the year. In winter the number of events is more limited, but in the summer months there can be several to choose from if one is prepared to travel. Some archers will drive a 100 miles to a shoot, and one well-known family living on the north-east coast used to travel well over that distance, since there was no club within 100 miles of them.

One ground may be flat, another very hilly, another swampy and muddy, and the type of woodland can vary far more than might be generally realized. Big pine trees can be wonderful to shoot amongst, while closely grown smaller conifers are quite different, being darker with low branches. Oak, silver birch or beech woods all possess different types of undergrowth. One may be full of ferns in summer, as high as a man's head, dying and turning to rust colour in winter, while another may be a nightmare mass of brambles to catch the legs. Whether the woodland is deciduous or coniferous can make a huge difference to its atmosphere as the seasons pass, since the coniferous wood will, of course, change far less than the deciduous. The latter will be far more open in winter and may develop so much foliage in summer as to become difficult to shoot. The sheer beauty of many pieces of woodland used as field courses can make the sport a pure delight. Summer sunlight filtering through leaves and patching the ground, early morning mist creating smoky rays of sunlight through tall pine trees, a carpet of bluebells in spring, the colour of the bracken, golden brown in winter, frost on tall grasses, the panoramic view of mountains, forest and lakes from the corner of a course in Scotland – these and many other experiences have made a lasting impression on one field archer at least.

Shooting field targets often has a subdued excitement which is difficult to convey. You come upon the target marker pegs, red first, then a few yards away the white. The blue is somewhere ahead hidden in the undergrowth. The pine trees tower, still and silent, overhead. The ferns are almost chest high, bright green and still growing. Patches of sunlight through the thin foliage create light and dark areas confusing to the eye; down the slope in front is a narrow gap in the greenery and at the end is the target, a 3D deer with tiny antlers, fitted the wrong way round. Its slightly shiny surface also betrays its artificiality. Part of it is in shadow at the moment, but the centre, where the high scoring zone is, is in sunlight. The scoring rings cannot be seen at this distance. How far is it? Your turn to shoot; one of the group has shot and scored with his first arrow, the second has just hit the target with his second shot, his first arrow falling short and between the target's legs.

You move up to the peg, settle both feet in place, leading foot against the rear of the peg, other foot slightly uphill. The target is big, about 4 feet long and over 4 feet high, but the body is only 16 inches deep, so there is really not a lot to aim at, especially at this distance. How far is it? Count the trees. Distance between trees, about 10 yards, about six trees to the target, not that far, maybe about 50 yards, far enough for the size. Slightly downslope, perhaps 10 degrees, add on – no, take off distance. At that gradient? Yes, let's try it at 48 yards. You wind the sight down, look at the deer again, the light is changing as the trees start to move in a slight breeze, the sunlight over the deer is moving, almost making it seem as if the animal is coming to life. If you hit it, at least it won't fall down in a bag of bones and dying flesh. If you hit it? Is there any question? No, you know you can hit it at this distance, it's a clear shot, no branches or twigs in the way. You look up – there are no hanging branches to foul the upper limb.

You slide an arrow out of the quiver and nock it on the string. Hook the cord of the release round the string. Now. Bring the bow up to above eye level, draw it parallel to the ground, draw the string back, your back muscles working, your shoulder blades coming together, feeling the power of the bow, the weight falls off as the wheels roll over the peak. It feels beautiful, you are in total control, you lock your right hand in place, it feels so familiar, the bow is under tension, the arrow in place, resting. The sight comes down over the target. The lens enlarges it, all you can see now is the body of the deer. Still. Hold still; the sight is moving slightly round the centre of the deer, your breath is still, you squeeze the trigger of the release, the bow jerks slightly and falls forward just a little. You are unaware of the sound of the bow, just right, your eye still on the deer through the scope – all this in the time it takes to think, faster than the arrow is moving as it shoots back into your line of sight and thuds into the target, slightly low from centre, but a good shot, good enough for a first arrow kill, a 20.

The speed of some arrows is astonishing. They leave the bow, there is no sight of them until they thud into the target; they are impossible to follow by eye. Some from slower bows seem to sail towards the target, taking their time to get there. The sound of the arrow striking is always a relief on these targets – no sound back, and you know you have missed and will have to look for the arrow, instead of seeing it proudly sticking out of the target. The sound, of course, takes longer to come back than your picture of the arrow in the target. There is sometimes a fraction of a second when you wonder if you have hit it, waiting for the sound. Moreover, very often you cannot see your arrow and you are not sure where it is. You walk down to the target with the others, in single file, but confidently knowing you have made a good score. You feel an inner smile, a bit smug, but why not? You are having a good day, the sun is shining, it's warm, there's a friendly feeling in the group and you are on form, shooting well. You just have to keep it up, keep your cool, not get screwed up if you make a bad shot. Don't even think about it! You gather round the target with the others, looking at the arrows clustered on it. Two in the kill, two wounds. You read off the scores, the scorer writes them down, someone pulls the arrows out and hands them back. You move off to the next target, not knowing what it will be or what the shot will be like, every shot part of a mystery tour. Why would anyone not want to do this?

At the time of writing, there is some concern that the Government might introduce legislation for the licensing of bows or similar measures to control them. Bearing in mind the Dunblane massacre, where a lunatic shot several small children, which led to the banning of handguns, is there a chance of bows being banned? Personally, I doubt it, since they have a totally different image in the public mind and are not seen as easily concealed weapons of violence. Many people are not aware of the advances in technology that have actually made bows potentially lethal, so they do not have the same mental image of bows as deadly weapons. Nor do many archers, who are only too well aware of the difficulty of putting a bow together and rigging it up ready to shoot. This cumbersome and clumsy device is difficult to conceal in use and takes time to shoot, so it is not the criminal's chosen weapon of convenience.

However, bows rarely feature in violent films and do not have the same appeal for those who feel that a gun would improve their masculinity and give them a sense of power. The psychology of holding, using, handling and owning guns is deeply suspect, and bows do not have the same effect. Rather they are seen as objects that are difficult to use with any accuracy and they rarely convey the sense of lethal power that all guns possess. It is difficult to imagine the tabloid newspapers whipping up a storm of adverse publicity to ban something that has only featured as a weapon to poach deer with, by a couple of irresponsible fools. Its use by bank robbers is laughable.

1 The Shoot

What happens when you go to a field shoot? What is it like? Well, it's not like anything else, for there is nothing comparable. What happens differs somewhat according to the national organization under whose rules it is held. If it is a GNAS shoot, there may be a tackle inspection to check that your equipment conforms to the rules, and if you are shooting with a compound bow, the draw weight will be tested to see if it is under the maximum permitted 60 pounds. My experience is mainly with NFAS shoots so the following description is based on those.

On arrival, you will be marshalled into a parking space on a field. You will find your way to the centre of events by following other archers. There may be tents, or even the luxury of a building for food and shoot registration. There is usually a queue for registration, which sometimes moves fairly rapidly. When you arrive at the desk, you should give your name, which is ticked off on the master sheet, where all the targets are listed with names against them. You should have booked in a few days previously, so your name should be on the target sheet under an allocated target number. You will be given a score-card with your name, class, club and the starting target number written at the top, and will pay your entry fee, which is amazingly cheap compared to prices for other sporting events.

Outside, fully armed archers mill slowly about, eating the traditional bacon butties, drinking tea from plastic cups, laughing, talking and getting in the way, with bits sticking out of them – clumps of arrows in quivers, bows that have to be avoided – dressed in a variety of clothing – leather shooting jackets, combat camouflaged gear, fringed buckskin jackets, jackets full of pockets for the outdoor man, huge belts containing knives, pouches and tassels, quivers, badges, hats (broad-brimmed, leather, woolly, bobbly). Is this a meeting for dressing-up people?

Somewhere nearby there should be some practice targets. There are only three, set in a gap in the trees. There is a line of archers, pouring arrows down towards them, and they are already stuffed full. There is no limit to the number of practice arrows you can shoot and no limit on the time you can spend shooting them. There is no one controlling all this, but everyone seems to know the rules. When all have stopped shooting, they stroll down to the targets to withdraw their arrows. Some will be hunting in the grass in front and behind. One can lose more arrows on the practice targets than on the course. There is also a much higher chance of damaging some, owing to the number being shot in each target. The archers trudge back to the invisible shooting line, some to have a few more shots, some to be replaced by others who have not yet shot.

A milling mass of expectant archers waits for a whistle to blow, the signal for the assembly and pre-shoot briefing. There is someone standing on a tree stump, waiting for everyone to gather together and be silent. He welcomes you to the shoot, tells you how many targets there will be, when the lunch break is, the peg colours and any local information that may be appropriate. The archers are divided into groups and guided to their starting points. You will end up at a marker peg with your starting number on it. There will be other people there, who may not be shooting in the same class as you. Sometimes you might get stuck for the day with someone who is difficult to get on with, but given what most field archers are like, this is not likely. Most are friendly and sociable.

You look at the first target, through the trees. You do a mental assessment of the distance before stepping on to the first peg. The target is about 30 yards away, a flat picture of a wild pig. A longbowman is nearest to the first peg, a red one. In the distance, you hear a whistle blow, the signal to start shooting. Nearby, there is a thud as the first arrow hits the target on another butt. The longbowman draws up and looses, all in one movement. His arrow misses the side of the butt by inches. He strides to the next peg, draws again, looses and this time his white-feathered arrow thuds into the centre of the target.

You move on to the peg, leading foot touching it. You look at the target. Here goes. Nock an arrow on the string, breathe out, bring the bow up above eye level, draw back as you bring it down to eye level, line up the target, steady, still, no breathing, loose, fingers off the string. The arrow disappears, you see it come down on to the target and hear it thud in. But you are not sure where it is on the target, only that it is scoring. You step aside for the next archer. He shoots, and his arrow also lands on the target, pretty near the middle. A lady steps forward, nocks an arrow on the string, draws up and looses quickly; her short hunting bow has a lot of power, but is too short to hold at full draw for long. Her arrow slides over the top of the butt. It is difficult to shoot barebow with no sights. She shoots again, from the white peg. Success. This arrow thuds into the target. A good shot.

You move down to the target and gather round it, looking at the arrow positions. Your first arrow is about ½ inch out of the kill, a bit disappointing but not too bad for the first of the day. The scorer writes down the scores as she calls the names of the group. You have a first target score of sixteen, for a first arrow wound. It was a clear shot, with no twigs or branches in the way. This is not always the case, since sometimes targets are deliberately placed so that trees have to be shot round or branches cleared, sometimes by crouching or kneeling.

The group moves forward, following a red plastic tape tied to a branch, indicating the direction of the next target. Of course, none of you have the faintest idea what it is, nor the distance, until you see it. It's a constant voyage of discovery. When the next red peg appears, you all look about, then find the next two pegs, which give an idea of the direction of the target. You spot it down a long slope, low undergrowth not quite concealing it; it is a 3D deer, head turned towards you. It looks amazingly realistic, apart from the sun shining on its light brown painted surface. It is a well-placed target, with a bank behind it to stop the misses. The sunlight through the trees is dappling it slightly. This makes it difficult to judge the distance, but it looks about 45 yards, slightly downhill. A straightforward shot. You set your sights at 45 yards – there is not enough slope to make it worth taking off any distance. You step up to the marker and stand with the side of your left foot jammed against it. You look at the target, studying the slope, the light, the distance, and nock an arrow on the string, draw up, into the anchor point, lock your string hand in place, move the bow down a fraction. The deer is all you can see, you can hardly feel the power of the bow in your shoulders, the loose happens with hardly a thought, the arrow is on its way; you see it land in the deer and then the sound comes back, a faint thud. Great, a good shot, in the kill area. A twenty scored. This is how it should be all the time, the pleasure of a good shot and a good score, the arrow flying steadily and speedily to the target.

At the end of the day, when you have shot the last target, the scorer adds up the scores and passes the score cards round to be checked. She has made a good job of it, very neat, all the scores are correct. Out of a possible total of 720 points, you have scored 650. There were quite a lot of first-arrow kills, for 20 each, not many second arrows and no thirds at all – the first arrows score more highly than the others. You shake hands with the group and thank the scorer.

Sometimes, at the end of a shoot, the target butts, 3D figures if any, pegs and numbers – 'everything except the trees' – have to be carried back to the start. If you are lucky, it may be a wood where the club can leave the targets out without fear of vandalism and they may want to shoot the course themselves later in the week, so nothing will have to be carried in.

Score-cards have to be handed in to the desk and you will have to wait for the prize-giving ceremony. It takes some time to work out the winning scores, since it has to be done for each of eight classes of bow, and for men, ladies, junior boys, junior girls, and, if any, under twelves as well – although there are not often all those categories in every class.

Eventually, an official blows a whistle and the throng of archers slowly coalesces into a semicircle round a table covered with raffle prizes and small trophies.

The Lady Paramount, often the wife of the landowner, presents the prizes, the club secretary wishes everyone a safe journey home, and you leave after a most enjoyable and satisfying day.

Excuses for use when you miss

1 The kill area was in the wrong place.
2 It's further/nearer than it looks.
3 The sun was in my eyes.

4 The rain was in my eyes.
5 My glasses were steamed up.
6 My glasses were in the line of vision.
7 That arrow was bent.
8 The target was in the wrong place.
9 The target was hidden/out of sight (and sometimes they can be!).

2 The Organization of Field Archery

Field archery in Great Britain is run under the auspices of three organizations: The Grand National Archery Society (GNAS), the English Field Archery Association (EFAA) and the National Field Archery Society (NFAS).

GNAS

The GNAS runs all target archery in Britain and also has some involvement in field archery. It has its own rules for the sport, and these are based on the international rules laid down by the Federation Internationale Tir d'Arc (FITA). Most of its field archery is on marked and unmarked distance courses which tend to be more open than those used by the other organizations. Marked distance means that the distance from the shooting peg to the target has been carefully measured and is displayed so that archers know the distance. Unmarked means that the distance is not given and the archer, if he or she is using sights on the bow, will have to estimate the distance. Marked distance targets tend to be at longer distances for their size than do those on unmarked courses. Target faces are nearly always the black and white ringed faces for the hunter and field rounds; animal targets are very rarely used, although they are permitted by the rules.

The GNAS supports a team for some international competition tournaments, and sends teams to the International Field Archery Championships shot under the rules of FITA. There are a few GNAS target clubs which also do some field archery, mostly in winter when outdoor target shooting becomes more difficult.

There are also some purely field archery clubs, but these appear to be few and far between. There are also a few clubs which indulge in field archery in the forms laid down by the GNAS and another organization, and who put on open shoots under the rules of one or the other, as they see fit. However, it must be said that there are not many GNAS open shoots. This may be due to the overwhelming influence of target archery in GNAS; it has been found that target archery enthusiasts very rarely have any interest in field archery; certainly it takes a different sort of person to enjoy field archery. The converse is also true: although the numbers of field archers are far smaller than those involved in target archery, very few are interested in target archery. There are many reasons for this, but one of them must be the greater sense of freedom in field archery as opposed to the highly structured and disciplined sport that is modern target archery. Field archery gives the opportunity for many people to shoot with the sort of equipment that would be inappropriate on a target field.

EFAA

The EFAA originally began as a comparatively small group of clubs, primarily in East Anglia, and was affiliated to the National Field Archery Association (NFAA) in America. The connection was a number of US servicemen stationed in Britain who had founded the Archery Association of Europe (AEE). The type of field archery practised at that time (the mid-sixties), was all unmarked distances, usually animal rounds with bushes and similar obstructions between archer and target. Consequently, the sport favoured both skill and the lucky shot and there was a healthy appetite for wooden arrows.

The Americans had other ideas. Their brand of field archery was to practise for what they considered to be the 'real thing'. Therefore, to achieve consistency, they used the best, most accurate equipment and shot at known distances with completely clear shots. This was a good formula for improving the skill of the archer, but could also be hard on the ego without the luck factor. However, those original English clubs were soon renowned for the shooting standard of their members, who always seemed to perform better than their rivals in the British Field Archery Association (BFAA).

By 1970, it was apparent that the two national bodies (EFAA and

BFAA) could not co-exist, principally because of the growing interest in field archery.

The NFAA concept had brought about the formation of the International Field Archery Association (IFAA), whose constitution recognized only a single governing body for the sport in each country. As the EFAA was already a founder member, together with the Scottish and Welsh associations, it was decided that the BFAA should amalgamate with the EFAA – hence the two bows on the badge of the 'new' EFAA, to represent the amalgamation.

At this time, the main shooting divisions, or styles, were Freestyle and Barebow, the former using the same equipment as target archers, with the addition of a peep, or string sight if desired. The Barebow archers used an accurate combination of string finger positions and anchorage positions (string and face walking) to cater for the different distances of the standard rounds, the best systems always using the point of the arrow for direct aiming.

The other division, Bowhunter, was not as popular, probably because it entailed 'gap' shooting (indirect aiming) and consequently may not have appealed as readily to the positive approach of eliminating the variables. Over recent years, the Bowhunter divisions have become more popular, owing to new shooting styles allowing the use of fixed five-pin sights and trigger releases. These devices, together with the compound bow, have made Bowhunter second in popularity to Freestyle, which now comprises Unlimited and Limited sections; the Unlimited is allowed the use of trigger releases. Also, the Unlimited Freestyle archer, from the earliest days of the style, was allowed to use a scope sight and, from a recent rule change, all Freestyle archers may now use a magnifying sight if they wish.

International interest has continued to grow, and the IFAA now has a truly worldwide membership, and European and World Championships are held.

There is a total of thirty-three clubs located throughout the UK, but mainly in the south of England and their rules are primarily those of the IFAA. Shooting is at marked and unmarked distances at a variety of targets, including animal targets and 3Ds. A wide variety of equipment is permitted – as is also the case with the other two organizations. A number of different rounds are allowed. There are regional representatives for different areas of the country, and courses have to be approved before being shot under EFAA rules. The association holds national championships and is involved in international competition through the IFAA.

NFAS

Probably the biggest of the three organizations in pure field activities is the NFAS, which grew out of the EFAA, in 1972, with the desire of some members to shoot with home-made wooden arrows. Within the rules of the EFAA at that time, this was not established as a separate class, and several of these archers decided to form their own society, which would permit a separate wooden arrow class. From this, the NFAS grew rapidly into a very successful organization. A high proportion of NFAS members still enjoy shooting with wooden arrows, and are classified as 'instinctive' archers if they use no sights, and 'non-instinctive' if they shoot with sights. It has a large number of competition shoots held under its rules. There are several major points of difference between it and the other two organizations:

- It is NFAS policy *not* to be involved in International competition.
- All shooting is at unmarked distances.
- Shooting is almost always at animal targets – the few exceptions are often 'novelty' targets such as cartoon characters.
- The emphasis is on shooting for the fun of it, and this means that members often seem to lack the seriousness that is sometimes apparent at other field archery shoots.
- Clubs are not affiliated, only club members, but some clubs ask all their members to join.
- National championship shoots are held annually, but they must be on ground that has never been shot before. This causes considerable difficulty every year in trying to find somewhere suitable which fits all the other requirements. For example, there must be a field for parking and setting up an administration area close to the woodland. It must be reasonably priced in terms of rental, and it must be in the right area of the country; there is a policy of changing the area each year to avoid enthusiasts having to travel long distances every year. Each region has its turn, to give advantage to members in that region.

- Shoots usually involve thirty-six or forty targets. This is possible because of the speed at which targets are shot. The great majority of NFAS archers shoot without sights and this enables them to shoot faster than those with sights. Thus the groups tend to move round the course much faster than in other organizations, and it is not uncommon for an NFAS shoot to start at 11 o'clock, break for forty-five minutes for lunch, and finish a forty-target course before 4 o'clock. Longer rounds are not unknown, such as fifty, sixty or even, on one occasion, eighty targets – although it has to be said that the eighty-target round was not completed by all competitors, some of whom decided that enough was enough at 7.30 p.m.!

The NFAS has been criticized for not doing more to raise the standards of shooting, since it has no shooting standard classification schemes and no system of national record scores, as the other two organizations have. However, this is in line with its policy of keeping the rules as few and as simple as possible and keeping the 'shooting for fun' policy at the forefront.

The sport is really in the hands of the clubs. Clubs which have suitable grounds are able to organize shoots when and as often as they please. Some will only feel able to do one shoot a year, while others may put on four or more. They can shoot under the rules of whichever organization they prefer. Any profits from open shoots are retained by the club and are not passed on to national organizations. A considerable number of open shoots are put on annually by clubs under NFAS rules – so many in fact that they do not appear in the fixtures lists of regular archery magazines such as *The Glade* or *Bow*. They can only be found in the regular NFAS newsletter which is sent to all members, and there may often be several open shoots on many Sundays through most of the year; although they tend to fall in numbers in the winter months, NFAS members think of their version of the sport as being active all year round.

Clubs consist of any number of members, of course, and a thriving and active club will always encourage beginners and perhaps even run regular courses of instruction. Most clubs will have qualified instructors or coaches who teach beginners and run courses. All clubs have a core group of members, some of whom have been shooting for years, and peripheral members who are rarely seen, but there is a constant turnover as members leave and new members join. There is no way of determining how long someone may stay in the sport; newcomers full of enthusiasm may last only a couple of visits while someone who expresses little interest initially may become a long-term stalwart. It might be thought that, once someone buys all their equipment they are committed, but this often turns out to be incorrect. It is very common for a newcomer to a club to buy all the kit, then leave, never to be seen again.

It is not essential to join a club; indeed, you may have difficulty in finding one within a reasonable distance. In that case, you may have to shoot as an independent – a somewhat despised and misunderstood life form. There is, it has to be admitted, a certain amount of prejudice against independent members. The common opinion is that archers become independent in order to avoid the responsibility and work that is often entailed in being a club member. However, this is very rarely true; most people prefer to be members of a club where they can enjoy all the advantages of having a club shooting ground, fellow archers to talk to, facilities to use and so on. Independents are such because of their distance from a club more than for any other reason.

Often, membership of a club should come with a health warning. Field archery clubs require a great deal of upkeep if they have their own ground, since they will often have to put butts out before shooting and bring them in when shooting is over. If they are out permanently, they will need to be moved occasionally, or at least the faces will require changing. If the club puts on regular open shoots, workers will be required to put out butts, target faces, shooting pegs, numbers, backstops and anything else required and perhaps act as marshals while the shoot is in progress, or as car park attendants, catering assistants, course clearers and so on. It is generally a core of club enthusiasts who commit themselves to these unselfish tasks on a regular basis, and they are the backbone of the sport without whom it would not be possible to continue.

There is an even more dedicated group who give up vast amounts of their spare time, travel huge distances and give up the right to shoot in order to assist in mounting and organizing the various national championships. These dedicated and hard-working few are the ones who sacrifice themselves in order to give pleasure to the great majority.

Local libraries usually hold details of all local organizations and should be able to help you find a local club. If not, contact one of the major field archery organizations whose addresses are given at the end of this book.

3 Equipment

This is the part which most surprises the beginner and causes the greatest confusion, since there is a wide variety of bows available. Where does one begin? Usually the best starting point is with members of a club, who will often have extensive knowledge of equipment and its availability, and who will also sometimes have some for sale, often at very reasonable prices.

Archery equipment dealers, who are all specialists in the sport, have extensive catalogues of their goods. These are sent free of charge and are well worth detailed study. In addition to goods for sale, they often include advice on bow tuning and setting up, as well as useful charts that show a huge range of arrow sizes and types and the bow weights and draw lengths to go with them. This will give some idea of the range of bows and other goodies available to a very small sport. Generally, the quality of archery goods is very high, but little is cheap. There is a great deal of high-quality and expensive equipment available, but reasonably priced goods that will do the job well can also be easily obtained. Attempts to purchase archery equipment in sports stores will usually fail, as there is little available other than from the specialist dealers.

Bows

An error made by many beginners is to rush off to the nearest archery equipment dealer and buy a very desirable bow which later turns out to be the wrong choice, despite all the advice received from the shop staff. Archery shop staff are usually experts who have a great depth of knowledge and who will rarely give wrong advice, but they will generally not advise someone not to buy the bow of their choice. Another problem is that beginners who are somewhat shy will often buy perfectly good equipment, but will not ask the club experts how to use it. Some archers prefer to shoot on their own and, when one encounters them in the woods, they are found to be using a totally incorrect technique for the bow they have just bought but they have been reluctant to ask the club coach or instructor how to use it.

Another minefield can be the second-hand bow market. Bows may be offered for sale by club members who may not have sufficient expertise to judge the correct bow weight or type of arrow for the buyer. It is possible that their advice is good, but how is the newcomer to tell? Sometimes it just has to be taken on trust; very few people would deliberately sell an unsuitable bow to a new club member since it would be only too easy for that person to complain. On the other hand, club members will often have bows for sale which are absolute bargains and it is a simple matter to ask others for their opinions. Equipment is often offered for sale at irresistible bargain prices, but if it is not right, do not buy it. Would you buy a bargain pair of shoes if they didn't fit? If it is a bargain, one must also sometimes ask why. Where did it come from? Is it from a car boot sale? If so, is it stolen? Sometimes ex-archers do sell their unwanted equipment off very cheaply, and bargains can be had, sometimes still in excellent condition. If it fits and it is what you need, then buy it by all means, but try it out first if at all possible.

On the subject of fit, there is no accurate formula for the ratio of bow weight to body size or strength. Do not expect anyone to recommend a bow weight that will be exact. It is entirely up to you to discover by trial and error what bow weight is most comfortable for you. A club instructor might suggest what he thinks could be suitable but he will be aware that this might be quite wrong. Some very powerfully built people have difficulty with average-weight bows at first, while apparently fairly lightly built archers shoot bows of surprising power – although, of course, there is a tendency for stronger people to shoot stronger bows. The most obvious example that springs to mind was a man over 6 feet tall and very powerfully built, who shot an 85-pound compound, a weight I thought was quite unnecessary, and even well beyond the permitted limit in some areas of field archery.

Of course, a bow should always be shot before purchasing,

unless the purchaser is a very experienced archer, and most of those would want to try it first. After all, this is often a major investment for many archers, bow prices being what they are, and most will want a bow which will serve them for several years, so most will shoot before buying. On one occasion a friend of mine was testing a bow on the range at a well-known archery dealer's shop and the lower limb of the bow delaminated – the laminations separated and a huge bulge appeared on the lower limb. Fortunately this happened before he had actually purchased the bow, since it was obviously unusable.

Field Archery permits the use of a wide variety of bow types:

- a traditional-style English longbow
- a American flat bow
- a recurve bow without sights, but with wooden arrows (hunting tackle)
- a recurve bow without sights, but with alloy or carbon arrows (barebow)
- a recurve bow with sights (freestyle), as in target archery
- a compound bow without sights (bowhunter)
- a compound bow with pin sights (compound limited)
- a compound bow with sights (unlimited)
- a crossbow

It is often a baffling choice. Let us have a look at each in turn.

The Traditional English Longbow

These are still available, made by hand of course, from a number of craftsmen. They are not always made from yew, the well-known traditional material, although it is still in use. Yew bows tend to be more expensive than those of other woods, probably because yew is more difficult to find. The English yew tree tends to be rather contorted and knotted, and even in medieval times yew staves were imported from the Continent for longbows. Today's longbows are made from several woods, often laminated together, including lemonwood, hickory, maple, greenheart, purpleheart, walnut and osage orange. Sometimes they have a mother of pearl arrow plate inserted into the wood where the arrow will bear against it, to prevent wear on the bow. Each end of the bow will have a horn nock glued to it which bears the stress of the string, while the handle will be bound with either leather or cloth. The bow should be of 'D' section with the flat facing forward.

Draw weights of modern longbows are far lower than those of the medieval period. The draw weight is the power required to draw the string to the archer's anchor point, this being the point where the drawing hand settles in the most comfortable position – usually somewhere on the face. Medieval draw weights were for a long time a matter for speculation, but the bows which were brought up with the Tudor warship the *Mary Rose* were carefully examined by experts and new bows were made by Roy King, a well-known longbow maker, to the same dimensions. It was discovered that many of the old war bows were of very heavy draw weights, many exceeding 120 lb, which few archer today could draw. In fact it took some searching before the researchers found an archer who could actually draw one of Roy's replica bows. This explained the state of many of the skeletons of bowmen found in the wreck, many of whom had deformed or injured shoulders, arm and necks.

Care should be take be taken to ensure that the bow is strung correctly, since a mistake can cause injury to the bow and/or the archer. There are three methods of stringing a bow. One is the 'step through' method (see illustrations), which is not recommended for recurve bows since it is liable to twist the limb, but is probably acceptable for a longbow. The second method is the centre pull, with the handle of the bow pulled up and the top limb pushed down, to slide the string in place. This method is normally used for longbows and is acceptable for recurves. The most painless method is by using a bow-stringing device which is placed on the bow limbs, the bow handle pulled up and the string then slid into place. This is a simple method, but rarely seems to be used by longbow archers.

Longbow arrows are of wood, preferably Port Orford cedar from the west coast of California. It is chosen for its lightness, straightness of grain and resistance to shock, which is equalled by no other timber.

Arrows can be personalized by cresting. This is done by rotating the arrow and running a paintbrush round the shaft. Any colour or combination of colours can be used, and some arrows become works of art. It is also a good idea, especially for field archers, to paint your name on each shaft. You will stand a much better change of getting lost arrows back if you do. It is true that at first you will lose arrows; this is inevitable and must be accepted, but if you shoot on a club field course which is shot frequently, arrows lost years before will reappear. Sometimes they are found remarkably quickly by others shooting the course. Unfortunately, unless they are found in time, they may be past being shot again. Even alloy arrows rot away.

Feathers are preferred for the fletchings (which keep the arrow straight) in wooden arrows, rather than plastics, and these require more care when applying them to the shaft because of their natural curves. Some longbow experts prefer, for extra authenticity, to bind thread round their feathers in the traditional manner, but this is hardly necessary with modern adhesives.

Arrow piles, or points, are usually made of steel in several weights and profiles, some specially designed for field archery, although brass piles can be purchased, so there is a range of choices for those wishing to make their own arrows. Many field archers do this and find it very satisfying. It gives them the opportunity to carry a range of arrows which may have different flight characteristics, for example arrows with heavyweight piles for shorter shots and arrows with lighter piles for long shots.

There is a new field pile available in Germany, made from brass with an internal thread that allows it to be screwed onto wooden shafts with quite a tight fit. This may eliminate the problem of tapered piles pulling off inside the butt. At the time of writing there was no news of when this might become available in the UK. Broadhead points are not available for sale within the UK. These are wide-bladed points used for hunting and designed to be lethal. They are in the archery dealer's catalogues, but for export only. These points are designed to kill animals, and since this is illegal in England, they are not for sale. All the field archery organizations ban their use and it is not difficult to see why, since they are extremely dangerous, and could cause death or injury to anyone hit by one. Apart from those obvious aspects, they could do horrendous damage to targets. In addition, they are difficult to shoot without considerable practice since their flight characteristics are quite different from normal arrows, due to the aerodynamic properties of the points themselves. One manufacturer will supply replica medieval arrows which have broadhead points fitted, but these are primarily intended for display purposes and each arrow costs about the same as a dozen wooden field arrows.

Shooting a longbow is not easy for the novice. Accuracy is not their strong point, and high scores are not likely, except for the very few truly gifted archers. They were originally intended to be shot at a large target such as a mass of horses and men, and it was far easier to shoot down the horses than to attempt to shoot down the riders. Longbows also gradually weaken to form a permanent curve – following the string – and their cast is inferior to that of other types of bow, so their draw weight is not an indicator of performance. It is often necessary for a longbow archer to shoot a higher poundage than he would really prefer for comfort merely in order to reach the longer targets. But the greatest problem on many field courses is the high trajectory of the arrow, causing it to disappear into, or be deflected by branches, where other bows can shoot under them.

It may be necessary to wear a leather glove on the left hand (if you use the bow in that hand) since it is used to support the arrow and feathers can make cuts in the skin.

The shooting technique for the longbow is straightforward; the string is usually drawn to an anchor point on the mouth or cheek, the bow moved up or down to the estimated height and the arrow loosed very quickly. (The anchor point is a point on the face where the hand customarily settles when at full draw, the bow being drawn to the archer's most comfortable distance.) Most longbow archers prefer not to hold on the aim for very long and some shoot with astonishing speed, drawing the bow, aiming and loosing with what seems to be one continuous flowing movement, which can be beautiful to watch when done by a real expert.

The longbow string is not quite like other bowstrings, since many archers still prefer the traditional type of string which has a permanent loop at one end while the other end is tied in a simple timber hitch which can easily be adjusted to change the length and thus the bracing height. (The bracing height is the distance of the nocking point on the string to the point where the arrow rests on the bow. It is sometimes measured from some part of the front or back edge of the bow handle.) This is critical on recurve bows, as well as longbows since the bracing height affects the bow's performance and if it is incorrect the bow will not work at its maximum efficiency. Longbows require some experimenting to find the most effective bracing height. This can be done by twisting and untwisting the string, and can also be carried out when tuning recurve bows, shooting arrows in between each adjustment to discover whether groups become tighter or spread out with each twist of the string. There is a limit to the number of twists that can be given to the string, usually about ten turns, before it starts to become more elastic and under more stress – and therefore more likely to break. Strings do break, but not often, and with care a good string of the right material will last for years.

When a longbow is purchased the only addition it requires is a nocking point. This is simply a marker on the string to show where the arrow should be nocked (the arrow fitted on the string in the correct place), and to hold it in that place when the bow is drawn. This is often made with twists of thread round the string, sometimes glued in place. Sometimes dental floss is used; this has been an old favourite for this purpose for many years. In structure it is very similar to bowstring material. It is vital on any bow that the nocking point is fitted in the correct place (see chapter 6). The nocking point determines the angle of the arrow when it leaves the bow and also the most effective position in relation to the arrow rest. If it is incorrect, the arrow may fly in an erratic manner, sometimes entering the target nock end down or nock end high, and often not where it is aimed.

Sometimes beginners express a desire to shoot longbows for a variety of reasons, including the historical romance attached to them. I have even known people who want to shoot them before they have even had their first lesson, saying that they want nothing to do with all those modern gadgets with bits stuck all over them. This is a rather mistaken attitude to take before learning the attributes and qualities of the other available types. An open-minded approach to the sport is far better than an initial bias.

The American Flat Bow

The American flat bow is a development of the traditional longbow, using modern materials to give it better performance. It is simply made from fibreglass laminated with wood to form a flat-section bow with tapering limbs and with a handle built up to a sufficient thickness. It may also have a narrow arrow shelf on the side so that there is support for the arrow rather than it having to be supported by the hand. There can also be a small cut-out, or window, to allow the arrow to be shot nearer the centre line of the bow than is possible on longbows. This means that the American flat bow can be more accurate, since one of the greatest problems of the longbow is that the arrow has to curve round the bow to produce any accuracy of shot.

There are no horn nocks on the ends of the limbs (the flexible working parts of the bow), and the string is simply fitted into grooves. It is essential that these nocks are carefully smoothed so that the string does not chafe on rough or sharp edges.

The same types of arrow are shot as with the longbow, and they are shot in the same way, so the only major difference is in the cast of the bow. For this reason they are shot in a different class in some field archery organizations. Those archers shooting with American flat bows instituted this new class some years ago. It should be added that in both longbow and American flat bow classes no sighting aids are permitted.

Laminate, Recurve or Composite Bows

Before the Second World War, bows were made of wood, for modern technology had not become part of the tiny sport of archery. After the war a new type of bow made its appearance, made from tubular steel. This was, perhaps, not the first steel bow since there is a record of steel bows being imported into England several centuries ago. Unfortunately, there seems to be only one reference and no other trace of such bows has ever been found. The new tubular steel bows were small, thin and tapered towards the nocks. Some were made in two parts which fitted one into the other at the handle, which was often made of cork. They came fitted with a primitive sight made of chromed steel and brass.

When shot, these bows were certainly more accurate than the wooden variety and possessed a far better cast, but they suffered from two major disadvantages. They had an alarming recoil up the bow arm and they could break without warning, sometimes cutting the archer across the face. For this reason, it was decreed that all archers should wear a peaked cap for protection, and some took the precaution of inserting strips of bamboo in the limbs in the hope that this would provide some help in case of breakage. Using a bow which might break without warning at any moment must have required nerves of steel.

Help was at hand. Realizing the limitations of these bows, a few enterprising Americans started to research the use of new materials combined with an ancient design using the principles of laminated limbs developed in Asia long ago. These bows had been made from flat sections of horn, wood, hide and sinew glued together very skilfully, with a tremendous recurve (a bow limb with a reverse curve from the major curve), making them light and short, so they were easily carried and shot from the back of a horse, and possessed of a cast which the makers of wooden longbows could only dream of. It has been said that the animal glues used in making these bows sometimes took a year to dry, and it took two or three men to string one, since they sometimes formed almost a circle when unstrung.

It was found that flap strips of fibreglass laminated with a suitable wood such as rock maple glued onto a wooden handle produced a totally new type of bow which made huge new advances possible in archery. The evolution of this bow proceeded at a rapid pace and it was soon found that it could be made into a thing of beauty with a sculptured wooden handle, long working curves to the limbs and shorter deflex curves in the opposite direction. These have come to be known as 'recurve' bows.

Many years ago I met a gentleman who claimed to have made the first laminate bow in England. When he took it to its first target archery tournament, he said that he was nearly laughed off the field, but after the tournament he was besieged by archers who had seen what it could do and wanted their own. He was kept busy for years developing and making the new bows.

The power of the new bow was in the sandwich construction of the limbs, with the inner layer of fibreglass compressed as the limb was bent while the outer layer was under tension. The rock maple in between created a gap between the layers. The new bows were relatively easy to make and not expensive, since the basic materials were cheap, and they had tremendous development potential. In addition, the handle could be made to fit the hand, unlike any previous type of bow. Part of the handle could now be cut away to allow the arrow to rest and to be shot on the bow centre line, a highly desirable situation since it would no longer be necessary for the arrow to bend round the bow, and it could be sighted directly on the target instead of having to make allowances laterally for the bow handle. Also, it was big enough to screw all sorts of bits on. Manufacturers of the new bows sprang into being and many discovered that, while little could be done to alter the basic design of the limbs once the optimum shape had been discovered, it was possible to make a number of models at a wide range of prices. The manufacture of accessories to fit on the new bows developed rapidly, with complex new sights, stabilizers and eventually adjustable and spring loaded arrows rests.

Thus cheap bows became available, while much more expensive models also appeared, with finely sculpted and polished risers or handle sections made from exotic tropical hardwoods. It was now possible to produce a superb piece of equipment which anyone would be proud to own and shoot. This new bow brought about a rebirth of archery and a slow but steady expansion, which is still continuing. For a time, these new bows were known as composite or laminate bows, but these terms seem to have died out and the word 'recurve' is now used instead.

From the single-piece bow, the take-down (a bow with limbs that can be detached from the handle when unstrung) was a simple and obvious step, then the metal riser arrived and from that came the computer-controlled machine process which was capable of producing the most complex and interesting designs as well as lighter but stronger bows. The metal normally used is a magnesium alloy.

Having see the effects of burning magnesium, with an intense white light, I have often wondered if anyone has ever had a bow catch fire and what the results were like. Presumably the alloy does not ignite as easily as the pure metal.

The take-down bow was, perhaps, an obvious step in design, since the long rigid riser or handle permitted the fitting of bolts and threaded inserts, while the limbs were now wide enough to drill through and bolt in place. This created bows which could be simply taken apart for easy transportation and fitted into a small case, which could also be made to carry arrows as well as other equipment. In time, the designers found that they could make the limb bolts and sockets in such a way that it became possible to adjust draw weights, within a narrow range, in the same manner as compound bows.

The simplicity of the recurve bow, with its obvious power and its sheer beauty, make it an attractive bow to shoot, and it is also suitable for beginners to use.

The Compound Bow

This was the great leap forward in bow technology, possibly the first major advance since the invention of the Asian laminate bow several thousand years ago. It is daunting in appearance; it can never be as beautiful as the recurve, and seems complex and diffi-

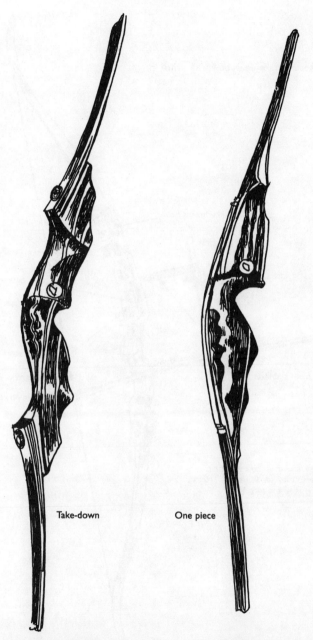

Take-down   One piece

Fig. 1 Traditional hunting bows made from exotic hardwoods, finely finished

Fig. 2 Recurve take-down bow with sights

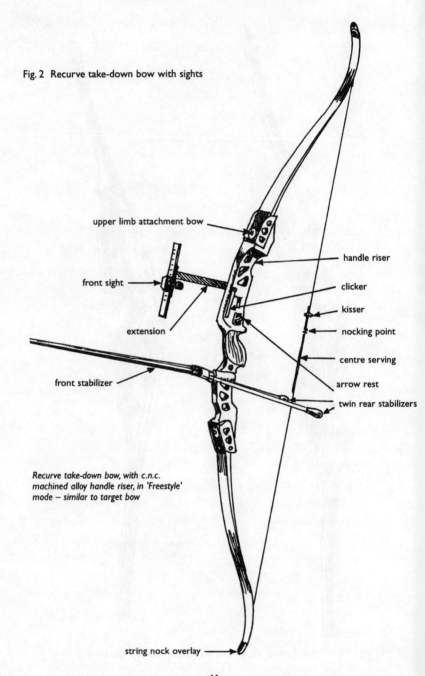

upper limb attachment bow

handle riser

front sight

clicker

kisser

extension

nocking point

centre serving

front stabilizer

arrow rest

twin rear stabilizers

*Recurve take-down bow, with c.n.c.
machined alloy handle riser, in 'Freestyle'
mode – similar to target bow*

string nock overlay

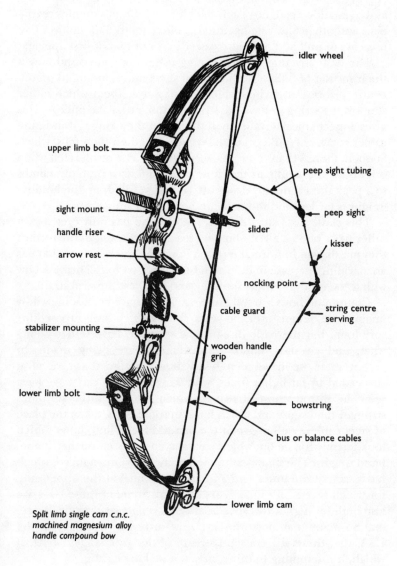

idler wheel

upper limb bolt

peep sight tubing

sight mount

peep sight

handle riser

slider

kisser

arrow rest

nocking point

cable guard

string centre serving

stabilizer mounting

wooden handle grip

lower limb bolt

bowstring

bus or balance cables

Split limb single cam c.n.c. machined magnesium alloy handle compound bow

lower limb cam

Fig. 3 A typical compound bow

cult to use, with its numerous cables and strings, pulleys and cams, as well as added gadgetry such as sights, stabilizers, complex arrow-rests and other bits. The beginner is often amazed to discover that it is easy to pull and hold and easier to shoot than it first appears.

The basic invention which distinguishes the compound bow is the insertion of pulleys at the end of short limbs, mounted on off-centre pivots and having cables running over them which either support the string or have the string running over the pulleys. This gives a mechanical advantage in that when the string is drawn, the cables rotate the pulleys and effectively lengthen the limbs, which are bent far less than those of a recurve bow. The result is felt when one draws the string, as the draw weight increases rapidly, climbs to a peak then suddenly drops off, so that at full draw, the holding weight is far less and the bow can be held far longer.

This comes as a surprise to someone who has only ever drawn other types of bow, all of which increase in draw weight the further they are drawn. In normal terms, a bow that 'stacks' is one that has an alarming increase in draw weight as it comes to full draw. A bow with a 'sweet' draw draws smoothy and with less physical strain.

Compound bows are still evolving. There have been some wildly imaginative designs over the years, few of which have survived for very long, but the basic design now seems to have settled some-what, and constant minor improvements are being made. In recent years we have seen heavy bows, designed for stability, succeeded by far lighter ones, which are easier to carry. We have seen the introduction of strings, which are said to be six times stronger than steel, and which have, in some bows, taken the place of steel cables. We have seen the arrival of split-limb bows, which look terribly fragile but which have served to lessen further the in-hand weight. The single-cam bow has also been introduced, which has a cam at the lower end and an idler wheel at the upper end, for which several advantages are claimed. Some of these bows are also built for high arrow speeds, another objective of many design-ers. So many manufacturers are now involved, especially in the USA, that there is a constant stream of design changes, some of which, it is tempting to think, may not be long lasting.

Compounds may not have the beauty of recurve bows but there can be no doubt that they have several advantages, one of which is that the techniques for shooting them can be quickly learned. A beginner may be able to reach the high-scoring ranks in far less

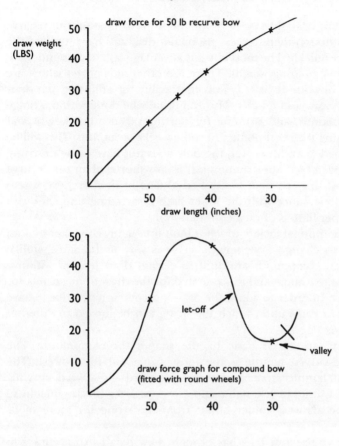

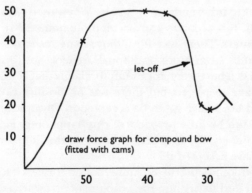

Fig. 4 Draw force graphs

time than it might take if he or she were to take up the recurve bow, although there too exceptional individuals have reached the top very quickly. The most obvious advantage, as I have mentioned, is the low holding weight. There are other advantages which are not so obvious at first. One is the facility for adjusting the draw weight easily and quickly. This can usually be done within a range of 15 pounds, and is useful for starting off at a low weight and increasing it after shooting for some weeks or months. This will be explained later. Moreover, the bow does not have to be unstrung or disassembled after shooting. It is also shorter than the recurve bow and this can be a positive advantage in field archery, where ground clearance with the lower limb or avoiding branches with the upper limb is often a consideration.

An additional facility which is built into many compounds is an ability to change draw lengths. This is very useful since, unlike recurves, compounds are built to certain draw lengths within a very limited range and it is essential for the draw to be correct for the user. In order to adjust the draw it is common practice to have wheels or cams upon which the string can be moved to different positions.

There are three basic handle shapes for compounds. The forward-curved handle is the most stable but the slowest. The straight handle is stable but faster, and the rearward curving-handle is fast but less stable and gives a shorter bracing height so that the arrow is under power from the string for more of its length.

The compound bow has brought new heights of accuracy to archery, being inherently more stable. When used with sights and release aids, this accuracy can become phenomenal in the hands of a real expert. There was, for a time, some resistance to the use of compounds from more traditional archers, but this has slowly been eroded. There were, for example, claims that compounds did more damage to targets but there was no positive proof of this. Compound bows have yet to be accepted in Olympic archery, and there seems to be little prospect of this happening. However, this need not concern the field archer, since all the field archery organizations have accepted it.

The compound produces more power for less effort. It can shoot faster and flatter and the problem of arrow trajectory is lessened. For example, most adult men will shoot recurve bows in the weight range of 36–42 pounds, but the compound bow gives an adult man a higher weight range, something in the order of 45–60 pounds, since the holding weight of the bow will drop off at least 60 per cent. Most men will be able to pull 60 pounds over its peak (the draw weight rises to a peak then falls off as the string is drawn further) after some experience and will thus be holding a weight of only about 20 pounds. The tremendous speed and flat trajectory this gives improves accuracy and thus enables scoring way over what might be achieved with a recurve bow. In part, this increased accuracy is due to the light holding weight, enabling the archer to hold the bow steadier for longer. It is not uncommon to see a compound unlimited archer, using sights and release aid, hold the sight on the aim for twenty seconds or more, almost without any movement, and then deliver an arrow right on the point of aim.

The release aid in itself is also an aid to accuracy, since it removes any variation in the loose which so bedevils recurve archers at times through variations of hand position and movement. It should be noted that release aids are only allowed for use with compound bows and were introduced because the light holding weight created difficulties for some archers in getting a good loose with the fingers. Despite that, some still prefer to use a finger loose.

The compound also works on the arrow in a different manner, since it accelerates the shaft from the low-power full-draw position past the peak of the power. This means that surprisingly thinner arrows can be used, since the shock of instant acceleration is somewhat less than that from the recurve bow.

Compounds are also equipped with several types of wheels or cams. The simplest type has round wheels, which vary in size according to draw length. Small wheels will be fitted to a bow for a short draw length, while larger wheels will be fitted to increase the draw length. These wheels will give a smooth draw, with the weight gradually increasing until it peaks at about half draw, then slowly comes down until the full draw position is reached. If it is pulled further, the weight will start to rise very rapidly until it appears to come to a stop. This is known as the wall. The area where the weight is at its lowest is called the valley, and full draw length should be in this area. Cams are another story. By clever design, they have added more power to the bow. They are sometimes extremely exaggerated shapes, but their effect is to act as levers which increase the length of the bow limb when they roll over; the longer the cam, the more it will increase this effect. The effect felt by the archer is that when the string is drawn, the weight rises very quickly to the peak and stays there for some distance (see diagram) before dropping sharply into the narrow valley of the holding weight. These bows can be fierce to shoot, since any relaxation of the draw will tend to snatch the string out of control, but the effect on the arrow is to propel it with astonishing speed since it now has the peak weight applied to it for longer. Manufacturers have competed against each other to produce faster and faster bows, but to choose a bow merely for the speed at which it will shoot an arrow can be a mistake, since these bows are often difficult to control and are not the most stable. They can also be difficult to draw even when of a relatively light draw weight, since the weight rises very rapidly to the peak.

Stability is a factor of major importance since it adds to accuracy, and the most stable designs can be a delight to shoot, although their arrows may be slower. It is perfectly possible to design bows for speed or stability and most manufacturers will include several types of bow in their ranges which will cover several different requirements.

Setting up a compound bow is a fairly complex business, as can be imagined, but it is not difficult. The techniques will be dealt with in chapter 6. Compound bows can be made with different levels of 'let-off', the most common being 60 per cent. This simply means that the peak weight will reduce by that amount when the string is at full draw. Some bows have an adjustment which permits one to alter the degree of let-off, but this is not very common. It is possible to find a range of bows that look almost identical, but careful examination might show that they vary in the size of their wheels or cams and in their draw weights. A badly assembled bow – which is not common, but I have encountered the problem – might have large wheels, intended for a long draw length, and a low draw weight. These two factors are usually incompatible, producing a bow which is too weak for a tall person to use. A badly adjusted bow could have much of its let-off removed so that its major advantage is lost.

Careful calculation is required to establish the correct arrow size for a compound bow. For any other type, there is a simple and straightforward relationship of draw length to bow weight, so that, for example, a 40-pound draw weight combined with a 28-inch draw length might require an alloy arrow of 1916 size, 28 inches long. There is a simple relationship of draw length to weight whereby the weight will be reduced by 2 pounds for every inch less in draw length if the bow is about 40 pounds or less, and by approximately 3 pounds for every inch if the bow is above 40 pounds. However, compound bows have additional complications, as might be expected. Wheels make the bow easier to draw and more stable, so lighter arrows can be used than with cams. Some of the more extreme cams being used will require stiffer arrows. Using fingers on the string requires a heavier arrow than a release aid. All these factors, however, do not add significantly to the difficulties of choosing the right arrow size since each size will be suitable for a range of draw weights and bow conditions. These are shown on the major arrow manufacturers' size charts, available in almost every archery dealer's catalogue. Although they are in tiny print, with a vast mass of numbers, a choice of arrows *can* be obtained for every bow weight and draw length.

Mass weight, the weight of the bow before any bits are added to it, is not normally a great consideration for the users of recurve bows, whose structure is such that weight is not a problem. However, the mass weight of compound bows is rather a different matter, since the handle risers can vary tremendously in both complexity of design and weight. Some years ago, the manufacturers of some compounds thought that more weight might be a good idea. Some heavy bows were produced, but they soon went out of favour. A heavy bow feels heavy only when being held by one hand; when held at arm's length, some are a considerable strain, but when drawn, the weight then disappears as it is distributed over the body. The bow becomes more stable to hold and to shoot – except that, once released, the weight comes back onto one arm.

Nocking an arrow on the string of a heavy bow becomes tiring after a while, and the bow arm starts to ache. Carrying one round a wood all day makes one more aware of its weight, too. Some people felt that the manufacturers had not really done their homework properly, and the heavy bows soon disappeared to be replaced with far lighter ones that might have lacked the stability provided by the weight but were far more enjoyable to shoot. The difference was only a matter of a pound or so, but when the bow was loaded down with sights and stabilizers as well, that pound was considerable, and could be felt easily.

The Crossbow

Crossbows are not common in field archery, but they do make an appearance sometimes, perhaps with only one or two at an open shoot. Although they are well known to the general public through myths and history, they are neither common nor popular. There is a British manufacturer, but the type of crossbows made by this company are not used in field archery.

Those which are normally used have heavy wooden stocks and are often fitted with beautifully made brass parts, but it is extremely difficult to obtain them. They are hand made to order, and few are being made any longer.

The prod, or bow section, was once made from duralumin, an aluminium alloy, but it was found that this sometimes broke, with disastrous results, so they were banned by the ruling body of crossbow shooting, and prods are now made of fibreglass or laminated fibreglass in the same way as recurve bows. The technology of the compound bow has also been applied to crossbows and it is now possible to buy a crossbow with eccentrically mounted wheels fitted.

Unfortunately, crossbows have acquired rather a bad name since they are easily purchased at some fishing tackle and gun shops and have been used for illegal purposes. Some years ago one archery shop owner declared that he would no longer sell crossbows because 'so many obvious nutters are coming in to buy them'. It should also be added that many field archers regard them as not being proper bows because they are not drawn and held by the strength of the body.

Their use is permitted by the NFAS and GNAS but not the EFAA or IFAA, and the British Crossbow Society usually holds it annual championships in conjunction with those of the NFAS.

Other Bows

In addition to the above, there are a couple of rare and unusual types of bow which are available, but which are difficult to classify. One of these has been available for several years, but it is not often seen. It is sold as the Classic Hunter and is based on the design of Middle Eastern and oriental bows, but made from laminated fibre-glass and wood. It is short, with large reflexes in the limbs, and is shot without sighting aids or arrow rest. It is said to have almost unlimited draw and so it would appear from its extremely flexible design. Probably the most difficult aspect of shooting it would be to establish a consistent hand position since the handle design does not give a positive position. There is no padding or binding in the handle position. These bows are said to be great fun to shoot, but few archers have shot them in serious competitions.

A similar bow which has appeared in recent years has been imported from Hungary and is a copy of the traditional Asian or Mongol bow, with long straight outer sections to the limbs, which give more leverage, and relatively short working curves. These bows are well made and pleasant to shoot, with performances similar to the Classic Hunter, but seem to be made primarily for display purposes, for which they are well suited, since they are decorative and attractive in appearance.

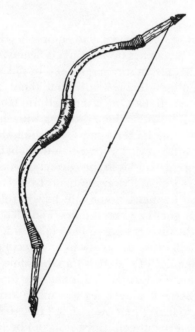

Fig. 5. Hungarian bow

Choosing a Bow

As can be seen, there are plenty of bows to chose from. And once the choice is made, of course, the archer is not obliged to stick to that type – except if one breaks during a competition, when it may be replaced with one of a similar type if there is one available. Otherwise you can choose a different style whenever you prefer or can afford a change, although most people stay with one style for many years, or never change at all. Success in shooting comes with constant practice with the chosen type, not in frequent changes in the hope that more success may be gained with something else. More often, a change is made to something simpler and less complicated. It is more common for someone shooting compound unlimited, for example, to change to hunting tackle, with wooden arrows and a recurve hunting bow, for simplicity, than vice versa.

Tabs, Bracers and Releases

Tabs

Before shooting, it will be necessary to equip oneself with a finger tab and a bracer. The tab lies on the fingers against the string and serves to protect them from soreness caused by the string. There is a wide variety, most of them simple, but there are types that perform different functions. One is the platform tab, which is used almost entirely by freestyle archers shooting with the hand under the chin, with the string locked against the chin. Made from plastic or aluminium and screwed in place on the tab, the platform is used to ensure that the hand is in the correct position beneath the chin; it helps to prevent the drawing hand from creeping up the chin, as sometimes happens. Some tabs have a rubber or plastic block inserted that goes between the first and second fingers and serves to prevent the fingers from squeezing the nock of the arrow. If this happens it will cause the arrow to fly inaccurately.

There is also a choice of materials for tabs, some of them being made from an imitation leather that is cheaper than the genuine article, but the better-quality ones are made from pony butt. Anyone who tries to make their own tab will find that the choice of suitable leather is very difficult, since it has to be the right thickness combined with the right amount of flexibility. Anything too

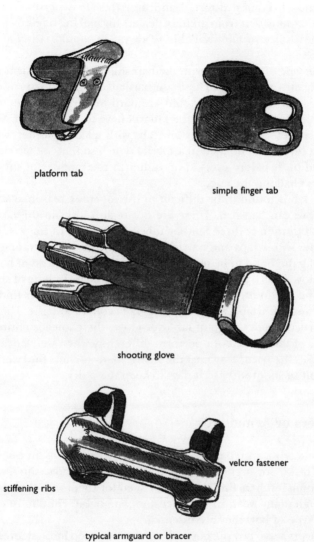

platform tab

simple finger tab

shooting glove

velcro fastener

stiffening ribs

typical armguard or bracer

Fig. 6 Gloves, tabs and bracers

thin soon becomes distorted and unusable. It is possible to buy pieces of pony butt from archery dealers for making one's own tabs but the choice of tabs available ready made should satisfy almost everyone.

One type of tab is sold with the hair still on the inner surface, to bear against the string. These are particularly good for providing less friction with the string, and are hard wearing, but eventually the hair will wear away and the tab will have to be replaced. Some archers prefer to lubricate their tabs with talcum powder, which can be carried on the belt in a special pouch so that the tab can be rubbed on it before every shot, rather in the manner of snooker players chalking the cue.

If a tab is found to be difficult to use for some reason, a shooting glove can be worn. These are not really gloves in the normal sense, but merely three leather tubes, tapered to fit fingers, held together with straps and a wrist band. They have the advantage of allowing the hand to be used for other purposes, instead of having to remove it, as is often the case with a tab. The technique of shooting is no different, but it has to be said that some archers find the glove uncomfortable when the fingers become too tight. There is no particular advantage of tab over glove; the choice is entirely a matter of taste. But both perform differently when wet, since this increases the friction against the string. Many archers find wet tabs difficult to shoot with, so it pays to keep them dry.

Bracers or Armguards

The bracer or armguard has always been regarded as an essential piece of kit for archers, but it is not always so now, since some compound archers find there is no need for them with their bows, although many wear one from custom and habit. For almost every other type of bow they are essential.

Bracers serve two purposes. The first is to keep loose sleeves out of the way of the string, the other to prevent the arm from being injured by the string. The first becomes obvious when beginners turn up wearing garments with very loose sleeves and the instructor discovers that they have only a thin t-shirt on underneath. The sleeves continually catch the string and throw the arrow off course. Or, as in a sudden rainstorm someone puts on their wet-weather top, which has the same effect. The other purpose is often discovered by beginners who have not yet got the bow arm position correct and find the string whacking their arm quite painfully.

Some bracers are vestigial or skeletal and are merely a narrow strip of plastic held in place by elastic bands. These seem to be favoured by only the very best freestyle target archers, whose body control is such that they are confident of never touching the arm with the string. It is possible to purchase extra long bracers that cover part of the upper arm as well as the lower, mainly for those lady archers whose arms have extra long ligaments that allow the elbow to bend inwards at full draw. Some archers, mainly those shooting longbow, like to use finely tooled leather bracers, while others go to the other extreme and just pull a length of tubular surgical bandage up their arms.

Release Aids

These are used only in the compound unlimited class, so a tab is unnecessary. Releases come in many forms, some supported by a strap round the wrist so that the strain of drawing the bow is taken by the wrist rather than the fingers. Most, however, require the fingers to take the strain, and there are many variations in which the finger can be used to trigger the device; some use the thumb and more sophisticated types can use back pressure and relaxation so that the fingers do not trigger it at all.

The let-off pressure required by the fingers is adjustable on nearly all releases to that the lightest pressure will operate it if required.

There are two main types of release. One has a mechanism that locks round the string with two steel balls. The other, by far the most popular, has a string loop passing round the bowstring and engaging in a catch of some sort which is released when triggered; the loop then flies round the string and lets it go. The newer string materials are not very tolerant of being bent round very small curves, so the string loop variety is kinder to them rather than the ball catch. One idea that relieves this is a loop which is permanently attached to the string round which the release rope or ball catch is fitted. This also saves considerable wear on the bow string.

Many release aids are very expensive for their size and you should try out as many as possible before buying.

Some releases have the advantage of being operable from any angle, so that the drawing arm need not be used in the normal position, but can be used with palm facing downwards, or even palm outwards, which seems to be popular amongst many of the top compound archers. Certainly the use of a release makes shooting far easier and far more accurate for most people. There is plenty of choice of releases in the archery dealers' catalogues.

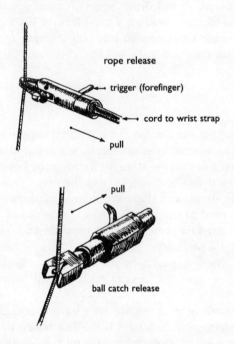

Fig. 7 Types of release aid shown without arrow on string for clarity

Arrows

'You can shoot good arrows well from a cheap bow, but you can't shoot cheap arrows well from a good bow.'

This piece of advice was given to me by a very experienced

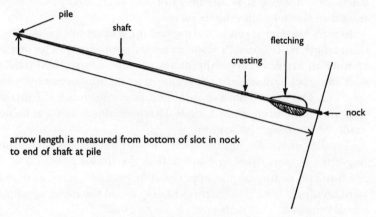

pile

shaft

fletching

cresting

nock

arrow length is measured from bottom of slot in nock
to end of shaft at pile

Fig. 8 Parts of the arrow

archer about a month after I started shooting and it proved over the years to be very sound. It was proved with my first set of good arrows, when I was astonished to see the difference they made. My scores improved by 50 per cent.

There are currently several types of arrow on the market, most of them except the wooden variety made by one manufacturer who possesses virtually a world monopoly on high-quality arrows. It has to be admitted that the archery world has been well served by them. There are:

- aluminium alloy tube arrows
- carbon tube arrows
- aluminium tube, carbon wrapped arrows
- fibreglass arrows
- wooden arrows

The most important factor in the choice of arrows is length, followed by thickness, then material and price.

It is essential for the arrow to match your draw length since if the arrows are too short they become dangerous. The reason for this is simple: if you draw an arrow which is too short – or if you draw it too far – it can fall off the rest on the bow, impinge on the belly, or the side of the bow facing you, and then virtually explode when loosed, since it is unable to go anywhere except sideways, usually in several high-velocity pieces.

Before you ever shoot an arrow, you must determine what your draw length is. This can be done in several simple ways. The first is to hold an arrow between the palms of your outstretched hands with the nock end against the upper part of your breastbone or sternum. The point where your longest fingertips touch the arrow indicates the correct draw length. However, this is not a reliable guide, only a rough indication.

Another method is to hold an arrow with the nock between the fingertips of your drawing hand and at the drawn position, with the fore end resting on the upper part of your bow hand as if you were holding a bow. If the arrow will not rest on the hand, a longer one is required. This is also only a rough guide.

The most accurate method is to hold the arrow in the full draw position – and it is preferable here, of course, to use an arrow which is obviously too long and to rest it on the bow arrow rest. Get someone to measure how much the arrow hangs over the rest. If an inch of shaft overhangs, this is a suitable length, since there will be a safety margin to prevent it from being drawn too far and off the rest.

If the arrow is too long it has two effects. One is that the bow will be propelling more weight than is necessary and the other is that the arrow will not have the right degree of flexibility.

The latter is vital for it to perform correctly for the draw weight of the bow. For this reason, arrows must be matched to bow weight, and the dynamics of arrow performance to bow weight need to be understood, if only on a simple basis.

When an arrow is shot, its inertia – its resistance to being moved – causes the rear, where the energy is being applied, to move before the front. This causes the arrow to bend into what is called the archers' paradox. It actually bends round the bow, then springs into a decreased bend in the opposite direction, and so begins its flight as a series of decreasing whipping bends. The thinner the arrow, the more it will bend. Therefore if a thin arrow is shot from a bow which is too powerful for it, it will shoot to the right of the bow. Conversely, an arrow which is too thick for the power of the bow will shoot off to the left. This is one of the reasons why arrows do not sometimes go where they are supposed to.

Aluminium Alloy Arrows

Arrow manufacturers have dealt with the problem of spine or flex-ibility by producing arrows in a huge range of thicknesses. Most aluminium alloy arrows are described by a four-digit figure, e.g. 1814, which is etched or printed on the shaft. The first two digits represent the diameter of the shaft in sixty-fourths of an inch, while the second two show the thickness of the arrow wall in hundredths of an inch. (All measurements concerning bows and arrows are in old fashioned Imperial style. The reason is that the vast majority of the world's archery equipment is made in the USA, where metrication has still not been accepted, which makes things easier for all us old-fashioned archers.) The thinnest shafts are in the 1511 area, suitable for a child's recurve bow, while the thickest are up in the region of 2514 which is suitable for an unusually heavy recurve in the long draw area. The range of sizes available in between these can be found in the manufacturer's matrix chart which is in all the dealers' catalogues. This enables anyone, with some care, to discover which size arrow they should choose for any weight of bow combined with any draw length. Each size of arrow can be shot in a fairly narrow range of draw weights, and arrows can also be selected from this chart according to whether one shoots a recurve or compound, whether the compound has round wheels, hard cams or soft cams, or whether it is being shot with fingers or a release aid, since all these factors will affect the arrow spine.

The straightness of the shaft is not quite as important as may be thought. It is perfectly possible, with a good arrow-straightening jig, to make an arrow shaft straight to within half a thousandth of an inch over its whole length. One manufacturer states the straightness on his boxes, but they are only to about .004 inches per foot, which is not very straight, and this is considered perfectly adequate. The accuracy of the arrow is affected by so many other factors that straightness is not critical, especially if all the arrows in a set are shooting to the same level of accuracy.

It may be necessary to shoot several types of arrow for a while until you find something suitable; the most expensive may not be the best for your requirements. The complex arrow selection chart produced by the Easton company makes it clear that it is not to be totally relied on for choice of arrows. Some of the archery dealers provide a computerized arrow selection service, where by giving details of the specifications of the bow being shot, you can obtain a range of suitable arrow sizes and specifications to match.

Aluminium arrows are made in several ranges, each with its own name and each of a specific colour. Years ago, all alloys were the same colour – aluminium – but for some time they have been made in anodized finishes so that each range can be distinguished by a specific colour. These ranges are important to know about, since each has different qualities and a different price. The main factor is their tensile strength. This is normally how much a metal resists stretching or pulling but in the case of arrow shafts it is an indication of the hardness of the alloy and its resistance to bending. The important of this was brought home to me very early in my archery career when a new set of arrows arrived in the post. I eagerly unpacked them, then took them outside to test them on my garden range. As I shot each one I was astonished to see it curve in flight and land 2 feet to the right in the target. On going down to the target, I saw that each arrow was now bent in a long even curve. The dealer and I concluded that arrows of the wrong spine had been sent and my bow had bent them.

In field archery, arrows sometimes hit trees instead of the target which often bends them. Good-quality arrows, with a high tensile strength, will not bend as easily as cheap ones. Taking your arrows every week to the only person in the club who has an arrow straightener can be embarrassing.

At one time good-quality shafts were swaged at the nock end. This means they were formed into a cone so that the plastic nock could be glued on easily. Today this practice has been discarded in order to keep the price down and now the ends are open but an alloy ring is inserted and the nock, of a different design, is inserted into that. This does not affect the performance of the arrows in any way, but once upon a time, if an arrow struck the nock of another, it usually split the nock and slid harmlessly off the tapered surface beneath. The new design means that there is a far greater chance of the point penetrating the shaft of the other arrow and possibly splitting that as well. However, since this is a fairly rare event it is not worth worrying about. Most damage occurs to arrows when others strike them and cause grooves. There is little that can be done about this, but using high-quality high-tensile shafts certainly helps to prevent too much damage. It has to be admitted,

though, that the most expensive alloy high-tensile shafts while difficult to bend, are also liable to crack, especially if hit by another
arrow which slides down it. They can also break where others
might only bend, but this again is a fairly rare occurrence.

A rather special type of arrow shaft has appeared in recent
years: a large diameter shaft with thin walls to reduce the weight as
much as possible. The purpose is to obtain higher scores, mainly
at indoor target shoots. The rules for scoring say that an arrow that
is actually outside the line defining a higher scoring area but
touching or breaking into it, gets that score. Thicker arrows will
therefore stand a better chance of gaining higher scores. However,
it must be said that these arrows are not very robust and are hardly
suitable for field archery although since the same scoring rules
apply, some people might find them worth a try.

A wide range of good-quality arrows, of whatever material, is
available from the archery dealers in several forms. They can, of
course, be purchased as fully made-up sets, usually of eight,
although in the USA they come in sets of a dozen. They can also
be purchased singly or in any quantity required. They can be
bought more easily as bare shafts, and all the other bits can be
chosen to your personal taste, such as nocks in a huge range of
colours as well as fletchings, also in a wide range of colours, in plastic or feathers. Points or piles can also be chosen and thus you can
make up your own arrows to your own specifications, which is why
any two archers' arrows are hardly ever identical.

Fletchings for alloys are usually plastic but feathers are also
used. Feathers have the problem of degradation when wet, when
they flatten to the shaft and become useless, although there is a
silicon spray available to waterproof them. Plastic fletchings work
well but some have to be replaced since they become distorted if
they go through a target butt. Some types are more resistant to
this than others. Only experimenting will tell you which ones are
best. They come in a range of sizes for different-sized arrows.
Generally, there is little point in fitting fletchings which are too
big for the shafts since these will only create more drag from air
resistance, without adding to stability. However, this can be useful
when shooting short distances, as large feather fletchings can
make the arrows stable and accurate more quickly than smaller
ones. This is a common technique at American indoor shoots.
The drag induced by the big fletchings can produce greater accu-

racy, by damping vibration, but over longer distances, they slow down the shaft.

Nocks are all plastic and are usually pretty tough. They do not crack easily, but it is worth checking them before shooting, as one may become cracked by being struck by another arrow. If an arrow with a cracked nock is shot the nock may break and the arrow fly off at an alarming and dangerous angle. Nocks are usually fitted to the shaft so that, with the arrow nocked on the string, one fletching is out at right angles to the bow while the other two slide flat across it. If you are using a compound bow with one of the highly advanced all adjustable arrow launchers fitted, however, you may need to pay some attention to the angle of the fletchings. Some launchers require arrows with one fletch pointing down through the twin prongs, while others require one fletch to be in the vertical position. Sometimes it is simply a matter of turning the nock slightly to get the required angle. Some nocks are made with an indicator on one side so that they can be fitted on the shaft aligned with the cock feather – the one at right angles to the bow. They are also usually made as clip-ons, with a slightly keyhole-shaped slot which helps to hold them on the string.

Nocks should not be too tight on the string as this will affect their performance when leaving the bow. Nor, of course, should they be too loose, but this is a simple matter to cure since it only requires some thread or dental floss to be wound round the nocking point on the bowstring to take up any looseness. Sometimes one can bite the nock and gently squeeze the sides together, but this is not really desirable since it may produce variations in the performance of the arrows. Correctly fitted nocks are the best answer. There should really be no difficulty about this, since they are available in a range of sizes to fit every size of shaft. A new type of nock that can be inserted in the shaft and tightened by a screw inserted into it seems a useful idea.

If you are shooting a compound bow, nocks need to be chosen with care since the shortness of these bows produces a sharp angle of string at full draw and arrow nocks can fall off the string if their slot is too short. This needs to be checked before shooting new nocks.

Distorted fletchings need to be replaced as soon as possible, since they do little for accuracy and can add considerably to wind resistance, as can be judged if an arrow with distorted fletchings passes nearby at high speed; the sound can be quite dramatic.

Piles, or points, come in different weights and here choice is entirely a matter of personal preference. Heavy piles can affect the performance of the shaft by making it more flexible and are thus suited to a lighter draw weight; conversely, lighter piles may make them suit a heavier bow. Surprisingly, this does not seem to be very widely known in the field archery world. Some experimentation may be necessary if you are inclined that way, but most archers are happy to stick with one size. A change to a different weight will, of course, affect the flight of the arrow; it will fly higher or lower than before.

When measuring the length of shaft required, it should be noted that shafts are measured from the lowest depth of the nock to the end of the shaft, excluding the pile. There will need to be a minimum of about ½ inch of arrow left to overhang the arrow rest or launcher for safety. Any less is risky since it is easy to pull the arrow further than usual and pull it off the rest.

Alloy shafts need to be checked frequently for straightness since they can easily become slightly bent without the archer being aware of the fact, and they will lose accuracy. An arrow-straightening jig is expensive, but it can be immensely useful over the years. If you suspect that your arrows are not quite straight, there are several simple methods of checking them. One is to roll them on a flat surface, preferably a mirror since this will double the effect of any inaccuracy and make bends more obvious. If they are badly bent, of course, it will be obvious, but even a slight bend will prevent them from rolling smoothly. Another method, usually used by experienced archers, is to spin the arrow vertically on the palm of the hand. This reveals wobble at the other end, which can also be felt on the hand. A straight arrow will spin smoothly without any sensation of movement. An arrow straightener takes skill and practice to use, since the shaft has to be bent back in the opposite direction to any bends and the differing strengths of different arrows make it very easy to overdo the bend and take it too far the opposite way. Only practice can overcome this. One type of straightener operates like a pair of pliers without any gauge but this too takes considerable practice to master and needs constant checking for accuracy.

It is surprising how badly bent arrows can be made straight and perfectly usable again. Archers sometimes regard a bent arrow as beyond hope but are surprised when a expert with an arrow straightener renders is shootable again. Dents are another matter. A dented shaft can sometimes be beyond repair because it will break easily on the dent when attempts are made to straighten it. Although I have a couple of times succeeded in removing dents by hammering a closely fitting steel rod down the shaft, this is not something I would recommend.

The anodized finish on most good-quality shafts not only serves to distinguish one type of arrow from another but also acts as an anti-corrosive. It is not simply a coating; if it is done properly it will have penetrated into the surface of the metal. This will take considerable use to wear away; in fact, on some arrows it hardly ever wears off, although it can be removed by scratching or rubbing. This means that if arrows are lost on a club's permanent field course they may well still be reusable if they recovered before they have time to start corroding. They may only need new fletchings, nocks and piles. But check the shafts carefully for corrosion before attempting to restore them. On some cheaper arrows the coating is not always of the best quality and may wear more rapidly than on the more expensive variety. If the shafts have been out in the open for some time, they may have started to form a white powder on the surface. This corrosion is not the same as rust on the surface of steel; it may well penetrate right through the wall of the shaft, making the arrow unsafe to shoot again. Try removing the pile and nock, scraping off the corrosion and filling the shaft with water. If it leaks, the shaft is not safe, and should be scrapped.

Carbon Arrows

Carbon arrows are another gift of modern technology, developed not long after the discovery that long strands of carbon were extremely tough and resistant to bending. This factor was applied to bow limbs first and arrows followed soon after. Some were of carbon tube, very thin and lighter in weight than alloy arrows, while some were of carbon laid round a thin core tube of aluminium alloy. These arrows have several advantages over alloys, the first being their strength.

Arrows can be purchased ready made to the required diameter and length, but the archer can also buy them uncut, in lengths of 33 inches, and cut them down to the required length. They are resistant to bending and shock, so they are very suitable for field archery. In normal use they do not have to be checked for suspected bends; they can be assumed to be perfectly straight at all times. Their thinner shafts have less wind resistance and some archers claim that they are inherently more accurate than alloy shafts. It is noticeable that they have almost entirely supplanted aluminium alloy shafts in use by top-scoring archers. Their one big drawback is their cost, since they are more expensive – some types very much more expensive – than alloys of even the highest quality. They can be a very worthwhile investment to a field archer who is shooting a compound bow and who has reached the stage of very rarely missing the target, but for the beginner they should be considered carefully.

Carbon arrows can be made up in the same way as alloys, but greater care should be taken when cutting them with a razor saw. I have found it useful to wrap masking tape round the shaft before attempting to saw through, and afterwards removing the tape very carefully so as not to pull carbon fibres off with it. It also helps if the shaft is slowly rotated while sawing gently, rather than trying to hack through it in one pass.

Care should be taken when working with carbon arrows or even when picking up broken ones, since the carbon fibres are very thin and sharp and can get into the skin very easily. They are often difficult to remove as well as painful.

Carbon arrows do bend, of course, but not often. When bent they are extremely difficult to straighten in a normal arrow-straightening jig, since great care has to be taken not to bend them too far. The carbon fibres break quite easily under the right conditions so only very slight bends are removable.

Great care should be taken when removing carbon arrows from wood such as trees. The wood should be cut away carefully until the shaft can be withdrawn with a straight pull. On no account should it be jiggled about to loosen it. It will not stand this treatment and will break far more easily than an alloy shaft.

Points or piles have been a rather vexed aspect of the design of carbon arrows. The thinness of the shafts means that it is easier to make points which fit over them, and this means that the points can punch a hole through a target which does not grip the shaft, since it is of a larger diameter, and the shaft will go right through and disappear – sometimes for ever. Fitting points that insert into the shaft can cure this problem. I would suggest that if the arrows of your choice cannot be fitted with inset piles, you choose another type.

Each type of carbon arrow comes with a wide range of points to choose from, all of different weights. The weights are expressed in grains. Bearing in mind that light points will allow the arrows to fly higher than heavy ones it is entirely up to you to choose which you prefer.

Some of the more expensive carbon shafts are barrelled, i.e. tapered from the centre towards each end. This is to reduce the weight while retaining the strength. It is noticeable that carbon arrows are more advantageous at the longer ranges since only then does their lighter weight become more apparent.

New carbon arrows now available have piles that decrease the spine rating, and nocks that can increase it. This offers new opportunities for fine-tuning arrows to match the bow weight. New types of carbon arrows are also appearing which offer greater strength and stiffness than previously known.

Fibreglass Arrows

Fibreglass arrows first appeared many years ago and were used by some field archers until they discovered that they were not strong enough for what was demanded of them. When striking branches they often disintegrated in a quite spectacular manner. In recent years fibreglass shafts have reappeared, sold as beginners' practice arrows. They are well suited to this task since the new ones are tough and difficult to break and they do not bend. They are probably unsuited to normal field archery since they lack the precision and uniformity of construction demanded of high-quality arrows. They are made in only one shaft diameter, but in several lengths. They are described in the dealers' catalogues as suitable for bow weights from 25 to 40 pounds, and are fitted with one size of brass pile and one size of nock, so they offer little scope for customizing to individual requirements.

Quivers

A quiver is an essential piece of equipment for the field archer, although no one will care what it is made from. Target archers can,

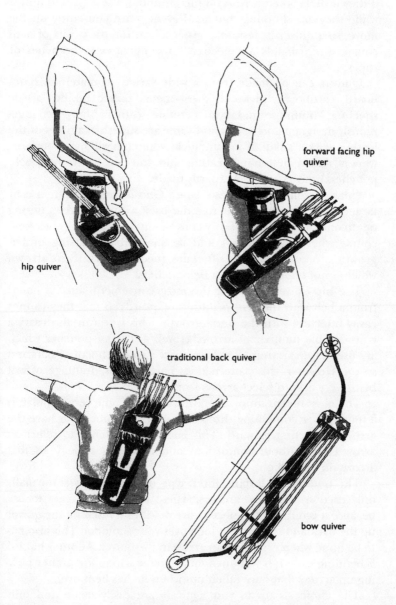

hip quiver

forward facing hip quiver

traditional back quiver

bow quiver

Fig. 9 Types of quiver

if they wish, lay their arrows on the ground or use a ground quiver while they are shooting, but field archers are constantly on the move, so a quiver is desirable, especially at the tricky bits of field course where hands are needed for clinging onto branches or ropes.

Quivers can be made from a wide variety of materials: hardboard, cardboard, plywood, sheet metal, plastic tubing, plastic sheeting, drainpipe and even genuine leather. Many are ingeniously designed and made, and some are superb examples of the leather worker's skill. If you are lucky your club will have someone who is skilled in tooling leather and you can get quiver, belt, pouches, bracers, etc., all expertly made.

Quivers come in four basic types. One is intended for use by target archers and hangs across the back with the arrows jutting out to one side. This is not very convenient on a closely grown field course where the arrows could be snagged on passing undergrowth. Moreover, they are often designed to hold only six arrows, which is not enough for most field archers.

The hip quiver is one of the most convenient since it hangs from a belt with the arrows jutting rearwards so that they cannot easily interfere with the undergrowth. This type can also carry a considerable number of arrows as well as having pouches which are useful for carrying Allen keys, spare strings, chocolate bars and so on. However, this pattern does have the disadvantage of not being very easy to select arrows from.

The most recent innovation, which has become very popular, is a long quiver containing three or four plastic tubes that have the arrows projecting forward. This enables the archer to select an arrow easily without contortions and it is long enough so that arrows do not fall out.

The traditional 'Robin Hood' type of back quiver is normally only used by longbow archers. These are not very easy to use because it is difficult to select an arrow without hitching the quiver up the back and straining to look over your shoulder. This also has to be done when replacing an arrow in the quiver. Another hazard is bending over. It is not uncommon to see a longbow archer picking up arrows that have fallen out when he has bent over.

The choice is up to you. Quivers are easily made and only require a little maintenance by emptying out rubbish such as twigs and leaves occasionally. One fitted with pockets will be most useful.

Bowsights

Relatively few field archers shoot with sights, many preferring to be as traditional as they can, without the encumbrance of gadgets. Some field organizations encourage the use of sights by shooting marked distance rounds in which sights are very useful; indeed, such rounds are not really appropriate for those *without* sights. Freestyle (recurve bows with sights, mainly target bows) compound limited and compound unlimited are virtually the only classes which use sights. The freestyle class is very small in some organizations and compound unlimited archers are not a large group.

Sights come in two major groups. The first are designed for use on recurve bows. The other are much more robust and for use on compounds, which have considerable vibration and thus require that all their bits are firmly screwed in place.

Good sights are expensive, since they are precision made, and have mechanisms for adjusting vertically as well as horizontally. Those with a quick-release device for the vertical adjustment are the most useful for field archery, since the sight often has to be moved for every shot. A good one will last for many years. Many have extension arms to push them well in front of the bow. This is a useful feature because it puts the sight further from the eye and thus makes for more accurate aiming. Some sights are equipped with a scale marked in inches or centimetres. If these are left in place the archer then has to carry a card with his distance marks on it and needs to refer to it to adjust the sight. This fiddly and time-consuming performance, it has always seemed to me, is quite unnecessary if one takes off the scale strip, which can usually be done quite easily, and substitutes a blank strip upon which distances can be marked in metres or yards or in any scale desired. I have found that a strip of thin polystyrene sheet is very useful. Distances can be marked on this in pencil, which will not be rubbed off easily or come off in the wet, but can be removed with an eraser if required, and which can easily be changed.

The scale can be marked in yard or metre intervals from 10 up to 80. This is likely to be sufficient since field targets further than 80 yards are extremely rare and the distances from 20 to 50 yards are most likely to be used.

It will be found that careful positioning of the sight is necessary. All metal risers or handles have drilled and tapped holes for fitting sights, all to standard sizes. Thus there is no choice of arm position for the sight, but if the scale is too far down it will soon become obvious that there is a lack of clearance beneath the sight for the arrow to pass. This may require an adjustment of shooting style by moving the anchor point further down in order to get the longer distances on the sight, which is only likely on a compound bow.

Sight marks will change if almost anything else is changed – arrows, anchor point, bowstring, release – so recalibration is frequently necessary. This is not a problem if a marked distance range is available, as in many clubs. But without a range, it is advisable to make as few changes as possible.

Sights come in several forms. Some are simple open pin sights, some are rings and the most sophisticated have magnifying scope lenses fitted as well as spirit levels. The latter help indicate whether the bow is upright, especially useful when shooting across slopes when the angle of the bow may be difficult to judge. Scope sights are usually only used on compound bows and there is a considerable variety on sale. Some have a black surround, designed to keep out unwanted light. I have not found these very useful since they also keep out light when it is needed and often make targets difficult to see. Probably the best is the type with a clear plastic mounting ring. The large ones that are now available are wonderful, since they present a very big view of the target and do not suffer quite so much when rain gets on them. They can be used in conjunction with a peep sight (see below).

Lens power is an important consideration when choosing a scope sight. Most have a range of lenses of different powers to choose from. They should be tried out before purchasing, because simply choosing the most powerful may not be a good idea. It will soon be found that the strongest lenses, like the strongest binoculars, are problematical in use since the slightest movement hinders focusing on the target. A middling size may be better, since it is easier to hold it on target.

It may be found that, on a field course, there is less requirement for the lateral adjustment of the sight, for wind is often not felt so strongly in trees and the shooting distances are shorter than in target archery, so once the lateral position is set there is often little need to disturb it.

A type of sight that is growing in popularity is the hunting or multi-pin sight. This is an American invention and takes the place of adjustable sights. They come with a number of pins, usually four but often more, which can be fixed at different ranges, e.g. 20, 30, 40 or 50 yards. They can be altered, but not easily. One draws up the bow after estimating the target distance and brings one of the pins onto the target. For example, if a target is estimated, on an unmarked distance round, to be about 40 yards, then the 40 yard sight pin is brought down onto the target. The gap between pins is usually not great, so it is easy to confuse them and practice is needed to avoid this. It is possible, of course, to shoot a target between pins. Normally bows with this type of sight are shot with fingers rather than a release aid, but if one wished to shoot with a release as well as pins one would be able to do so in the unlimited class. The NFAS rules permit a separate class for bows fitted with hunting sights, as 'compound limited'. Some unlimited archers have taken up this type of sight, claiming that it is easier to use and requires little fiddling about during the course of a shoot.

Peepsights

If you intend to shoot a compound with sights, it is useful to fit a peepsight into the string. This acts as a rear sight through which to view the front sight and is a considerable aid to greater accuracy. It serves to avoid the problem of seeing through or round the string. This is easier on a recurve bow since the strings are thinner, but because of its power, the compound needs a thicker string, which therefore becomes more difficult to see round. A peepsight should be chosen which is easy to see through. Some have very small holes which may be suitable under good lighting conditions, but this is not always the case in woodland. Peepsights reduce the available light, so choose one which is suitable for the intended purpose. They are fitted into the string and bound tightly into it when their optimum position has been found by drawing up and looking through them at the front sight. This binding into the string is most important since it both prevents the peep from pulling out of position when the bow is drawn and avoids it causing an accident. One well-known American archer has a horror story about someone losing an eye when an unsecured peepsight shot out of the string, bounced off the bow limb and came back at him with tremendous force.

Some peepsights are attached to part of the bow by a rubber

tube. This intriguing device is for turning the sight into line at full draw. The tube can be a nuisance and can wrap itself round the string, gradually causing wear, unless the string is protected by something such as plastic tape. The rubber tube needs to be carefully adjusted for correct length so that it is not under too much stretch when at full draw. If this type of peepsight is used, it is advisable to carry a spare length of tubing, since breakages are common.

There are other types of peepsight, but they need to be tried for effectiveness. One type has a facility for changing the size of the viewing aperture.

Bowstrings

It might be imagined that bowstrings are a simple subject and could look after themselves. This is not so, for they get worn in various ways and sometimes need replacing.

It is vital for a bow to be fitted with the correct length of string. If it is too short the bow will be overstressed and may well break, as well as being unable to work efficiently. If the string is too long, the bow will again not work efficiently, but might give you some unpleasant sensations along the arm where the string will strike. The string length affects the bracing height, the distance from the nocking point to the arrow rest. For every bow the bracing height is different, but there is sometimes a manufacturer's recommended height or at least string length. On recurve bows, a string that is too short will soon be obvious by being difficult to string on the bow and the archer will, if he has had very much experience, soon be aware of something not quite right. The bracing height has a great effect on both the bow and the arrows, and the draw length will not be correct either; it will affect the feel of the bow. For most recurve bows, the bracing height will be somewhere in the range of 8–10 inches, while for compound bows the height may be more specific for each model, owing to the variation in handle designs. A bow with a stable, forward-curved handle riser will have a high bracing height, while those designed with a backward-curved handle will have far shorter bracing heights, which will deliver the bow's power to the arrow much more quickly, and thus give a faster arrow flight.

Longbow strings were traditionally made of hemp and are still sometimes made from linen but it is more common now to make them from Dacron which is less subject to wear. This material is also used for recurve bows and compounds, but more man-made fibres are appearing so the choice is becoming wider. Some of these fibres have different qualities, such as low stretch, but they need to be used within the recommended limits since some have limited lives and need to be replaced after a specified number of shots. It is advisable to discover what type of string is on a bow when you purchase it. When Kevlar strings first appeared they had very short lives and had to be replaced frequently, so they soon fell out of favour. Fastflight soon replaced them and has proved to be more durable. Some of these new materials have been described as stronger than steel – so strong in fact that bows could be tested to destruction when fitted with them, whereas when fitted with Dacron and steel cables, the cables broke first.

It was found to be possible to use thinner and lighter strings with the new materials, with fewer strands, which means that the problem of seeing round or through the string is reduced.

Dacron B50 is a standard material for beginners' bows. For bows up to 34 pounds draw weight, ten strands, and for those over that weight 12 strands, are more common. Fastflight is now the most popular bowstring material. It has minimal stretch and is durable, strong and fast. On many compound bows it has replaced steel cables, which broke more easily. A blend of HMPE and Vectran is 450 Premium, which will not stretch or creep. Use two or four strands fewer than Fastflight to get the same diameter. Dynaflight will have the same durability as Fastflight but with less creep. S4 bowstring material is a composite blend of Fastflight, Vectran and Kevlar, which will settle approximately $1/16$ inch and then show no further creep. It will last about 25,000 shots, by which time it may have outlasted the bow! A field archer shooting about 100 arrows a week will be quite satisfied with such a performance. Ten or twelve strands will give the equivalent of eighteen to twenty strands of Fastflight. A thinner string is an advantage on a compound bow since it may enable the archer to dispense with a peepsight. Angel Dyneema has slightly more stretch than Fastflight and is more forgiving in giving a softer shot. It needs to be 5 millimetres shorter than Fastflight and because each strand is lighter, two to four extra strands will be needed to give the same weight string.

For those archers who enjoy making their own strings, these new materials have the disadvantage of being far more expensive to purchase in reels. However, bowstrings of any of these materials are available from all dealers in any size the archer specifies.

Strings require maintenance, which should be done by frequently examining them for wear and chafing. If any is found, treat the string with suspicion and attempt to assess how serious the problem may be. If it is not too bad, try rubbing the string with beeswax or an equivalent preservative made especially for artificial fibres, to minimize the effect. However, this is not advised if the wear is in a critical area such as the end loops, since a break could easily occur there, or in the centre where the nocking point fits. The centre area of a string is always bound with thread or nylon monofilament to reinforce it and prevent wear from the arrow nocks and armguard. Nocking areas do wear, and centre serving made from hard nylon monofilament can eventually be worn right through, so this needs to be replaced at times.

It is perfectly possible for a handyman archer to make his own bowstrings by making or buying a jig for the purpose. Such a jig is easily made and simplifies production of bowstrings. However, although strings for recurve bows are relatively simple, as are compound strings of the type which hook onto steel cables, those that run round cams and wheels are more tricky since they often need considerable lengths of serving to reinforce them. If this is not applied properly it will creep and separate on the wheels and expose the string beneath to wear. It is also important to get the string the correct length, which can be tricky when attempting to calculate how much it may stretch and how much the serving will shorten it.

Bowstrings are delicate and need careful handling. Never lean a bow against a tree with the string touching the bark. It is possible for some tree bark to cut like razors through strands of string, and ruin the day. Never put any sort of cutting edge near a bowstring – it is only too easy to make one careless move with it, and the string will be gone. Remember that, when under tension, it will be far easier to cut through it. Even one cut strand will weaken it. A good Dacron string will last for years if it is looked after, and will only need the serving replaced once a year or so.

Even string colours are important. Try shooting with a brand new white string with the sun high behind you and you might soon decide that black is more practical. Some of the newer strings are being made in very colourful mixtures which are useful for seeing the twists in them.

A string should be twisted to give it some extra strength but only for a maximum of about ten turns. The number of turns is critical to the performance of the bow, as mentioned previously, and if you aspire to really accurate and consistent shooting, it is worth spending some time experimenting with your bow's performance at different twists of the string, since there is an optimum number. Twisting the string will shorten the bow and put more stress on it, as well as changing the bracing height. On a recurve bow, 1 inch difference in string length will alter the bracing height by a similar amount, and this will alter the performance not only of the bow but of the arrow as well, since it will not be drawn the same distance as before.

Some of the compound bow string systems, in which steel cables have been replaced by man-made fibre strings which pass over the wheels, have some degree of stretch in them because of their sheer length, so the use of low-stretch strings is somewhat negated, or so it is thought by some experts. For compound bows, strings are critical and it is worth ensuring that they are bought from a reputable source or maker and looked after with care. A recent idea for compound strings is designed to prevent them from twisting as the bow is drawn by making the string in two equal thicknesses but twisting one in the opposite direction from the other, so that any tendency to twist is counteracted. This is most useful for some types of peep sight that require a non-twisting string in order to be seen through.

Stabilizers

Stabilizers are allowed on different types of bow according to different rules, so it is wise to check what is permitted on your choice of bow by your favourite governing body before buying them. All the three governing bodies permit any sort of stabilizer with both freestyle and compound unlimited classes, and some allow them in other classes with some restrictions in length.

Stabilizers serve several purposes. One is to balance the bow, another is to absorb shock, recoil, vibration and other undesirable movement when the string is loosed. The balance can be felt at full draw, but the other aspects can be felt on loosing. A good stabilizer system needs some experimentation. The huge range of equipment available today gives much to choose from. There are stabilizers of varying lengths. Some are tubes filled with foam, powders or liquids, while others are simply rods with removable weights that can be changed according to taste. The most recent type, which is said to be very effective in absorbing vibration consists of a number of thin rods joined at the ends. These often have sliding weights fitted so that they can be moved according to preference.

Stabilizers can be fitted to bows in several positions: top and bottom of the riser, back below the hand, in front below the hand etc. The most effective and popular system seems to be a long rod, lightly weighted and balanced by two shorter ones out to the rear. This works very well to balance the bow so that, on releasing, it stays where it is and does not fall forward or, worse, fall backwards. The rear twin stabilizers can also, when adjusted to the right angle and if long enough, serve to stand the bow on when it is not in use. It seems to be another case of 'You pays your money and takes your choice', but without doubt stabilizers can add to the comfort of shooting a bow despite adding extra weight to it. Some experimenting may be necessary to see which arrangement suits you best, but can usually only be done over a length of time by borrowing from other archers.

Some archers feel that a long stabilizer is an encumberance when working through vegetation, undergrowth, bushes and trees, and there is no doubt that care must often be taken to hold the bow in such a way as to reduce snagging, but you soon become accustomed to it. Most compound bows are uncomfortable to shoot without a stabilizer system, but many recurves can be shot quite well without them.

Falls are possible on field courses, and it is best to fall without damaging the bow or other equipment. So, if an archer falls, he throws up his arms to save the bow, rather than putting his hands down to break the fall. If stabilizers are fitted to the bow, there is a good chance, when falling forwards, of the stabilizer hitting the ground first and being bent or even breaking off completely. This can ruin a day's shooting, so it is wise to attempt to throw up the bow before your body hits the ground. Some archers have developed this into an art form. In addition, it has been known for an archer to hurl his bow to the ground in rage. This is frowned upon, and can also have surprising results, since a strung bow is somewhat like a coiled spring, and on hitting the ground at a suitable angle, it can rebound skywards to an astonishing height, shedding string and stabilizers as it gains altitude. A request for an encore is usually not greeted by a positive response!

Bow Slings

A bow sling is not essential for most field archers, and is mainly confined to those who shoot freestyle class. Slings are used to prevent any muscle tension in the hand transferring to the bow by shooting with an open hand. The sling prevents the bow from falling forward when the arrow is loosed. There are three basic designs. One is a leather strap buckled round the bow handle below the grip, with a sling that passes over the wrist. The hand has to be inserted into this before taking a shot, so it can be a nuisance until one becomes accustomed to it. The second type is similar, being a cord fastened round the bow handle and hooked round the wrist. The third type is a sling of leather or similar material that has a loop at each end, one loop going over the thumb of the bow hand, the other over the forefinger when holding the bow. I have never seen this third type used by a field archer.

The technique for shooting with a sling requires that the archer is relaxed when the shot is made and does not snatch the bow back as it starts to move forward; the sling is adjusted to prevent this movement. It should not be too tight so that it pulls the hand down. Slings can be very useful to freestyle archers and could also be used by compound shooters, but few seem to favour their use.

Arrows Rests and Launchers

For some bows arrow rests are simple and may consist merely of a plastic 'tongue' stuck onto the side of the bow for the arrow to slide over, without there being any means of adjustment. For target bows and freestyle class, rests may be more complex and consist of not only the plastic rest but a plunger that is screwed through the riser and bears sideways against the arrow. This plunger is usually spring loaded so that it absorbs some of the sideways energy imparted to the arrow when it is loosed from the fingers. It helps to minimize the effects of a poor loose. It is most useful for adjusting the spines of arrows and taking up a change from one spine to another (i.e. changing from one thickness of arrow to another with a different degree of flexibility). It can be screwed in or out to push arrows to shoot further to the left or to allow them to shoot to the right. In fact, it is a most useful device. Often they come with a set of springs, one of which is fitted internally and this too can be adjusted to increase or decrease the pressure on the arrow. In this way, there are two methods of adjustment allowing the use of a wider range of arrows with one bow. If you intend using one, it is better to choose a good-quality plunger which is not likely to stick and possibly cause arrows to start shooting at the wrong target.

Arrow rests for compound bows have naturally developed much further. They are bolted onto the bow riser, and many are adjustable sideways and vertically, some with measuring scales. Many of those intended for shooting with release aids have spring-loaded hinged arrow supports that move vertically. Some have devices for moving the support away from below the arrow when it is moving over the bow, to create clearance. There is a choice of supports, some being forked or pronged, some merely a single narrow arm. There is a wide range to choose from and it will take some time to discover which you might prefer or which is most suited to your style of shooting. It is a good idea to ensure that you obtain the right type – whether it is for use with a release or with fingers – since the two are quite different. The most important aspect of the release-type launcher is its design for shooting an arrow straight with no side play. Try to choose one that will give the arrow positive support and prevent it from falling off too easily or being blown off. Some are tricky to hold the arrow on if a bad draw is made.

Since these launchers have arms that can be adjusted for vertical position this means that they can change in relation to the string nocking point, so before making any adjustment it is a good idea to measure the position in some way. This may ensure that the relationship is not changed, otherwise it may be necessary to check all the arrow flight conditions again, or recalibrate sightmarks.

Clickers

Clickers tend to be used only by those who are shooting in the freestyle class. They are properly known as draw-check indicators, meaning that they are devised to tell the archer when he has reached his correct draw length so as to prevent under- or over-drawing, either of which will result in the arrows not flying a consistent height. The clicker is simply a thin metal blade screwed to the bow handle. The arrow, when nocked on the string, lies beneath it. When adjusted to the correct position, the clicker falls off the point when the arrow is drawn the desired distance. This tells the archer when he has reached full draw. The majority of people who use them find them useful as a signal when to loose, so they are used as a trigger device, as an audible signal.

They are most useful for helping with target shyness, when an archer develops the habit of loosing too soon. The clicker tends to prevent the arrow from being shot prematurely, before it is drawn through. The archer comes to nearly full draw, holds his aim on the target, gradually draws the arrow from beneath the clicker, then looses when the sound is heard. Usually the clicker will be set so that the arrow only has to be drawn an extra $1/8$ inch or so. However, it takes considerable practice to get used to one, and at the commencement of shooting, before the muscles become tired, it is easy to draw through the clicker prematurely. Later, when fatigue has started to set in, the effort required to draw that arrow just another $1/8$ inch becomes almost superhuman. Nevertheless, the clicker is a very simple and effective bit of equipment. Unfortunately, they are far more difficult to use when using release aids on compound bows. The technique required for drawing through a clicker, then triggering a release, is difficult to learn. Moreover, a compound, by the manner of its working, with the arrow at full drawn when the string is in the valley, rarely needs a draw check indicator anyway. As a means of curing target shyness with a compound, therefore, it becomes less useful.

Chestguards

Chestguards are triangular pieces of fabric, often nylon net or leather, which are designed to protect the chest from the string.

They are held in place by a strap over one shoulder and another round the chest and back. They are used more often by target archers than field archers, to allow the string to slide smoothly across the chest without catching on items of clothing or the body. It may only be necessary for a style of shooting which involves standing very straight upright and holding the bow in such a way so that the bowstring slides over the chest.

Other Equipment

There is a vast range of other gadgets available. The dealers' catalogues are full of them, and so, of course, are their shops. They are all very fascinating, and sometimes baffling, and new bits for the bow are constantly appearing. Some are worth a try and some are too expensive to buy just to see if they work. Moreover, what works for one archer may not work for another, so be careful of other people's recommendations.

A good knife is always useful, often for digging arrows out of wood, whether it is trees or target supports. A stainless steel blade is best so that you do not have to keep cleaning rust off – field archery can often be wet.

Clothing should be a serious consideration for the budding field archer. Big baggy jackets with lots of flaps and lapels are out, as is anything else that can catch on the bowstring as it springs forward. Shooting jackets are fine, again so long as there is nothing to catch the string. Those with lots of pockets are very useful for carrying spare bits such as strings, glue, tabs, releases, score cards, pencils etc., and if there are pockets big enough to keep hands warm all the better. I find a thick one for winter and a thinner one for warmer weather is a good arrangement, with a sweater or two underneath when necessary. One of these should be thick but not loose-fitting. Jeans are not a good idea since they are not very warm, but the outdoor trousers that are now available, often with lots of useful zip pockets, are very good. One type I have found especially useful is made from a thin cotton material that is both very tough and also has amazing drying properties. Another type has a very warm lining and is excellent in cold weather.

Hats are useful in the cold, and broad brimmed hats that keep the rain out are amazingly good when shooting in the wet, since they keep rain off the face and this makes one feel better and helps the vision.

Boots are important. Field shoots often cover considerable distances and often the terrain is difficult, wet and muddy. Wellington boots are not a good idea since they do not keep the feet warm and often cause excessive sweating, as well as not fitting too well. The best answer seems to be a pair of good-quality walking boots that will keep out the worst of the water, provide a good grip on muddy slopes and feel comfortable for many hours. If they are worn with two pairs of socks, one thin with a thicker pair over them, cold feet should no longer be a problem. This also helps to prevent getting sore feet and blisters.

Some archers prefer to wear thermal underwear when it is really cold, and this may be a good idea.

Gloves are a problem when shooting, since there are few which are really suitable and they can take away all the necessary feeling. One answer might be woollen mitts that have a removable finger section. This can be taken off for the actual shooting and replaced afterwards. Certainly there are conditions when gloves are essential so it is my belief that a pair that can be worn between shots can be most useful. The modern metal bow handles have exacerbated the problem of shooting in cold weather.

The decision on what to wear for field archery is made more difficult by the fact that on some shoots movement is very slow and there may be long cold waits between targets, while on others there may be a constant steady movement, sometimes a very active uphill movement; overheating then becomes a problem. Sometimes the day starts cold and rapidly warms so one is never sure of being suitably dressed. Some wet-weather clothing is necessary, and only good quality stuff will do. Some archers carry large umbrellas and these, though cumbersome when added to everything else being carried, seem to be an excellent idea.

One piece of equipment which some archers find essential is a rake, for working through undergrowth or ground looking for lost arrows. These do not ever seem to have been available in the dealers' shops and are always home made. It is a simple matter to make one by bending a thin steel rod over in a vice to form an arm about 2 inches long and hammering on a wooden handle. A long screwdriver might serve. It can be carried easily in the quiver but it is not advisable to carry it hanging from the belt, especially if it is a long one; it can be an accident waiting to happen.

One last item of equipment, which has been traditional for many years, is a woollen tassel hung from the belt or quiver. These were originally intended for wiping arrows clean after plunging into something other than a target, but evolved into a pure decoration. Target archers traditionally preferred green tassels, but field archers often chose more colourful wools for theirs. They seem to have gone out of use in recent years and are not seen as often now. For field archers, they often slowly disappear as strands of wool get caught on thorns and twigs.

In place of these, many archers carry a piece of cloth such as a small towel for wiping arrows and bow. These can be especially useful for cleaning sight lenses when they are wet.

4 Learning to Shoot

I have serious doubts about the practicality of learning to shoot from a book. It can really only be done in person; anything a book can say can only be a rough guide to a complex process. A good instructor is far better than a book, no matter how much experience the writer has had in teaching beginners. There are always subtleties only an instructor can see, and the best instruction is one-to-one. I have always found it difficult to instruct a group, and the larger the group, the more difficult it is. This is mainly because of the problem of trying to watch too many things in too many people. So this is intended only as a basic guide, to back up and reinforce the teaching given by a real live, preferably qualified, instructor.

The process might best be considered from both sides, that of the beginner and that of the instructor. One is attempting to learn a process with many aspects and the other to impart a skill he already possesses. Both require patience and forbearance. One is involved in the process for the first time and may be overwhelmed by a mass of new sensations and information, the other may be involved in a process repeated many times but with highly variable individuals. The instructor needs to approach the beginner with sympathy. Learning to shoot is not easy; there is a lot to remember at the same time, as in learning to drive. Everyone who learns has come to the situation with different feelings, some with doubt, a few with eagerness, some with determination, some simply with curiosity. Some – and these often are the most difficult to deal with – lack self-confidence and are convinced beforehand that they cannot learn. There are also some who are over-confident. They are rare, but are convinced that they will do well without the aid of the instructor. Thus they are difficult to teach because they do not want to listen or take note.

Most people are eager to learn, however, and it can be difficult to restrain them from shooting far too much at their first session. Some will stand and shoot dozens of arrows in succession if given the chance, and they will soon tire. You need to be aware that there is a limit to what is sensible to shoot at first, and that, normally, most forms of field archery do not require more than four arrows to be shot at one target. You need to take a short break between every few shots. The best way of ensuring this, of course, is to have only four arrows; you will then have a break every time you are obliged to go to the target.

Almost anyone can learn to shoot, even people with physical disabilities. Occasionally one comes across someone who is really weak or not well coordinated, and whose limbs take impossible angles when holding a bow. Every instructor has had one or two pupils he has thought would never learn to shoot, although sometimes this judgement has proved to be wrong.

The basic shooting technique, in simple form, is as follows:

1 Take up the shooting position, sideways to the target, feet apart, about the same width as the shoulders.
2 Bring the bow round to the front of your body, laying it horizontally, window side uppermost (i.e. the cut-out on the bow handle facing upwards).
3 Nock an arrow on the string, at the nocking point, with the arrow on the arrow rest.
4 Place your drawing hand under the string, forefinger above the arrow, the next two fingers below, the string just above the first joint.
5 Bring the bow round to the side and raise it above eye level.
6 Extend your bow arm, without locking it rigid, above eye level, and bring it down to eye level while drawing the string with the other hand, in a movement parallel to the ground.
7 The drawing hand should now be on your face, with the forefinger in the corner of your mouth.
8 Move the bow down so that the target appears high in the bow window.
9 Relax your fingers on the string and let your drawing hand move back on release.

10 Hold the bow in place until the arrow strikes before relaxing and letting the bow down.

11 Continue doing this until you win a national championship.

That is the theory, anyway. Now let us examine it in detail.

You should be welcomed to the club – after all, it is in constant need of new blood and no-one should ever be turned away or treated with disdain. It should have at least one qualified instructor who is prepared to give up time to beginners, explain the basics of field archery, show them round the course, and let them watch others shooting. After this introduction, do you still want to shoot? After all, there is not much point in visiting a club to investigate what is done without learning to shoot. A demonstration of shooting at a couple of field targets should precede the instruction.

Dominant Hand and Eye

The instructor should select a bow of a suitable draw weight and length for your size, first ascertaining whether you are right- or left-handed. A simple test for him is to hand you a bow. It may seem odd, but even a person who has never picked up a bow in their life will usually reach out for one with the hand they would use to hold it when shooting. This is usually the left hand. A left-handed person will usually reach out with the right hand, but just occasionally someone will be undecided. This is probably because they are really left-handed, and many left-handed people have learned to become ambidextrous to differing degrees. Some left-handers are perfectly happy to shoot right-handed, and fewer left-handed bows are sold than the number of archers who write left-handed. It can be difficult for a right-hander to teach left-handers, not because left-handers are innately more awkward, but because, when demonstrating a technique, the instructor has to reverse everything so that the pupil can fully understand.

Many people are not aware of having a dominant eye, but everyone with two normally functioning eyes has one that is dominant, and this is the eye that will do the aiming. The dominant eye is affected by the dominant hand. Before even giving you a bow, the instructor should find out which is your dominant eye. There are a number of simple methods of doing this. One is to extend your right hand in front then gradually bring your forefinger towards your nose until it drifts towards one eye, as it nearly always will. That will be the dominant eye. There are other methods, such as looking at an object down a tube or through a hole in a sheet of paper, but they all work in the same way.

Normally the right eye will be the dominant in right-handed people, and the left in left-handers, but this is not always the case. It is important to discover which eye is dominant because if you are given a right-handed bow to shoot and you have a dominant left eye, there will be some difficulty. There will be a powerful tendency to lean the head over to the right in an attempt to see through the sight. This will make shooting very difficult. To overcome this problem I have sometimes recommended shooting with a left-handed bow, but this has seldom been successful and I cannot recall any beginner who continued shooting for very long with this problem.

Stringing a Bow

The instructor may think it is a good idea to show you how to string a bow before proceeding further. After all, if you cannot string a bow, then you have to rely on someone doing it for you, which puts you in an inferior position and induces a feeling of inadequacy. Being able to string a bow correctly can give a feeling of independence that is important in the early stages.

There are three basic methods of stringing a bow, as shown in the illustrations. The first is tricky at first and can be quite dangerous if it is not done with care. If the hands or bow limb are wet, as can be the case at the end of a shooting session, the limb can slip out of control and spring upwards with disastrous results. It is possible to be hit in the eye with such force that it can be permanently blinding. Hold the bow so that it is facing upwards and stand with your legs well apart. Ensure that the limb and your hands are dry, then place the lower nock of the bow in your right instep, pull the handle up with your right hand and push the heel of the other hand down on the upper limb so that your fingers are free either to slide the string into the groove or to twiddle it out. Relax the pressure on the bow gradually; do not allow it to spring up suddenly. If you have been stringing it, carefully check whether

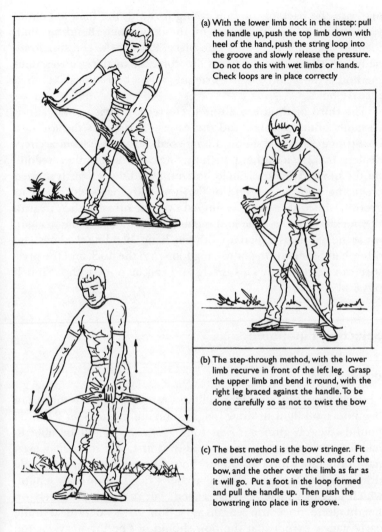

(a) With the lower limb nock in the instep: pull the handle up, push the top limb down with heel of the hand, push the string loop into the groove and slowly release the pressure. Do not do this with wet limbs or hands. Check loops are in place correctly

(b) The step-through method, with the lower limb recurve in front of the left leg. Grasp the upper limb and bend it round, with the right leg braced against the handle. To be done carefully so as not to twist the bow

(c) The best method is the bow stringer. Fit one end over one of the nock ends of the bow, and the other over the limb as far as it will go. Put a foot in the loop formed and pull the handle up. Then push the bowstring into place in its groove.

Fig. 10 Methods of stringing a bow

the string lies correctly in the grooves. Draw the string to see if it feels right. This manoeuvre can be difficult with some older bows designed with a large reflex in the limbs.

The second method has never been popular because of the possibility of twisting the limbs. Place one limb in front of your left leg, with the back of the bow facing forward, the handle behind your right leg, and both hands on the upper limb. Bend this limb forward and slide the string into place. Release the pressure gradually and check that the loops are correctly in the grooves. This method is more suitable for stringing a longbow than flat-limbed recurve bows.

The third method is the one preferred by most archers and is certainly both the safest and the easiest. It requires the use of a bowstringer, which is simply a long cord, obtainable from archery dealers, that has a leather pouch on one end and a leather 'saddle' on the other. The bow is held horizontally and the pouch slipped on to the nock at one end of the bow, with the bowstring in its groove, while the 'saddle' is slipped over the other limb as near to the nock as possible. One foot is placed in the loose of the stringer, while the handle is pulled up with one hand, bending the bow. The other hand then fits the bowstring loop into the nock and the pressure can be released. This is safe and can be done without much physical effort.

Selecting Equipment

Bows

Any self-respecting club should have a range of bows for the use of beginners, all light in draw weight, ranging from about 24 to 36 pounds. Few beginners, even fully grown men, will be able to handle anything heavier comfortably at first, and some may even have difficulty with a 26 pound bow. The selection of a suitable draw weight bow relies on the archer's height and draw length, which are, of course, closely related, but it is unwise to rely on height alone, since arm lengths vary. Bow size is not critical in the early stages, except that the bow should not be too heavy or too short. A simple formula that is easily applied for adult men is:

$$\text{draw length} \times 1.5 = \text{draw weight}$$

For example, 27 inches draw length times 1.5 equals 40.5 pounds. For ladies, the formula is slightly different: the weight is 1.1 times the draw length. This means that a lady drawing 26 inches would probably require a bow of about 28–29 pounds draw. Most will increase this after some months' experience.

The type of shooting involved in field archery needs bows of greater power than in target archery, since, although they are being shot at shorter distances, the trajectory of the arrow is more important, in order to shoot below branches and reduce error in arrow height on target. A very light bow may not reach some longer targets if there are branches in the way, and aiming becomes more difficult, so that the point of aim can often be over the top of the target. Many modern compound bows are built to shoot arrows very fast, with the flattest trajectory possible in order to reduce the gap between height of arrow over target, thus reducing possible height errors.

It is possible for a beginner to overdraw the bow, pulling the string back to the ear as he thinks he may have seen in films. This is dangerous for several reasons. If the arrow is too short it may fall off the rest, drop on to the hand and then be shot into the hand – all this happening so quickly it cannot be stopped in time. There is also the possibility that the arrow point will impinge on the face of the bow (the side facing the archer) and when loosed it will be unable to go anywhere and will explode in the archer's face. Other possibilities are that the arrow will fall off the rest, be loosed and go in almost any direction, or the bow may break. Most bows have a draw limit based on their length. A 72-inch recurve bow has a draw limit well beyond what most people would be able to draw, but shorter bows must be checked by reference to the draw length stated on the label, on the lower limb. The majority will be safe at 28 inches, about the maximum for most people. However, shorter bows, such as a 62-inch may approach danger point when drawn by anyone who is 6 feet tall. So it is important to ensure that you are shooting a bow of sufficient draw length for safety.

If you have bought a second-hand bow, it may not be the bargain you thought if it is the wrong size. It is not uncommon for club instructors to be approached by people who have obtained a bow, only to find that it is totally unsuitable for them, because it is either so light that it is useless or so heavy that it cannot be easily drawn.

Buying bows for children can be a problem. Do you buy a bow that fits now and will be outgrown in a few months, or buy a larger one for them to 'grow into'? Most parents will try to compromise by opting for the latter course, and choose something cheap that will serve well for a couple of years – not only will the child grow out of it eventually, but he or she might also have given up archery by that time. The danger is in choosing something cheap that might be far too big for the child to handle.

Beginners' fibreglass practice bows are cheap, but they should really be avoided if anything better is available. They do have the advantage of being virtually unbreakable, but have considerable disadvantages. The arrow rest is generally inadequate. It is usually formed from a ledge on the upper part of the rubber handle moulding, and this wears away so that it is difficult to balance an arrow on it. In an effort to hold the arrow in place, the beginner will often squeeze the nock or attempt to keep it on the rest by gripping it.

I have found that in France it is common practice to teach beginners to shoot by using the 'three fingers under' method. This means that all three drawing fingers are positioned below the arrow, and therefore cannot grip it, thus eliminating one of the problems many beginners have in the UK. It seems to me that there must be considerable advantages to this method of drawing, but because it is forbidden by the rules of most shooting classes, where the Mediterranean draw, with one finger above the arrow and two below, is required, it is not used for beginners. Moreover, it is often noticeable that many archers place so much pressure on the arrow with the top finger that it can easily be seen to curve when held at full draw. A proper bow, even if it is old or cheap, is far better if it has a serviceable arrow rest.

Tabs and Bracers

Tabs and bracers should also be of a suitable size. Tabs are available in three sizes, and a club should have a selection. A two-finger tab fits on the two middle fingers and lies on the inside of the hand. The bracer should be fitted on the bow arm so that it is on the inside, with the broadest end uppermost.

The purpose of the tab is to protect the fingers. Sometimes a beginner will say, 'I don't need one of those, I've got tough fingers.' So they may have, but they will usually find that a tab is a good idea after all, a bowstring can be remarkably effective at making even the toughest fingers sore after only a few shots.

The bracer has two purposes. One is to keep loose sleeves out of the way of the string and the other is to protect the arm from the string, which can cause impressive bruises. You might think that because the string is moving along the arm rather than at right angles to it, it would not be a problem, but it is astonishing how much bruising it can cause. Some instructors think that telling beginners of this may tend to put them off shooting, but I have never found this to be the case. It is possible for the string to strike the skin just above the bracer and make a pinched bruise, but moving the bracer higher up the arm can soon cure this. If you hit your arm, there is a problem with your arm position, for which there is a quick solution: alter the arm position so that your elbow is slightly bent and your arm not locked rigid.

Arrows

Club arrows are often a collection of old and battered wooden shafts of different lengths and weights, some with loose fletchings hanging off, and rainbow hued, so that the beginner thinks he has been given inferior rubbish to shoot with. No self-respecting club should allow this; durable beginners' arrows are now available at very reasonable prices, made of fibreglass with brass piles. The piles almost never come off and the shafts are difficult to break, and certainly do not bend. Beginners will appreciate being given the use of arrows that they cannot damage easily.

The relationship between arrow length and bow length is important because a short arrow drawn in a long bow would not be utilizing the full power of the bow, since it would not be drawn sufficiently, while a long arrow in a short bow might overstress the bow – not to mention the archer – and cause some danger. The following chart shows the relationship.

Length of arrow	22–24 in	24–26 in	26–28 in	28–30 in	30–32 in
Length of bow (recurve)	62 in	64 in	66 in	68 in	70 in

The instructor should ensure that you are equipped with arrows of sufficient length before being allowed to shoot. Some clubs ensure that their arrows are of a safe length by purchasing only arrows 30 inches long. There will be very few beginners who need anything longer.

A measuring arrow is very useful for determining correct draw length. This is simply a long wooden shaft, perhaps 32 inches long, which will accommodate the tallest archer, with a nock fitted to one end, and a scale marked along it from about 22 inches up to 32 inches. when this is drawn up into the shooting position, the scale can be used to find the correct draw length. It is important to ensure that the arrows are long enough to give a safety factor of at least an inch at full draw. You should draw up the arrow across the rest, to the anchor point, while the instructor checks how much arrow is in front of the rest. If it is not sufficient, then find some longer arrows.

Before actually shooting any arrows, it is a good idea to get the feel of a bow by drawing up up a few times, partly to get the drawing action right and make any corrections without the danger of arrows going off in all directions. When this is satisfactory, so that you have an idea of the power of the bow and feel that you are capable of drawing it to the anchor point, the instructor will usually let you shoot a few arrows into the ground a couple of yards in front, without drawing the bow to full draw. This shows you how to lay your fingers on the string, with one finger above the arrow and two below, leaving some space between your fingers and the arrow, with the string in the first joint of the fingers. This can be done with the bow across the front of the body in a horizontal position. Drawing the bow from this position for a few inches and letting go of the string will give a feel of the string tension on the fingers and how to loose it without holding the arrow.

These initial preparatory moves will give you more confidence when raising and drawing the bow at a target for the first time.

Holding the Bow

A firm grip on the bow is unnecessary; it can be held lightly between thumb and forefinger, when the pressure is in the fork of the hand with a high wrist and on the palm with the low-wrist position. One can see that a grip is unnecessary by shooting an arrow with the bow in the open-hand position; it will fall to the ground on loosing. Many freestyle archers prefer to shoot with the fingers extended forward so that they are not gripping the bow, and the bow is prevented from falling by a wrist sling. A firm grip is likely to set up undesirable muscle tensions that may extend into the bow and cause inaccurate shooting. When the arrow is loosed, the bow should be free to move. If it is properly balanced or stabilized, it will not move far except perhaps for a tendency to fall forward. If it is not properly balanced, it may well fall quite violently backwards, causing the archer to grab at it, sometimes before the arrow has passed over the rest, again causing an inaccurate shot. Some archers are taught to let the bow gently rotate forward in the hand after loosing. This seems to work quite well, and is popular among target archers.

There is also the question of how the hand should be placed on the bow handle. It might be thought that it would be obvious, but it is of vital importance to develop a consistent hand position. The hand can be held in several positions, some of which are dictated by the form of the handle. For example, the longbow has a straight handle and the most comfortable position is the dropped wrist so that as much hand as possible is in contact with the handle, bracing it against the pull from the other hand. However, recurve and compound bows have handles designed to fit the average hand and it is perfectly possible to shoot these with a high wrist position, having the wrist straight and the bow merely pulled into the fork of the thumb and forefinger. This can work quite well if you are using a bowsling of the variety which braces the bow against the high wrist. The design of the handle allows a fairly straight wrist, and is more comfortable than the straight handle of the longbow.

Wooden handles tend to be fat and fill the hand, shaped so that the thumb curves over a shaped portion; the 'wrong' hand does not fit at all well. Sometimes total novices pick up a bow the wrong way up and are baffled by the complex shapes, unable to see the handle until the bow is turned right way up. Modern alloy bow handles do not need to be as thick as wooden ones, for strength, so they can be made slim and have, over recent years, become more comfortable. Thick wooden grips have given way to slim wooden panels, sometimes inserted into the alloy structure, with a minimum of grip, but supported on some bows by a flatter area resting on top of the hand. These can be far more comfortable to shoot with, but on cold days, gloves are needed. There is some similarity to the handle of a Japanese sword in these bow handles.

It is possible to 'customize' bow handles by purchasing special pastes to build up a handle to fit one specific hand. One can also stick a special pad with a groove formed in it on the handle. This can be felt, so that the hand always falls into the same position. Very few archers seem to find these measures necessary, apart from the fact that the build up of paste on a handle spoils the appearance of a bow. Attempts have been made, with a variety of methods, to create bow handles which allow some angle on the hand away from the vertical, and these may possibly be more comfortable, but again, most archers do not seem to feel that this is important. A consistent grip, not too firm, seems to work for most.

Stance

When you start to shoot, begin close to a large target butt, no more than 10 yards or so. The exact distance is not important, but if it is too great it will be difficult to hit the target at all, which is frustrating. A beginner needs to be able to develop his confidence as his ability improves, and hitting the target occasionally with the first few arrows is a great help.

The correct shooting position, or stance, is not natural at first. Standing sideways to the target just does not feel right and many beginners have a compulsion to turn towards the target or at least have their feet pointing towards it. Stand sideways and raise both arms to shoulder height, so that the bow hand is pointing at the target. The feet should be apart, about as wide as the shoulders; this gives a stable base. The feet should be planted firmly on the ground, and should stay in contact with it throughout the shooting process, not raised on the toes when loosing, as if to give extra power to the bow. It is important to realize that the 'feet apart' stance is not always possible on a field course, where some target pegs are positioned in such a way as to make this difficult, by being on logs, tree stumps or steep banks. In addition, watching some compound archers who had adopted a feet-together stance can cause confusion about correct position. There seems to be no particular reason for this beyond the fact that they feel more comfortable.

The weight should be balanced evenly on both feet, the legs straight but not locked rigid. Relax the body, let the arms hang down the sides and take up the bow.

The foot always has to touch the rear of the shooting peg on

NFAS shoots, but on GNAS shoots, there is more flexibility and one only has to stand in a position behind an imaginary line drawn between two pegs for most shots. Shooting down- or uphill demands changes in body position. As far as possible, the body should bend at the waist to accommodate changes in bow angle. However, it is possible to find some shots so steep at times that this method is insufficient, and it is impossible to bend at the waist sufficiently, so the bow has to be shot by raising or lowering the bow arm in relation to the body, but this should be avoided as much as possible. In any case, these shots are relatively rare, so there is no need to worry about them.

Nocking the Arrow

The arrows should be on the ground in front of the archer, or in a ground, or belt quiver. If there is no quiver and the arrows have to be placed on the ground, a beginner will invariably place them behind him, presumably in an unconscious effort to avoid standing on them. This means that he will have to disturb his standing position after every shot in order to pick up the next arrow. From one point of view, this is not important, since field archers do not often shoot more than one arrow from one place, but from the point of view of learning to shoot, it is a problem: it is unnecessary movement, breaking the rhythm of shooting. Therefore, it is better to place them within reach on the ground in front. There is little chance of standing on them, since they will all be shot before you move your position. A ground quiver is safer, but these useful devices are almost unknown in field archery clubs, since they are rarely needed. They usually consist of a steel rod with a spike at one end and a horizontal loop welded to the other end; the arrows are placed in the loop with the spike in the ground.

The arrow is picked up by the fletching end, with the forefinger and thumb between the fletching and the nock, or just below the fletching, and pushed onto the string nocking point. The cock feather, the one which stands at right angles to the slot of the nock, should now be uppermost, standing out from the bow so that the other fletchings can clear the bow window. At this stage, the bow should be held horizontally across the front of the body, with the bow hand over the top.

The Draw

There are four basic methods of drawing the bow: drawing from a low position, bringing the bow up slowly until it is at eye level; the T-draw, where the bow is brought to eye level, then the string is drawn back parallel to the ground; the high draw, where the bow is raised well above eye level and brought down while drawing; and the high parallel draw, where the bow and the drawing hand are raised above eye level and moved down while drawing, with the arrow kept parallel to the ground.

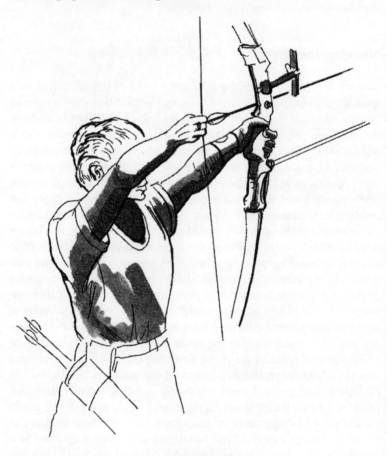

Fig. 11 The high parallel draw

Drawing the bow while moving it up from a low position does not, it seems to me, allow the back muscles to come into use right away, and might result in a poor position for the drawing arm when at full draw. However, some Olympic-level archers seem to prefer it, so it cannot be entirely wrong.

The T-draw is popular and works well to bring the vital back muscles into use, but it seems to require more effort, and it can still not get the drawing arm into position correctly every time. But it works well for a great many archers who find it effective and comfortable.

The high draw can be dangerous. It has a very stylish appearance, by bringing the bow up, drawing as it pivots down to eye level. It may be safe enough for most types of bow, but for compounds with release aids it is downright dangerous because of the risk of premature release of the string. The power of the compound will send an arrow a long way when it is shot into the air at a high angle, with possibly fatal results. The obvious danger of this method has caused it to be banned from use in some areas of archery.

The high parallel draw, as I learned it from a visiting American expert, was a revelation. It solves several problems with teaching and learning to shoot. It has several advantages. It gets the back muscles into play immediately, which gets more power into the draw, thus making it appear easier than if you are drawing with the arms as most beginners do. It gets the drawing arm into the correct shooting position easily so that the arm is well back, preventing the elbow from pointing outwards, and in line with the arrow, forming the 'draw force line' easily. It avoids shooting in the half crouch, with the back rounded, as some beginners also do. It creates an upright stance, well balanced and stable, and is generally easy to teach. Since adopting it myself, I have found drawing the bow easier, being able to get more strength into the draw. Beginners find that they can get to full draw more easily and soon are able to shoot from a consistent anchor point. The rules of the International Field Archery Association state: 'No archer shall draw a bow with the bow hand above the top of the head, when drawing on a horizontal plane', so some care is necessary to avoid prematurely loosing an arrow that could be dangerous.

Shoulder position can sometimes cause difficulty in some beginners, who may allow the bow to control them rather than the reverse, and they may allow their bow arm shoulder to rise as if it is pushed up by the power of the bow. This can happen to such an extent that the string will strike the shoulder. Again, the high parallel draw seems to cure this tendency, but if not, you will need to push the shoulder down. You need to understand the opposing forces of the drawn bow, pulling with one hand while pushing with the other, and give some thought to how your body is learning to adjust to these forces. The push-pull system is used with all methods of drawing the bow, so the shoulder is part of this mechanism and must not be allowed to collapse when some pressure is put upon it, but must resist the power of the bow.

It is most important, when drawing the bow, not to squeeze the arrow nock between your forefinger and second finger. There is an unconscious tendency to do this, partly perhaps because beginners do not trust the arrow to stay in place on the string and feel that it ought to be held in place. This makes it very difficult to keep the arrow on the rest, as one constantly attempts to juggle it back in place every time it falls off, as it does when full draw is nearly achieved. Because of the importance attached to the Mediterranean draw, with one finger above and two below the arrow, learning to shoot is actually made more difficult than it needs to be. The cure for this problem is to discover for yourself that if the fingers are kept apart when laid under the string, so that the arrow is not in contact with them, the draw can be completed without the arrow falling off the rest. The arrow is clipped on the string and should not, if the nock fits correctly, fall off or need your help to stay on. If you cannot cure the problem, it is possible to buy finger tabs fitted with a block that fits between the fingers and prevents the pinching of the nock.

Another aspect of this problem is the hand position. The drawing hand should be kept so that the fingers are at right angles to the string. If the hand changes position so that it is angled on the string, then the fingers cannot work properly to get a proper loose, since the string will lie across them at an angle, and the amount of friction on the string will be greater than it should be, as well as the hand not coming off correctly, in a straight back motion.

The Anchor

There is an excellent method of establishing where to anchor, and it is useful if you learn it. Simply extend your drawing hand

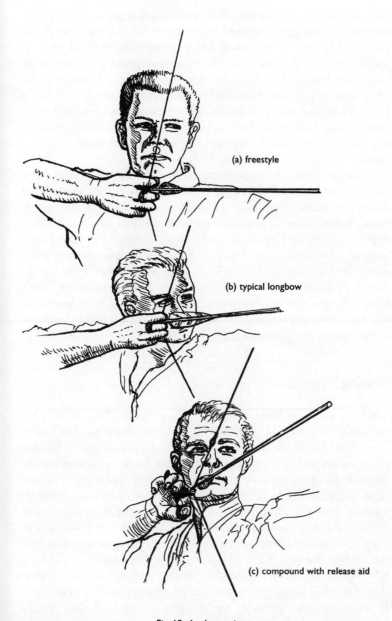

(a) freestyle

(b) typical longbow

(c) compound with release aid

Fig. 12 Anchor points

outwards, then pivot at the elbow to bring it in towards your face, with the forefinger extended; that finger will usually end in the corner of your mouth, thus giving a relaxed and natural position for it. This can then be used as a reference point for drawing the string, so that the forefinger is always drawn to the same position. The draw length then remains constant, as does the height of the hand, so the position is established in three dimensions and consistency can be built from that point. No degree of accuracy in shooting the bow is possible without the use of a consistent anchor point.

Other anchor points can come later when you have progressed on to other styles of shooting, such as freestyle, with the anchor under the chin. This, I have found, is difficult to teach and to learn, but it is useful for those freestyle archers who need to get sight marks up to 100 yards. Compound unlimited archers shooting with release aids use a variety of anchor points, many of them along the jawbone or on the cheek, while some other styles use the corner of the mouth anchor point. At this stage, however, 'KISS' should be the motto – 'keep it simple, stupid!' In other words, do not allow yourself to be overloaded with excessive information, or try to absorb everything at once.

Aiming

This is a cause of some concern to beginners. If the bow is not equipped with any sort of sight, then you will have no idea how to aim. The instructor should be able to show you that a sight is unnecessary at this stage and sighting can be done by viewing the target high up in the bow window. A few shots will soon show how high the bow needs to be held. The arrow cannot be used for aiming. There is a natural tendency for beginners to assume that the arrow point should be aimed at the target, but if it is, it will go high over the target. The simple reason is that the arrow is held well below the eye, but if the point is on the target it is pointing too high. It should therefore be pointed well below the target so that it is more parallel with the line of sight, instead of crossing it. If you point the arrow at the bottom of the butt, you will be surprised how high it shoots. So use the bow to aim with, not the arrow.

Point blank, as it is known, when the arrow is shot with the point on the target, is for most bows somewhere between 35 and 45 yards, but aiming with the point becomes difficult further than that since the arrow has to be raised higher than the target in order to reach, and thus obscures the target from the archer's view. This difference between eye and arrow can also cause difficulty on the field course when there are branches close to the archer. It is entirely possible not to notice branches between you and the target, especially if they are not directly in the way. They can be a few inches below the eye line, but directly in the path of the arrow, and any branches in such positions should be examined for arrow marks if others have got there first. If any branch or trunk has arrow marks on it, beware and take avoiding action. If a branch, for example, lies a few inches below eye level, but has fresh arrow marks on it, it may be advisable to attempt to shoot from a kneeling position, so that the arrow flies under the branch. If a tree has fresh marks in the vertical plane, that means taking extra care to shoot straight down the centre. Do not take avoiding action by shooting deliberately away from the tree, since this will often mean going off the centre of the target.

As you improve, you can move further back from the target, and the bow will need to be held slightly higher in order to achieve a greater trajectory of the arrow.

If, of course, you are having difficulty with sighting, by looking at the target past the bow window, a simple sight can be made by sticking a strip of tape on the back of the bow window, i.e. the side facing away from you, and inserting a pin sideways in it. It may take a few shots to find where the pin needs to be, but once this is done, there should be little more difficulty.,

The Loose

This is one of the most critical aspects of shooting. The apparently simple act of releasing the fingers from a string under tension without causing that string to go off line and throw the arrow off centre has baffled archers for centuries. The position of the string on the fingers is critical. Many beginners find it impossible to loose at first because they have the string gripped in the fold of the fingers and are terrified of letting go. The string should lie in the first joint of the fingers, with the thumb and little finger tucked towards each other, and you will soon discover that this is enough to press the string back so that letting the fingers relax causes it to be released. There is no need to hook your fingers firmly round the string. The little finger and thumb should be curled in towards the palm to keep them out of the way. The principle behind using three fingers is simply to spread the load as much as possible. Two fingers may be used, but you will soon discover that three work far better. However, the hand must be in such a position that all three fingers are doing an equal share, since if the hand is twisted slightly there may be an imbalance of load and a good loose will be difficult. The hand should be as relaxed as possible so that no unnecessary tensions cause it to come off the string in anything other than a direct backwards movement. The string should be allowed to pull itself off the fingers as soon as they relax sufficiently. If this is done correctly the fingers will still be bent behind the anchor position after the loose is completed. Throwing the hand violently backwards, snatching at the string or jerking the hand off will not produce an accurate loose.

Even the use of a release aid with a compound bow requires care, and they are not really appropriate for beginners to learn with, since the technique, though simple, is dangerous. The release trigger needs to be pressed gently rather than snatched or jerked. The surprising thing is that although many releases work in similar ways, they can have different effects on the bow. Some will enable higher sight marks to be used, while others may shoot the bow to the left.

Your wrist position is important in that the wrist should be relaxed, without any tension except that from the bow, and should therefore be straight, in line with the forearm and the arrow. This should enable a good backwards movement on the loose without any undesirable side movement that may affect arrow direction. Again, the high parallel draw will help to achieve this position. An outward-jutting elbow will often result in a crooked wrist adversely affecting the draw.

The finger tab may prove a little troublesome at first, but will soon become an accustomed part of the shooting process. The loose may not be too good for a while, but when you are able to release the string with confidence, part of the initial battle is won.

A backward loose, with the hand dropping as it relaxes, is important. A forward loose, the subconscious attempt to unhook the fingers from the string is to be avoided. There are beginners who never conquer this urge and it remains with them until they give up archery altogether. There are a number of methods of trying to cure this problem, and some of them have been known to be successful. One is to keep the back muscles under tension so that they pull the string hand back on loosing, but without snatching at the string, and another is to ensure that the fingers hold the string as far towards the tips as is practical.

One problem that sometimes emerges is creep. This takes the form of the string hand gradually moving forward, while supposedly being at full draw, so that when the arrow is loosed, it drops low or short, since the bow is no longer under full power. Pulling the hand firmly into the anchor point can help to prevent this. Even some experienced archers can be prone to this problem at times, often when their concentration lapses. Shooting correctly requires total concentration and no external thoughts should come into the mind while at full draw; the aim on the target is all that should be in the mind. One well-known American compound archer said that he draws up, using a release aid, comes onto the aim and holds still 'until a non-archery thought comes into the mind', then releases.

The Follow-through

After the arrow is loosed, you should endeavour to hold the bow up in the shooting position until the arrow has landed to prevent premature movement of the bow. Very often, there will be a strong desire to watch the arrow in flight and to see where it lands. This can develop into an unconscious movement of the bow so that you can see past it, moving it out of the way. This can lead to the bow being moved as soon as the arrow is loosed but while it is still passing over the arrow rest. The arrow is then encouraged not to hit the target. Do not attempt to watch the arrow in flight but keep your eyes on the target. A good shot will come back into the line of sight. The bow can be allowed to rotate forward during the follow-through, but it can still be kept upright from the side.

Fig. 13 The follow-through

Breathing

This is a good idea. There is a natural tendency to fill the lungs before drawing up and to hold one's breath until the shot is made, but this can set up undesirable tensions in the body. The best approach is to attempt to relax the whole body when shooting, so that there is a lack of tension that might affect accuracy. Exhaling just after drawing the bow seems to work quite well. The breath can be held for several seconds without any difficulty and this will assist aiming. Most archers will probably be unaware that they are even doing this.

Practice

Most archers are convinced of the need to practise in order to improve performance. This seems logical and sensible. However, it can happen that bad habits will develop without you being aware of them, and they will become ingrained, preventing you from developing your full potential. Therefore a thorough knowledge of the correct shooting technique is necessary in order to develop a consistent and effective method. A good instructor will not interfere with anyone's day-to-day shooting unless requested to do so, but he may politely suggest that the archer ask for advice or that a little coaching may not be out of place.

The mere twanging of arrows will not improve shooting unless the correct technique is applied, and some knowledge of more advanced aspects is necessary. This will develop into techniques which are applicable to different types of bow, since obviously the technique used by, for example, a compound unlimited archer is quite different from that for shooting a longbow. But some aspects are common to several types. The shoulder of the bow arm should always be kept down. It is common to see beginners allowing the bow to take over the body and their bow arm shoulders will rise until they are attempting to view the target in a most difficult manner, round or over the hump formed by the shoulder. The whole body must be as relaxed as possible and you should be in control of the bow, rather than the reverse. The high parallel draw can also help here, since it is difficult to use this method without the shoulder coming down into its right place.

The shoulders should be level and relaxed, and when the bow is raised there should be no undue tension. The bow arm should be slightly bent at the elbow, not locked rigid. If the bow is of a reasonable draw weight, the arm should be strong enough to work as a prop without locking the elbow, and can even be turned outwards slightly if you find that the string is striking the bracer too often. There is often a problem with lady archers in that their arms have longer ligaments than those of men, and if they lock the elbow, the arm will not be straight, but will form an inward angle, allowing the string to strike the arm frequently and painfully. Making a slight outward bend of the elbow should cure this. It was once said, during an instructor's course, that any instructor who allows a beginner to strike his arm with the string is not doing his job properly. If a beginner arrives at the next session with huge bruises on the bow arm, the teaching has been at fault, since this can only happen if the bow arm is allowed to protrude into the path of the string. Poor shoulder position, locked arm and generally poor body control can all contribute to this.

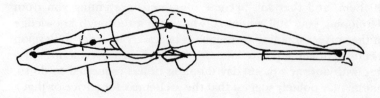

(1) Good stance. Straight line from elbow to arrow
rest, feet in line with shoulders

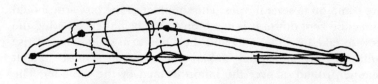

(2) Good stance. Straight line from elbow to arrow
rest, feet parallel to shot line

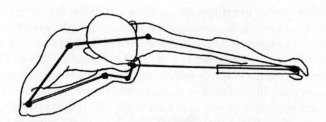

(3) Poor stance. Elbow out, wrist cranked – almost
impossible to shoot an arrow straight from this stance

Fig. 14 Draw force lines – body geometry

The elbow of the drawing arm should be pulled as far back as necessary to get the forearm in line with the arrow, to form what has been called the 'draw force' line. This means that, if it is formed correctly, a straight line will run from the elbow, through the wrist, and the arrow to the pile. This enables the force exerted on the string to be released in a direct line so that the arrow will fly straighter. A protruding elbow, with the hand on the string at an awkward angle, will often make the arrow fly off at all sorts of angles because it prevents a good straight backwards loose and pulls the string sideways on release. Again, the high parallel draw prevents this problem. It is almost impossible to get the elbow to stick out at an ungainly angle with this method.

Allowing the bow to do the work when loosing is the aim in the early stages, not necessarily hitting the target. Some beginners seem to lack confidence in the bow's ability to project the arrow, and think that extra physical effort is required, by thrusting the bow forward, leaping up on the toes, unhooking the fingers from the string, pushing the arrow forward and similar actions. All these are unnecessary; simply allow the bow to do all the work.

Understanding the need for good body position will help you to shoot well. Many people adopt a good upright stance with head up and bow held correctly, with a good drawing action and good anchor point, almost without any assistance from an instructor. Others have difficulty in adopting the proper stance, and present a challenge to the instructor.

Shooting techniques can be studied at length; there are excellent books that go into considerable detail and are well worth reading. If you want to progress far, then reading a couple of these books will certainly be worthwhile, since they concentrate on the subject of technique at some length. There will inevitably be some differences between them, but the basic shooting technique remains the same for all types of archery as does the necessary mental disciplines that go with it. Archery demands control above all else; it is not wildly energetic or physically demanding, but it requires a high level of mental control of the body if success is to be achieved. Many field archers have no concern about this level; they just want to enjoy their shooting. But it becomes more enjoyable when one has confidence in one's ability to hit the centre of the target with reasonable regularity. The pleasure of seeing the arrow shooting towards the target and striking the centre repays all the study and practice, especially on a long and difficult target.

Safety

When withdrawing arrows from the target, never stand behind the arrows being withdrawn, but always to one side. Archers have been injured by arrows projecting nock end first. The nock is perfectly capable of penetrating the body although it may seem too blunt to do so. The force required to release an arrow from the target butt can be quite considerable – sometimes it takes two people to pull one out – and it will often come out suddenly and very forcibly. Carbon arrows in 3D animal targets are often difficult to get out. As an aid various rubber pads are sold for this purpose in archery shops. They are easily carried in the quiver and are a great help, especially when the shafts are wet. There is a type of thin rubber disc used for opening jars in the kitchen that is also useful. A new device is a tube containing a silicone-based compound into which one can push arrows before they are shot; it lubricates the shaft so that it can easily be withdrawn. The question, of course, is whether it helps the arrow to penetrate the target further. I have no information about that yet.

When withdrawing arrows from a target, it helps if the target is braced against the pull, so the accepted method is to place one hand on the target face, with the fingers spread on each side of the arrow, and pull straight back with the other hand. Waggling the arrows to loosen them is frowned upon, since it is easy to break them. It is astonishingly difficult to pull arrows out without bracing against the target – the target tends to come with the arrow. Some field targets can be made of such difficult material that it can be almost impossible to draw arrows out, especially when they are wet. This sometimes happens when someone in a club discovers a new material that seems ideal for making butts but it is not always satisfactory. Breaking arrows trying to extract them makes for bad-tempered archers. Carbon arrows especially seem to be prone to friction heat welding them to some target materials, so the effort needed to withdraw them is considerable.

Other safety precautions to take when a number of people are shooting on a practice range, perhaps with more than one target, include the fact that while one person is shooting, no one should go down to the targets; everyone should finish shooting before anyone moves forward of the shooting line. Everyone should shoot from the same line, even though that line might not be marked but only exist by virtue of the position of the archers themselves. They can shoot at targets placed at different distances, which is common practice at open competition field shoots, but everyone should return to the shooting line before shooting recommences. These are common-sense precautions, but there is usually no one in charge of safety at the practice targets during events, so everyone should know the accepted procedure and be aware of the dangers.

The Shooting Area

If you are trying to teach yourself to shoot, the choice of where to shoot must be dictated by several factors, one being the availability of a suitable ground. One of the best places would be a vast, open beach with unlimited space, in which distance would be of no consequence and arrows that missed the target would be easy to find. However, this is not very practical since such beaches are few and far between. In place of this, you may be able to obtain permission from a friendly farmer to set up a practice target and shooting area on his land. Safety, of course, is the first consideration, and you must bear in mind that any arrows that miss the target may easily travel over a 100 yards if shot too high, and the outer limit of your safe area should be that sort of distance away. It is also advisable to shoot somewhere where you cannot be seen too easily. Local children may become curious about your activity, with all sorts of dangerous possibilities. You should not shoot near a road where drivers can see you easily. A former archer of my knowledge upset local traffic when shooting while standing on the pavement outside his house and shooting down the side of the house into the garden. This caused a few complaints to his club.

You should also consider whether there are any livestock in the field, of course – and not only for the obvious reasons. Horses are strange animals and some, it seems, are not without a sense of humour, they have been known to seize bits of archery equipment and run off with them! On the other hand, I was told of a farmer who gave a friend permission to shoot in one of his fields, saying that it wouldn't matter if he shot any of the sheep, since at current prices they were virtually worthless anyway!

The length of the grass in your field should also be considered. Try to choose an area where it is not too long. Even very short grass can hide arrows, so use the biggest target butt or boss you can carry and try not too shoot so far away from it that you cannot guarantee hitting it, otherwise you may spend more time searching for lost arrows than shooting, and your attrition rate for arrows will be very discouraging.

In choosing the material for your practice target, make sure that arrows cannot penetrate completely and disappear behind it. Some large cardboard boxes, flattened and lashed tightly together, to a thickness of at least 4 inches, will serve very well and have the advantages of being free and easily available. Local television shops or motorcycle dealers can often be a useful source. You will also need a couple of stakes about 3 inches thick to hammer into the ground to support the target butt. Ensure that it is firmly held to them, since an unsupported butt has a large wind area and can blow over quite easily, or even fall over without any wind. It will always fall when you have a few arrows in it, and it will always fall forward. This does not do much to prolong the life of your arrows. One of the advantages of the modern foam-layered targets is that many of them are thick enough to be almost self-supporting and will stand on level ground on their own. However, as a precaution, they are always staked.

If you can find a field with a high bank in it, this will do very well as a backstop behind your target, and after some practice you might find it useful to reverse the positions and shoot from the top of the bank down at the target, which would make good field course experience. Never, of course, shoot in a direction where there might be people somewhere behind the target you cannot see.

Many archers practise in their gardens, which is fine if you have one long enough and no houses at the other end. If there are, take great care about your safety precautions. Arrows can go astray from the most unexpected causes, not just shooting errors. A towel flapping on a washing line, for example, can suddenly blow across the path of your arrow and divert it into someone else's garden. Cats can appear suddenly in front of a target and throw your shot off. If it is your own cat, it will often decide to sit in front of the target without regard for safety rules, probably just to annoy you, and will sit admiring the garden and ignoring you.

You may find that, if there are any objections to your shooting in your own garden, it is difficult to convince neighbours of your accuracy – the fact that you are intending to get all your arrows in a 4-inch circle and not spray them in all directions. They will only be convinced by seeing that you do not behave dangerously and irresponsibly, and that your arrows do actually land in your target all the time.

Up, Down and Sideways

Mastering field archery requires the ability to judge distances, on the flat and on slopes. Many newcomers to the sport say that they are unable to judge distances. This is not because of an innate mental problem; it is merely that the majority of people have no need to learn how to do it. Anyone who anticipates shooting with sights will need to learn how to judge distance. For unsighted classes, it is not so important, in fact many unsighted archers declare that they are unable to judge distance simply because for them, there is no need. They merely adjust the height of the bow when drawn up on the target to what they *think* may be correct. This is called instinctive shooting, but it is just as much learned as any other aspect.

You can start to learn distance assessment almost as soon as you start shooting. If you are learning to shoot on your own, you can make estimates of target distance, then pace them out. This does not have to be done over very long distances, bearing in mind that the average target distance on a field course is probably only 30 yards. Beginning at 10 yards and progressing to 20 would make a good start. You may find that the estimates are way out, but this can soon be corrected. Ten yards may sound a lot at first, but it is not far. Twenty yards is a useful distance, which could be measured out quite easily by counting how many of your steps equate to that distance. A lot of practice shooting at 20 or 30 yards will help to fix a picture of that distance in your mind. This can then be used as a mental reference thereafter. Many field archers do this, and will often say that, when they come across a strange target, they make a mental picture of a specific target which is well known to them, such as the 25-yard target in their garden. Other distances can be added on to this basic distance, and a mental 'file' built up of a variety of distances. Eventually, with sufficient attention and practice in different surroundings, the skill will develop. Practising while elsewhere can be useful, even if it is impossible to check the estimate for accuracy; making judgements while out walking, for example, gets one into the habit. Top archers using sights seem to be superb at judging distance. 'Counting trees' is one method while in woodland – not actually counting them, but merely estimating the distances between them, and adding them together.

The judgement of distance uphill and downhill becomes more difficult. Slopes, especially when they vary in gradient, are more difficult not only to judge, but also to shoot when using sights because gravity starts to have unexpected effects. For example, most people expect to shorten the distance when shooting downhill; this seems logical and sensible, but what many field archers do not know is that this also applies to uphill shots. Estimates of uphill distance usually involve an 'add-on' factor based on the difficulty of walking uphill. However, this does not apply to arrows, whose trajectory curve is different from on the flat. The curve, on the flat, is like the shape of a fletching over the length of the arrow's flight. This can easily be verified by observation; it is easy to see with a low-powered bow and heavy arrows. But on an uphills shot the curve formed in flight is different, and the arrow will fly fairly flat for a considerable part of its flight, then form an increasing curve, and this cannot easily be observed. The deduction of distance for uphill shots is rather surprising, and when I first read about it in Don Stamp's excellent book *Field Archery*, I queried it with him. He assured me that it was true and had been tested at varying gradients and distances. The problem is, unless one has conducted such tests oneself, it is almost impossible to say by how much one should reduce the distance, when and where. Generally it might be better not to take off very much unless the slope is unusually steep. It is well known that it is necessary to take off distance when shooting downhill, but distance is notoriously difficult to judge downhill, and the most frequent result is that everyone in a group will find their arrows landing too high on the target. The steeper the slope, the more likely this is to happen. It even happens to those shooting without sights and not making any distance estimates.

Tests have been conducted to discover what actually happens to arrows at various degrees and distances of slope, and it is possible to work out a chart that will indicate how much to deduct for a given degree of slope and distance. The judgement of angle of slope also requires practice; it is another skill few of us require. Bear in mind that 45 degrees of slope would for most of us, be virtually unclimbable. There is no road in Britain as steep as that. Anything from perhaps 20 degrees upwards might be regarded as steep, that being what used to be known as one in five. So most slopes being shot will probably be 20 degrees or less. Shots over 50 yards uphill will be very unusual.

Heavy arrows will be more difficult to shoot uphill, but shortening the distance would still apply if the slope were steep enough. It has been suggested that, on a downhill slope, at 60 yards on a 30-degree slope, it would be necessary to take off about 8 yards, shooting it at 52 yards. It is probable that considerable practice would be required for the average field archer to discover just how much to take off when shooting uphill or downhill, and if your club course is flat, the opportunity may never arise.

The phenomenon that occurs when shooting across slopes is well known. Arrows seem to strike downhill on the target, following the slope. It is almost as if gravity has changed direction slightly and now acts parallel with the slope. It has often been suggested that this is actually caused by the archer, standing on a slope, canting the bow over at an angle. This may be possible some of the time, but using a compound bow fitted with sights that have a built-in spirit level should prevent this. In addition, the presence of trees should give a vertical reference, since most of them grow upwards, however steep the slope. Is it possible that the archer may be slightly misled concerning his own angle to the slope, since there is a natural tendency to lean into the slope to prevent falling over. The bow will tend to follow this and the arrow will then be pointing down the slope. It is necessary to check your position before taking the shot and make sure you really are upright. So when shooting across slopes, make sure the bow is vertical. The target butt will probably not be level, but on a slope as well, and this may cause a misjudgement of the vertical, too. It may be wise to aim slightly up slope of the target centre; I have often found this to be effective.

Positive Thinking

Archery has been described by a lady Olympic archer as a very psychological sport, and she should know. Many sports have a powerful psychological aspect, but archery requires less of the physical than many others, and therefore more of a mental component. There seems to be a common factor among top archers that might be described as 'steadiness under fire'. All of them seem to possess the ability to concentrate totally on the shot and to cut out all thoughts of external factors. One ability that they must possess is to ignore mistakes or bad shots. It is not worth getting upset over a couple of bad shots, an attitude which is often seen among those who are relatively new to the sport. They need to learn that it is self-defeating and negative. They start to worry after two or three bad shots, and sometimes, in a really bad case, they can gradually go to pieces. Watching this process spiral out of control can affect others in the group. It is well known that shooting with very good archers can pull one's score up, and shooting with those who are noisy or careless and who are not really trying can have a disastrous effect on one's own success. There is also the problem of shooting with someone who is not easy to get on with for some reason or another. I once had the most unpleasant experience of shooting a national championship with a spectator, accompanying his competing girlfriend, who constantly and loudly broke wind from both ends. I tried not to let this affect my shooting, but it was difficult. I changed groups the next day and shot with a group accompanied by a dog – which was far better behaved.

When things are going badly, they can be corrected. It is only necessary to think that all the bad arrows can be forgotten, that a change can and will be made, but most of all that the only arrow that matters is the one in the bow that is about to be shot. But this requires total concentration. All the previous arrows cannot possibly affect this one; it is the only arrow there is. This method of thinking does work. I have used it on other archers when they have started to believe they are doing badly, and it has worked for them too. Depression must be defeated.

When shooting with a poor group, it is necessary to cut oneself off from them and concentrate on one's own shooting. Setting a points target may help. There is a fixed number of targets, the maximum possible score should be known or be easy to calculate, and you should, after a few shoots, know what you are capable of. Therefore, setting a scoring target should be simple. Achieving it should be possible.

The Plateau

Most archers feel they have reached a plateau after some time. When one starts shooting, there is, of course, a natural tendency to expect a gradual improvement in performance. It would be strange if there was not, but there are a few beginners who never master the art of shooting with a bow and it soon becomes evident that they have some problem which cannot be solved, and that they will never be any good. They are rare, but they exist, and they soon realize that they will not improve and drop out. The average person will find that his performance will improve gradually, depending on what bow class he is shooting in. Progress may be slow in one of the more difficult classes, such as longbow, but shooting something with sights on will help. Scores will climb slowly, but after a while one finds one has stopped, having reached a plateau. You may stay at this level for years, until something drastic is done, or some minor improvement in technique, style, or equipment makes a difference.

Many archers constantly struggle to beat the plateau and make, or find, something to improve their performance. In some field organizations, there are classification levels that will provide incentives for improvement, such as the GNAS classes that lead up to the dizzy heights of Grand Master Bowman, leading archers up in gradual stages of score increases. Many archers constantly try to improve their performance in order to move on to the next class level. This is one of the most satisfying aspects of the sort, in that one is always striving to improve a personal best rather than attempting beat someone else – although there are those who know someone, perhaps a personal friend, whom they are trying to beat at every shoot. Incentive works.

Those who enjoy plodding round the club course without ever bothering about the struggle to improve scores, without ever worrying about going to competition shoots, but just like shooting with a couple of like-minded friends, may get as much, perhaps even more, pleasure from shooting as those going to competition shoots every weekend. In most clubs, there is no compulsion to do competition shooting and some people are happy to go round every Sunday, shoot round the permanent course without ever scoring – and who is to say that they are less keen or less supportive of field archery?

5 Aiming Techniques

This is a contentious area for some field archers, since there are preferred methods of aiming which do not have official approval and are banned in some classes. The use of sights is permitted by all organizations, but there is a handful of clubs who do not allow anyone to shoot at their open shoots or in their clubs with sights fitted. These presumably prefer to think of archery in a 'pure' form without the corruption of modern technology, and only instinctive shooting is permitted by them.

Sights on bows are a comparatively recent innovation, dating back perhaps only about sixty years. The use of sights brings about greater accuracy, of course, and very few unsighted archers have been able to equal the scores of those shooting with sights. The basic problem is gravity. The arc of an arrow in flight is a parabola, with the arrow curving up then down – simple, of course. Much of the art of archery is based on how to deal with this phenomenon. The weight and speed of the arrow combined with the power of the bow produce a curve which can be precisely calculated and sights can be set up with a considerable degree of accuracy. Since the arrow is usually positioned below the eye, when at full draw, the resultant gap will create another difficulty that has to be taken into the equation. The further the bow is tilted upwards, the further the arrow will travel until, at almost 45 degrees to the ground, it will travel furthest. Any increase in angle over this will produce a curve that will bring the arrow closer. We all know this, and it is the reason why high angles of shot are so dangerous – not in themselves, but because it is unknown where the arrow might land. The average weight of recurve bow will shoot an arrow, at maximum elevation, about 250 yards. A 45-pound peak weight compound will reach further, somewhere over 300 yards perhaps. Few archers have ever shot their bows to maximum distance, so when small boys gasp, 'Cor, that's a good bow, mister – how far will it shoot?' most of us have no idea, and it is galling to have to admit that. So we tell them, 'Bloody miles, mate.'

As a matter of interest, one of the more esoteric forms of archery is flight shooting, which is little known in England perhaps because of the limited space available for this shooting-for-distance sport. The bows are specially built, and very short; the arrows are tiny and are usually shot through a hole in the centre of the bow handle. They are barrelled – tapered from the centre towards the ends – and the fletchings are equally small, to reduce the weight as much as possible. These arrows can be shot for hundreds of yards, with the bow held at maximum elevation.

There is an old record of a Turkish sultan, in the early nineteenth century, having shot an arrow for over 900 yards. Stone pillars marked where this took place, but there has always been considerable doubt about the truth of this account, some being of the opinion that servants rushed out to measure the distance and exaggerated it for the sake of their health.

The American Harry Drake specialized in flight shooting and set several world records, one of well over a mile, shooting a foot bow, that is, one shot when lying on the ground with the feet braced against the bow while hauling the string back with both hands.

This is largely irrelevant to the field archer, however, since ironically there is virtually no aiming involved in flight shooting, merely pointing somewhere down range and getting the maximum angle of elevation correct.

For field archers, there is a number of techniques for aiming without sights. Some prefer merely to judge the height of their bows in relation to the target, coming to full draw then moving the bow up and down until they think it is about right. The key to this method is ignoring any estimation of distances; indeed, many who use it say that they cannot or do not make any distance estimates. Although one of Britain's finest field archers, Roy Mundon, shot barebow, as it is called, for many years and was very skilled at estimating distances, even the longer distances that become progressively more difficult to judge.

Barebow archers – and by this is meant virtually anyone shooting without sights – look at the target and judge its height in the bow window or, in the case of longbows, against the side of the bow. If it is a long target, they lift the bow higher so the target moves down the window: if it is a short target, the bow is moved down until the target is high in the window. Although this is called instinctive shooting, and compared to throwing a ball, which if it has to be thrown a long way is thrown higher, it is not really instinctive but learned. Each archer who shoots without sights has first learned how high to hold the bow on short targets, then progressed on to learning how high to hold it on longer targets. It may be that some do not think in terms of how high to hold it, but only how it feels, but this becomes more difficult when targets are set at different heights and are uphill and downhill.

I once watched a barebow archer aiming at a target about 40 yards away and about 15 feet below his eye level. I was surprised to see that, on the aim, his arrow was absolutely horizontal. I thought, 'He'll never hit that', but the arrow flew from the bow, curved gracefully down and struck dead centre. It was surprising how much the arrow dropped when shot horizontally.

Many of the rules of the field archery organizations are framed in such a way as to prevent barebow archers from using any part of the bow as a sight system or mark. Strings must be of one colour, so that coloured strands cannot be used, nor laminations on the bow, nor marks or blemishes. One archer of my acquaintance found that the camouflage paint design on his new bow handle could be used for sighting, and claimed that this was acceptable because the rules did not mention camouflage paint. However, this still contravened the spirit of the rules and their intention, as well as being an unfair advantage over others in the same class without such handles.

When shooting barebow, the technique is to draw the arrow into the corner of the mouth, using the cheek as a cushion and steadying area for the hand, and locking the hand into place so that the forefinger can be felt in the corner of the mouth. The bow is held upright, and the target viewed in the bow window with the string running down the centre of the bow and the centre of the target. The arrow should be pointing somewhere below the target centre, and the head turned somewhat more than when shooting freestyle. The reason for this is that the nose can get in the way when this anchor point is used, and the string can whip past it and make it very sore.

If an arrow is shot from in front of the eye, so that the archer is aiming down the arrow – 'gunbarrelling' it – directly at the target with the point in the centre, the arrow is not given any extra height to counteract gravity, and it will inevitably drop lower than the target centre. Therefore, it will have to be aimed higher than the target and will thus obscure the target from the archer's eye. It makes more sense, then, to place the arrow below the eye, so that the target can be seen. The lower the arrow is positioned, the higher it will fly. Freestyle archers shooting target archery, are often shooting at 100 yards, distances very rarely shot in field archery. It therefore makes sense for them to position their arrows below the chin in order to get the greater distance within the range of the sight fitted to the bow.

Some barebow archers adopt a shooting position with the bow canted. This does not seem to make aiming any easier, since it means they have to judge two components, lateral and vertical. Experience is the only way to learn to shoot in this manner, and it often seems as if it is only being done for dramatic effect, or to keep the arrow on the rest.

One method of aiming by changing the angle of the bow according to the distance of the target is known as string-walking. This uses the corner of the mouth as an anchor point for the hand, but moves the arrow nock up when the distances are shorter. When fully refined this method uses the turns of the string serving as a means of setting the distances. The idea is to count the number of turns for a specific distance – placing the forefinger on the string twelve turns under the nocking point may be the position for shooting a 20-yard target, while six turns might be counted for 40 yards. This method can, of course, only be used if the archer is permitted to use the 'three fingers under' method, i.e. three fingers under the nock of the arrow. It is easy to see if anyone is using this method, so many of the class rules state that the bow must be shot with the Mediterranean loose, or one finger above and two below the arrow nock. There is only one class in one set of rules permitted to use this method, the Barebow Class in the EFAA.

A similar, but also doubtful method is known as 'face-walking'. This simply involves moving the hand up or down the face according to the target distance. In a very refined form, this would mean establishing exactly where the anchor point would need to be on the face for any given distance, which would require considerable practice and research – all to produce a method of dubious accuracy. The longer distances would be shot with the hand further down the face, and the shorter ones higher up. I have never seen this method used and only once seen string-walking, perhaps because both are banned by most sets of rules and permitted only for barebow in EFAA rules.

The barebow archer shooting in the usual way, judging the height of the target in the bow window, will find it very useful to know where his point of aim is. This can be done simply by shooting on a measured range, starting at about 20 yards and working back in increments of 5 or 10 yards. The bow will have to be moved up progressively in small increments, using the point of the arrow as an aiming point, and eventually it will be found that the point will cover the centre of the target, rather than being below it as it has been up to that point. This is called point blank, when no allowance has to be made for height of arrow. For many bows, this will be about 40 yards. It can be used as a datum point from which all other aiming points can be measured by eye. What this point blank distance means is that any targets over that distance will have to be shot with the point of the arrow covering the target, so that an estimation of its height becomes difficult. Many barebow archers will say that on especially long targets, they are actually aiming with the point on some object over the top of the target, such as a particular branch. If, however, they are aiming by using the height of the target in the bow window, this is not such a problem. Any targets under the point blank distance can be shot using the gap method, which uses an estimated distance of point of arrow below the target centre, so that, for example, at 20 yards the point might appear to be 18 inches below the target centre, while at 15 yards it might be 20 inches. This method needs considerable practice and refinement, and is probably best used in combination with other methods, such as the instinctive feel of the bow height and the view of the target in the sight window. Many barebow archers prefer to feel that they are shooting more by instinct than calculation, which is why they shoot that way.

The question of whether to shoot with both eyes open is entirely for the individual to decide, but many archers shooting with sights find that they can only aim with one eye shut, since the dominant eye is not sufficiently dominant to ignore the image being received by the other. Many barebow archers may find that it is easier for them to shoot with both eyes open, but this again is for the individual to decide.

Strange things happen at very short distances. Many archers with sights find that at 10 yards or less they cannot get an arrow in the target because they are shooting, not too high, as one might expect, but too low. This has to do with the relationship of height of arrow to sight against height of anchor point to eye. Some find that they have to go down to a 20-yard sight mark to get the arrow the right height at 6 yards, for example. This reversal seems odd, but any movement of the sight to a higher point will make the arrows go lower. Of course, there is virtually no drop in arrow due to gravity at these distances, but a complicating factor is that such very short targets are usually low on the ground and not at eye level. The barebow archer will find the same problem, but, again, only practice and experience will show how to deal with shots such as these.

An understanding of the geometry of bow movement against target distance and arrow height is a great help in making adjustments to bows. The leverage of the bow against the target and the arrow against the bow sometimes becomes confusing. Again, experience and practice will enable you to grasp these points. The bow is a lever pivoted from the shoulder when moved to adjust for target distance, but when the arrow is moved laterally for shooting too far to one side, it is pivoted at the nock when the arrow rest or the sight is moved.

Normally, when adjusting for side winds, the sight would be adjusted sideways, but this is not required as often on many field courses as on a target archery field, since many courses are sufficiently sheltered to make wind effect rare except in exposed corners of a wood. Barebow archers merely try to counter the wind by aiming slightly off centre of the target, the degree depending on distance and the strength of the wind, so it becomes a bit of guesswork. Often the wind will be found to have more effect on the archer's arm than on the arrows, and at shorter distances it often has very little effect, which is what one would expect.

There is no specific aiming technique for barebow; most archers have to develop their own methods. Archers using freestyle sights can use a peepsight in some situations, but often they prefer not to. However, relying on the front sight and rear alignment will

An understanding of what moves where when making adjustments to the bow may help to avoid confusion

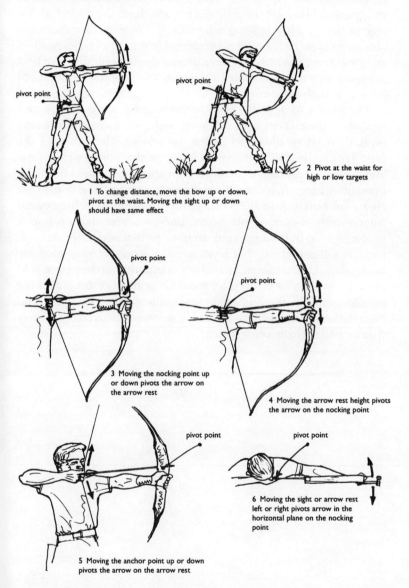

1 To change distance, move the bow up or down, pivot at the waist. Moving the sight up or down should have same effect

2 Pivot at the waist for high or low targets

3 Moving the nocking point up or down pivots the arrow on the arrow rest

4 Moving the arrow rest height pivots the arrow on the nocking point

5 Moving the anchor point up or down pivots the arrow on the arrow rest

6 Moving the sight or arrow rest left or right pivots arrow in the horizontal plane on the nocking point

Fig. 15 Bows as lever systems

depend on the setting of a kisser on the string. Compound unlimited archers can use a front sight with a lens, a peepsight in the string and a kisser on the string. They also have the added advantage of having a low holding weight on the bow and are therefore able to hold on the aim for a considerable length of time, producing great accuracy. I have frequently timed some unlimited archers at twenty seconds on the aim, which may not sound very much but is an amazingly long time.

The idea is to draw the bow, containing its stored energy, and hold it on the target centre while the sight pin floats gently about on it, then, when all is ready, press the release. The bow does the rest. This technique and the accuracy of the bow enables quite inexperienced archers to achieve high scores very quickly. At the time of writing, there are four Britons amongst the top seven compound archers in the world, which is quite an achievement. Interestingly, they have no coach, since it seems that no one is qualified to coach compound archers at that level. So they are entirely self-taught. At that level, perfect scores or very near are being shot. One national champion compound archer once told me that, at a shoot in Italy, he was four points off the maximum possible score at the end of an international championship and thought he was in line for a top place, but was dismayed to discover that he had actually come fourth!

6 Bow Tuning and Setting Up

When a bow is purchased new it is not in a shootable condition; it will not be fitted with two essential items – the arrow rest and the nocking point. Before either of these is fitted, the correct string length must be established. On a new bow, the manufacturer will have supplied a string of the correct length to produce the right bracing height, i.e. the distance from the nocking point to the arrow rest. On most recurve bows, this will be from about 8 inches to somewhat less than 10 inches. This sounds rather inexact, but it will vary from one design of bow to another. There will be a correct bracing height for each bow. If it is wrong the bow will not shoot at its most efficient. This can become critical for very high-scoring archers, who can sometimes be seen altering their bracing height while in the middle of a shoot by unstringing the bow, twisting or untwisting the string and then refitting it. This is only done in extreme circumstances when the bow is felt not to be working at its best, and most archers will not interfere with their string length unless they are desperate.

It is not uncommon for beginners to be given bows that have been fitted with incorrect strings so that the bracing height is too low for the bow to shoot well, and the string may also keep striking the wrist. Or the bow may be overbraced so that it is stressed far beyond what is acceptable. Any club instructor dealing with beginners should ensure that all bows are fitted with strings of the correct length. There is a simple method of discovering this without stringing the bow; if the string is looped on to the end of one limb, then on to the other with the bow the 'wrong' way round, it should fit between these two points without needing to bend the bow.

A bracing height gauge, as its name implies, is used for measuring bracing height. It clips on to the string and the distance to the arrow rest can then be measured. If the bow has the correct string length and is shooting well, grouping the arrows, then it is at the correct bracing height. This is essential not only for recurve bows but for all other types. Bracing height should be checked before shooting. If it is not as it should be, the string can be given a few twists to shorten it – but no more than about ten turns over its whole length – or twists removed to lengthen it, but not to the point where there are no twists at all, since this will separate the strands and thus weaken the string.

The arrow rest on a recurve bow will normally be positioned directly above the hand pressure point of the handle riser. I prefer not to call this the 'grip' since gripping the bow will affect performance – it is held rather than gripped. On a compound bow, the arrow rest may be above the pressure point or further back, giving

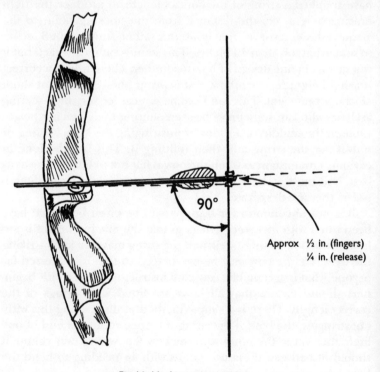

90°

Approx ½ in. (fingers)
¼ in. (release)

Fig. 16 Nocking point position

an element of 'overdraw' so that a shorter arrow can be shot. The advantage of this is that a lighter arrow can be shot.

When the arrow rest of one's choice has been fitted, the nocking point position can be selected. This is important because it balances the bow limb forces and if it is positioned incorrectly the arrow will not fly properly and will appear unstable in flight. Using a set square or, better, a bracing height gauge, fix a marker on the string so that its lower edge is about ½ inch above the 90 degree position on the string to the arrow rest. This marker can be a piece of thread (or dental floss is an old favourite), but better yet are the brass clips with soft plastic linings that are sold for the purpose. Place another marker lower down the string slightly more than the width of the arrow nock down. It is better to allow the nock a slight amount of movement between these points, since when the bow is drawn, the changing angle of the string will either jam the arrow nock too firmly or will force the nocking points further apart. On a compound bow, being shorter than the recurve, the string angle is far more pronounced and the position of the upper point may be moved unnecessarily. It is the position of the upper point that is important, since this is the one against which the arrow nock is forced.

Shoot several arrows at a fairly short distance and observe their flight. If they appear to wobble vertically, 'porpoising', then they are unstable and the nocking point will need to be moved. Observe how they have entered the target, whether tail high or low. If they are tail high, then move the nocking point down, if tail low, then move it up, but only by $\frac{1}{16}$th inch. Work in increments of that size until the unstable flight seems to have disappeared and the arrows are entering the target straight. Once this point is established, it should not need to be moved again unless the height of the arrow rest is changed.

Next deal with the arrow's horizontal flight characteristics. This can be more difficult since more factors are involved, but if the arrow spine is correct for the bow's draw weight, adjust the arrow-rest assembly or plunger so that the arrow is angled slightly outwards from the bow, i.e. pointing slightly to the left. On a recurve bow this adjustment will be only very slight, from ½ to $\frac{1}{16}$ inch measuring the arrow point against the string when viewed from the rear. It is probably better to use the plunger position for this than to attempt to adjust the plunger spring pressure, since

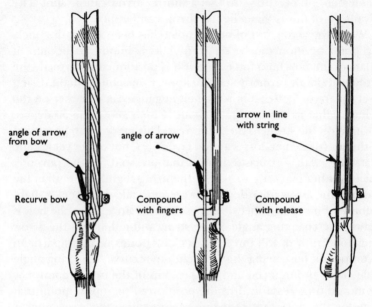

Moving the cable guard can affect these positions

Fig. 17 Arrow angle settings

that is more suitable when fine tuning. For a compound bow, using fingers, this distance should be about the same, and for a compound using a release aid, the arrow should be in line with the bowstring. This is because the release aid shoots the arrow straight rather than imparting slight side movement on it as the fingers do.

The Bare Shaft Planing Test

When setting up, one useful method is the bare shaft planing test. Shoot at least three fletched arrows at a target about 10–15 yards away. Then shoot two or three identically aimed unfletched arrow shafts of the same type and weight. If the unfletched shafts plane up or rise above the point where the fletched shafts impacted, move the nocking point up the bowstring until both fletched and unfletched shafts land in the same area on the target.

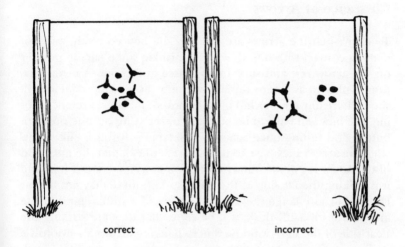

correct   incorrect

Fig. 18 Bare shaft planing test

If the bare shafts land below the fletched ones, move the nocking point down the string until both sets of arrows are landing at the same height.

To check that the porpoising effect has been eliminated, repeat the test, shooting the fletched shafts first, then the unfletched ones. Note that it is important to deal with this vertical setting before going on to the other adjustments.

For the next stage it is essential, if you are using a bowsight, to have the lateral adjustment of the sight in the centre. This test can also use the bare shafts in conjunction with the fletched arrows. If the bare shafts land to the left of the fletched ones, the spring pressure in the pressure plunger will need to be decreased, thus allowing the arrows to move to the right. If the bare shafts land to the right of the fletched ones, then the plunger or cushion pressure needs to be increased. When correcting for fishtailing (moving from side to side), using the bare shaft test, it may not be possible to make the two types of arrow land together. This may indicate that the arrows are slightly weak for the weight of the bow and will tend to shoot to the right. If the two shafts can be brought within 4 inches of each other at 15 yards, this is acceptable and good arrow performance should now be possible.

Clearance of Arrows

To check that the arrows are clearing the bow correctly, and not making contact with it as they pass, sprinkle some talcum powder on the arrow rest and surrounding area and shoot. An examination of the areas where the arrow might be making contact will show where any powder has been removed. If arrows are not clearing, the bow will have to be adjusted by screwing out the pressure button and testing once again for fishtailing. If this is still occurring, the arrows may have to be changed. Check that the nock end of the arrow is still in contact with the bow as it is shot. If it is, and it is striking the far side of the bow window, there may not be any choice but to change the arrows to a set of a stiffer spine. If the arrows are too stiff, there will be signs that they are striking the near side of the sight window. Since changing arrows is obviously a drastic step, ensure that nothing else is causing the problem, such as the string catching on clothing.

Shoot several arrows again and observe their flight characteristics. If they appear to fishtail, or wobble from side to side, adjust the spring-loaded plunger above the arrow rest or adjust the spring pressure. An observer standing behind you can be useful in these tests.

It can also happen that the fletchings may brush against the handle riser. If this is suspected it can be checked, again by lightly dusting the area around the arrow rest with talcum powder, shooting and checking if any marks have appeared in the powder. If they have, the arrow plunger needs to be screwed further out to push the arrow away from the bow, or the spring pressure needs adjusting. Some plungers are equipped with several springs of differing pressures and it is possible to change the spring.

In the unlikely event that none of these adjustments have sufficient effect, it may be that the arrow piles need changing to a different weight. Heavier piles will dampen the flexing of the shaft and so will have the effect of making it stiffer and shooting more to the left, while lighter piles will, of course, have the opposite effect.

Paper Tuning and Walk-back

Paper tuning seems to be very effective and is a relatively simple method of checking a variety of adjustments. It can also be carried out in a restricted space such as a back garden. The walk-back system is better, but requires at least 40 yards to be effective. Both tests can be done. It should not be necessary, but interesting results might be gained from comparing one with the other. A degree of accuracy in shooting is required, otherwise both tests are useless. If you are not a brilliant shot, you may find it necessary to shoot more arrows to get consistent results.

Paper Tuning

Fix a sheet of paper to some sort of frame – an old picture frame will do very well if you have one about 2 feet square, and support it at normal shooting height about 6 feet in front of a target butt. Shoot an arrow through the paper and observe the shape of the hole. If there is a hole with fletching slits arranged symmetrically round it, go no further for you already have perfection. However, this is unlikely and there will probably be an elongated hole with only two fletching slits showing. Depending on the angle of the hole, make the adjustments indicated in the illustration.

Walk-back

The walk-back or dropping arrow system requires a large target boss, preferably with a blank sheet of paper pinned to it. Then follow this procedure.

1 Start by using an aiming spot about 15 inches from the top edge of the target.
2 Set the sight at 15 yards then, without adjusting the sight, shoot one arrow at each of these distances, moving back for each one: 5, 10, 15, 20, 25, 30, 35 and 40 yards. Ideally, your arrows should result in a vertical straight line down the target (diagram 1). However, other patterns are possible, in fact likely.
3 If the pattern makes a curve to the left, as diagram 2, the arrow rest plunger should be screwed in.
4 If the pattern makes a curve to the right, as in diagram 3, the plunger needs to be screwed out.
5 If the pattern forms a slanting line to the left, as in diagram 4, the plunger spring is too stiff. This can be relieved by screwing the spring-retaining screw out slightly or by changing the spring

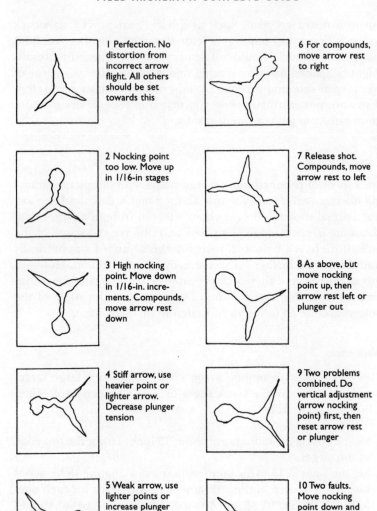

1 Perfection. No distortion from incorrect arrow flight. All others should be set towards this

2 Nocking point too low. Move up in 1/16-in stages

3 High nocking point. Move down in 1/16-in. increments. Compounds, move arrow rest down

4 Stiff arrow, use heavier point or lighter arrow. Decrease plunger tension

5 Weak arrow, use lighter points or increase plunger spring tension. Move arrow rest to left for finger shot compounds

6 For compounds, move arrow rest to right

7 Release shot. Compounds, move arrow rest to left

8 As above, but move nocking point up, then arrow rest left or plunger out

9 Two problems combined. Do vertical adjustment (arrow nocking point) first, then reset arrow rest or plunger

10 Two faults. Move nocking point down and arrow rest or plunger to right

Fig. 19 Paper tuning

for one of a lower pressure. The original plunger will have been supplied with three springs of different stiffness.
6 If the pattern forms a slanting line to the right, as in diagram 5, then the plunger spring needs to be stiffened.

Slight adjustments only are needed; make a note of what you have done, since it is only too easy to forget which way something has been adjusted. Distances need not be exact for this test, since they are irrelevant.

It is also important to realize that these instructions are for right-handed recurve bows fitted with spring-loaded plungers. Left-handed bows should be adjusted the opposite way. If you are shooting a compound with a release aid you will probably only encounter the last two situations. It would be unusual for it to form a curving pattern, since there is no side spring loading on its arrow rest, and if the slanting line patterns emerged, it might be that the arrows are not suited to the bow peak weight. Side adjustment of arrow rests will generally only produce a vertical line somewhere on the target, so that it only needs adjusting to bring the line down the centre.

Patterns of arrows formed by moving back 5 yards for each shot, without changing sight distances

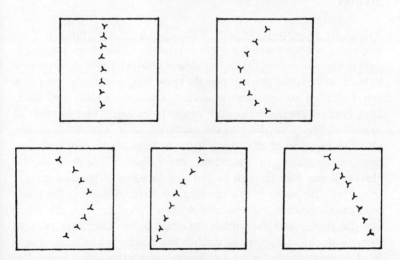

Fig. 20. The walk-back method of tuning

It is a useful exercise in another way, for it will give an excellent idea of the amount of arrow drop on the target for a given distance. Incorrectly estimating the distance by 5 yards may still result in the arrow reaching the kill or it may be way out, but this will also depend on the total distance; there is more chance of it being in at a longer range than a shorter one. If, through inaccurate shooting, no consistent pattern emerges, you may need to shoot a group of arrows at each distance. But do not expect too much if your shooting career is still in the early stages.

This test is not very useful for determining the correct nocking point height. That will still have to be done at short range, preferably with the bare shaft planing test or the paper test. A lot of time can be spent happily testing and adjusting if that is what you enjoy, but it is only a means to an end, and that is to set your bow up so that it is shooting as accurately as you can make it. The rest is up to you. It is not a good idea constantly to be adjusting this, resetting that, fiddling with bits that are never quite right. Once you feel that everything is at optimum setting, leave it alone to perform its function while you concentrate on the really important part of shooting, which is to enjoy it.

Strings

Strings are an important part of the tuning process, but are often neglected. Correct string length is vital, as I have said, but thickness is also an important aspect. Many archers pay little attention to their strings, but the top people know how important the properties of their strings are for stretch, elasticity, length and thickness. Some have them specially made by experts. The number of strands differs according to the material, so it is of some importance to know what the string is made from, especially with new mixtures appearing on the market more often. Once there was no choice, it was B60 Dacron or nothing but now there is a greater selection. The number of strands in the string will affect the bow's performance, since the power of the bow drives not only the arrow but the string and everything attached to it. Therefore, a light string with the minimum of strands will enable a heavier arrow to be shot, since more power will be going into the arrow instead of the string. Conversely, of course, a thicker string may require a thinner and lighter arrow. The addition of string silencers and other attachments will degrade performance, but perhaps not enough to be important to the average field archer.

Setting Up a Compound Bow

Compound bow peak weights are calculated differently according to whether they are fitted with round wheels or cams, and whether they are being shot with fingers or a release aid. If Dacron string is being used, *subtract* 3–5 pounds from the draw weight to find the peak weight. If Release aid is being used, *add* 5–7 pounds. If over-draw devices are being used, the draw weight will increase according to the increase in overdraw length. A 1-inch overdraw, for example, will increase the draw weight by 1 or 2 pounds. For bows which are under 43 inches long, but over 28 inches draw, *add* 4–6 pounds. For heavy arrow piles, *add* 1–2 pounds for every 10 grains over the recommended arrow weight.

These calculations should be used when selecting the correct arrow size for a bow, using Easton's arrow selection chart. You will also need to know which arrows you wish to shoot, since there are several sizes suitable for a given weight range of bows, and you may be able to shoot two different types at the same weight, although it may be necessary to use two sight mark ranges if you are using sights. This is quite easy; just make a sight mark range from, say, 10 to 80 yards, down one edge of a bowsight for X7 arrows and another range down the other edge for ACCs, since you may not be able to shoot both on the same sight marks. Theoretically, since the ACCs are lighter in weight, they may be expected to be shot on sight marks slightly higher than X7s, but in practice they may need lower sight marks, as if for a heavier arrow.

There are several ways of setting up and adjusting compound bows. To ascertain which to use for a specific bow, refer to the manufacturer's handbook. If you have bought it second hand, however, you may not have the book, so here is a general guide for setting up most compounds.

There are several points of adjustment:

• the main limb adjustment bolts
• the string length

- the nocking point
- the arrow rest
- the peepsight, if fitted
- the bowsight, if fitted
- the kisser, if fitted
- the degree of let-off
- wheel rollover

The list may seem daunting, but many are simple to adjust and the important thing to remember is that many of them are interrelated; one cannot be adjusted without affecting others.

Adjusting Draw Weight

The main limb bolts control the draw weight. On most compounds, the weight can be adjusted within a range of 15 pounds. Bows are made to lie in a certain weight range, e.g. 45–60 pounds, or 55–70 pounds. The weight is altered by screwing the main limb bolts in or out. Screwing in the bolts will increase the weight, while unscrewing will decrease it. It is important that this is done evenly on each limb, making one turn at a time, but never more than four. It is worth bearing in mind that the manufacturers state that the bows are working at their greatest efficiency when at their top weight.

The limb bolts on some bows can turn while in use, without the archer being aware of it, and thus the bow may go out of adjustment, the tiller (the balance of the bend of the limbs) will alter and the performance will change, so the bolt head position may need to be marked by a paint line to check whether this is happening. If it is, the bolts will have to be turned to their correct positions, or locked in some way to prevent inadvertent turning. A small indentation lightly hammered into the line between the bolt head and the housing with a centre punch may work.

After setting the limb bolts, the tiller should be checked. This is a vital measurement of the relationship between the limbs, and is done by measuring the distance of the string from the point at which each limb enters the handle riser. The distance should be the same for both limbs. If it is not, check the number of turns of the limb bolts and adjust until the tiller is correct. When adjusting bolts, it is a good idea to tighten them as far as they will go, with-

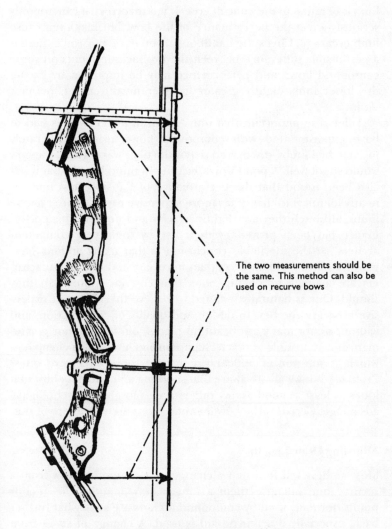

The two measurements should be the same. This method can also be used on recurve bows

Fig. 21 Measuring tiller on a compound bow

out overtightening, then screw them out to the desired position, if necessary.

Tiller measurement is vital on all bows, even longbows, since it is a check on the even balance of power from the limbs. It is carried out during the manufacturing process to check that each

141

limb is bending to the same degree. If it is incorrect, it can not only seriously affect the performance of the bow, but may even cause limb breakage. Check the handbook if you have one, since there is a permissible difference between the two measurements on some compound bows, and performance may be improved by having the lower limb slightly greater in tiller measurement, perhaps ³/16 inch.

Tiller is so important that one American expert who is said to have experimented with compound bows, using deliberately mismatched limbs, discovered that if the tiller was correct, the bow would shoot well. A point worth bearing in mind here is that it has also been found that the performance of flat fibreglass limbs is nearly identical to that of far more expensive carbon fibre recurve limbs, although they are slightly heavier and noisier. This performance has been proved by their use by some very competent archers, so the inevitable conclusion is that many archers have paid far more for their bows than necessary and that manufacturers are actually producing bows that cost far more than they should. One is naturally inclined to believe that the most expensive bows are the best in design and quality of construction, and without doubt many are beautiful pieces, but what about performance? Is it possible to reach championship level with a cheap bow which is inferior in appearance to the more expensive ones? Probably, but we all are aware that shooting an up-to-date bow that looks as least as good as any others seems to give a psychological advantage. Certainly the bow manufacturers are well aware of this.

Adjusting Draw Length

Most archers will find that a change to a compound bow from a recurve one will give them a longer draw length. The anchor points normally used by compound archers are somewhat further back, especially if a release aid is used. A change of styles from freestyle to compound with a release aid will need about 2 inches more in arrow length.

Draw length adjustment is not possible on all compounds, since some have no provision for it apart from changing the length of the string. This is usually the case with the cheaper models. The most common method of adjustment is on the wheels, where there may be alternative positions for the string loops. On most quality bows there are three string loop anchor points and moving the loop from one position can alter the string length by about ½ inch, and the draw length by the same amount. On most bows it is possible to alter one end without the other, but altering both will double the adjustment.

It is essential to get the draw length correct for comfortable use. If it is too short, you will feel cramped and unable to draw the bow properly, while if it is too long you may not be able to draw the string into the lowest let-off point, the valley, or you may feel that you have to make too much effort to achieve full draw, and your body is being stretched too much. Many compound archers shoot with the bow arm slightly bent at the elbow and do not adopt the straighter arm preferred by most freestyle recurve bowmen, so the draw length may appear to be shorter, but in fact the drawing hand is further back.

It is worth bearing in mind that changes in string length will also affect draw weight so this will perhaps need checking after any changes in string length. Do not attempt to make any alterations in string length without relieving the tension on the string. This can be done in several ways, depending on the make and design of the bow. It can often be done by using a strong cord or cable, which is made for the purpose, and which hooks onto the limbs or cables so that the bow can be drawn, the cable fitted to take the tension and the string can then be removed. On some bows it is possible to draw the bow, lock the wheels by inserting a rod such as a screwdriver through holes in them, then remove the string or cables. I have only once seen anyone do this in the field, in order to replace a frayed cable, and it was remarkably simple. It is possible to purchase these cables with fittings which can be used as a bow press to remove cables and wheels.

Any bow work at home will often require the main limb bolts to be screwed out to relieve all the tension in the bow and enable it to be stripped down. This will, of course, mean that it will have to be set up for shooting all over again when it is reassembled. It is possible to change the string loop position on the wheels, to change the draw length, by unscrewing the limb bolts, relieving some of the tension and screwing them back up. With many bows, totally unscrewing the bolts may still not relieve all the tension and some difficulty may be encountered in refitting cables or strings. The method of dealing with this problem will vary from one make to another, but locking the wheels will work for most.

The best device for servicing compounds is a proper bow press, preferably one of the double-pull variety that pulls evenly on both ends of the handle riser, but these machines are too expensive for the average archer to purchase for occasional use and are normally found only in the archery dealers' shops. They allow bows to be taken apart and rebuilt speedily, and any servicing and repairs to be done. Older types of bow press may have only a single-pull system which pulls the handle down against the arms which hold the bow limbs in place, and it is easy to overstress the handle with this type.

Cheaper bows often do not have any means of altering the string or draw length and thus the only means of doing so is by fitting a string of a different length. It is best to consult your nearest archery dealer before venturing into this, since the bow may not be able to accommodate a different string length without overstressing it in some way.

Drastic changes of draw length can sometimes be made by changing the size of the wheels or cams used. Smaller wheels can be fitted to decrease the draw length while bigger ones will increase it, by changing the length of the string wound round them. This is a considerable change to the bow, and, again, should not be done without a dealer's advice. Compound bow limbs move very little compared to recurve bows, so any large change should be carefully considered. New wheels are often expensive and the cost of new cables and string to fit must be added on.

Fitting the Arrow Rest

There is a wide variety of arrow rests available for compound bows, some of them quite complex. They fall into two main groups: one provides for the arrow to shoot round the rest, and is designed to be used by finger shooters, while the other type is intended to be used by release aid archers.

When fitting a rest for finger shooters, it should be set so that the point of the arrow is slightly out from the bow, i.e. on a right handed bow, it would point slightly to the left. This is to accommodate the slight side movement of the bow string when it is released from the fingers. The arrow fletching should be arranged in the normal configuration of cock feather horizontal, at right angles to the string. Shooting will soon show where the arrow rest needs to be adjusted in order to get the shot centred.

On recurve bows, the handle is so designed that the string should lie exactly on the bow centre line, but this cannot be done very easily on compound bows because of the necessity of having the balance cables wound round the wheels. Stresses on the limbs must be balanced, so the actual bowstring is positioned to the left of the cables (on a right-handed bow). The arrow rest will still relate to the position of the arrow on the string rather than the position of the string in relationship to the bow limbs.

Most of the shoot-around rests do not have any provision for vertical adjustment and are somewhat simpler than the release-aid type. The shoot-through or release-aid types are more complex and sometimes have provision for vertical and horizontal adjustment, as well as falling away when the arrow moves over them. To set them correctly, start by adjusting side position until the arrow, nocked on the string, lies in line with it. Set the vertical adjustment in relation to the nocking point in the usual way, so that the arrow is positioned slightly above a right angle to the string. If, when checking the nocking point position by shooting, the arrows appear to be flying as if the nocking point is too low, it may be easier to adjust the arrow rest height than to move the nocking point, by moving it down and shooting again to check. The fletchings should be positioned so that, for fork-type rests, one lies vertically downwards in the fork. For the 'lizard tongue' type rest, or loop types, the vertical fletch will lie upwards so that there is no interference of fletchings with the rest. The fork-type rest appears to be rather better for holding the arrow in place in side winds, but support with all these rests is delicate and the arrow has to be drawn gently so as not to pull it off the rest. The modern insert type nocks can often be rotated quite easily to match the fletching position to the arrow rest. Some of the more sophisticated arrow rests incorporate a mechanism that drops the rest out of the way when the arrow is shot.

Adjusting the Nocking Point

The nocking point position is vital. The position where the arrow fits on the string must be carefully placed to even out the stress on the limbs and to ensure that the arrow flies correctly. The procedure for this is the same as for the recurve bow, but there is more latitude on the compound bow. Because the bow is shorter, the more acute angle formed by the string when it is at full draw, must be taken into account and the two nocking point markers must be positioned slightly further apart to account for this, or the arrow nock will simply force them apart. If dental floss is used, it may need to be kept in place by a couple of drops of superglue, but most compound archers prefer to use the brass clip type of nocking point, especially those with a soft plastic liner to grip the string.

There is also a type of nocking point which is useful for cushioning the release aid against the arrow nock; it has a thick rubber cushion held in place with a brass clip. This can be fitted if difficulty is found with the release pushing the arrow nock off the string, as can sometimes happen.

Finger shooters may find that their fingers, combined with a tab, inflict some wear on the nocking point. Dental floss tends to stay in place better than most types of thread, and the application of superglue will help, but not until the nocking point position has been clearly determined. When shooting with fingers rather than a release, the bow adjustments for correcting fishtailing and porpoising are similar to those for a recurve bow. An additional adjustment is possible in the form of the bow poundage adjustment bolts, and if it is suspected that the spine of the arrows is incorrect, it may be possible to adjust the draw weight until the arrows are performing correctly within the bow parameters. This can be done in increments of 1 pound at a time, since it would be very easy to overdo the adjustments to the point of making the bow unshootable, or at least uncomfortable.

If arrows are fishtailing and landing too far left, try adjusting the arrow rest in or increasing the bow weight. If they are landing too far right, try moving the arrow rest out or decreasing the bow weight. This is true of right-handed bows, but the effect will be the opposite for left-handed bows, and the adjustments will accordingly also be the opposite. At one time springy rests were very popular for compound bows and if one of these is fitted to the bow being set up, springs of different strengths may still be available.

Calibrating the Bowsight

If you intend to shoot with a sight which is adjustable, moving on a vertical track, you will need to calibrate it before doing any serious shooting.

Calibration is straightforward if you have a marked distance

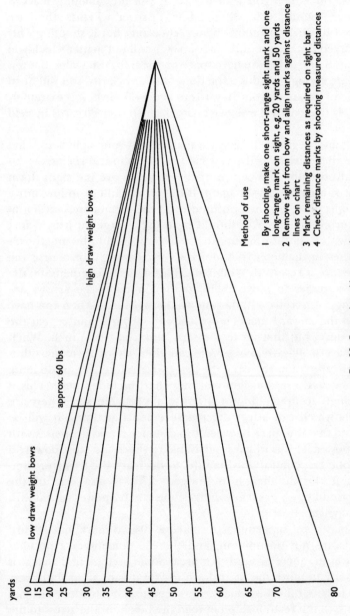

yards

low draw weight bows

approx. 60 lbs

high draw weight bows

Method of use

1 By shooting, make one short-range sight mark and one long-range mark on sight, e.g. 20 yards and 50 yards
2 Remove sight from bow and align marks against distance lines on chart
3 Mark remaining distances as required on sight bar
4 Check distance marks by shooting measured distances

Fig. 22 Bowsight calibration chart

range available, preferably marked in both metres and yards so you can choose which you wish to use. If you are shooting marked distance rounds, you will need to discover whether they are marked in yards or metres before choosing, but if shooting only unmarked distance rounds or courses, it will not matter which you choose. Some sights will have space on them for two scales, but few are wide enough for this to be done with any clarity. You will need a scale of distances from 10 yards to about 80 yards; it is extremely unlikely that you will ever see a target much over 80 yards in field archery.

To start, begin at the 20-yard marker, put your sight somewhat above the halfway of the vertical bar, and shoot three arrows. If they drop below the centre of the target, move the sight down about ¼ inch and shoot again. If the arrows still drop low, move the sight down again. Continue until the arrows are landing at the correct height. You should be using a target at least 3 feet high with a spot for aiming that does not need to be much over 2 inches in diameter. If the arrows fly too high, of course the procedure is reversed. When adjusting sights to compensate, the trick is always to move them in the direction the arrows are moving, i.e. arrows left, then move the sight left. When you have found the 20-yard mark, move back to 40 yards and repeat the procedure, but first move the sight down about ½ inch. When you have a 40-yard mark, you can then shoot as many other distances as you wish, using the first two as references, or do it the easy way and use the sight-marking chart included here. This is amazingly accurate, but not always totally reliable, since there are factors which can affect the measurements at times. It will be noticed that the space between two distance marks decreases with bow power. This is why it is advisable to shoot the most powerful bow one can comfortably handle, to decrease the trajectory and error if the distance is misjudged. This is also one of the compound bow's great advantages, the greater power stored with less physical effort.

It may seem superfluous to make a 10-yard mark, but 10-yard targets are not uncommon, and there is sometimes a peculiar effect at distances around that area. Some archers find that it is necessary to move the sight down to 20 yards or so to shoot very short targets, otherwise their arrows tend to shoot too low. This has to do with the relationship between the height of the arrow to the height of the eye, and this to the height of the sight above the arrow. When moved too high, the sight effect will reverse and the arrow will shoot too low. Targets are placed at these seemingly silly distances in order to catch out those who do not know about this phenomenon.

If you prefer to mark distances on the sight track, a thin strip of polystyrene card stuck to it with white PVA glue can be used, and the distances marked on it in pencil. This will allow marks to be removed with an ordinary eraser, but the pencil will not wash off when wet. Some sights come equipped with a measured strip attached, so you then have to make a chart of distances and what their measurements are on the strip, and this has to be consulted before moving the sight. Some prefer to do this, but it has always seemed a cumbersome method to me.

When you have become accustomed to your bow, you may find it easy to make new sight marks when any alterations are made, since you will have learned roughly what the spacing distance is on the sight bar. Alterations have to be made for wide variety of reasons, since many things can affect sight marks – a change of arrows, for example, with a change of weight, or a new bowstring.

Fitting a Peepsight

If the bow is to be shot with sights, a rear reference point may be desirable. This may be in the form of a kisser, a peepsight, or both. The kisser is merely a plastic or rubber disc fitted round the string so that it can be felt by the lips when at full draw, usually in the corner of the mouth as it is used by most compound archers. When it comes into a predetermined place the archer knows that he is at full draw.

A compound string is generally thicker than that of a recurve bow and if the archer is unable to see round it to the front sight, a peepsight fitted into the string is a great help. The position is critical, since it should align with the front sight. It can easily be set up by fitting it into the string, but without serving it in, then lining it up with the front sight and moving up or down until it is in a comfortable position. Do not, ever, try to shoot the bow without the peep being bound in place.

One type of peepsight has a rubber tube connecting it to the bow so that at full draw, the tube tightens and pulls the peep round into the right position for looking through. These tubes can be troublesome and break or pull off frequently, so their length has to be carefully adjusted. Some archers find that binding or attaching them to one of the cables works well. Another type is bound into the string, which is split into three parts, and this seems to work for some people, since wherever the string is twisted, the peepsight can still be looked through. It must be said that some archers find it tricky to use, but for others it is an advantage. Perhaps it depends on the quality of one's eyesight.

The position of both the peepsight and the kisser will depend to a great extent on the hand position, but with a compound, there is a great variation of hand positions. Many top archers prefer to shoot with the hand along the cheek, while other prefer to have it along the jawline, and some tend to hold it under the jaw. Too high a position will, however, mean that there may be difficulty in getting the longer distances as the sight is moved down, since it will come to a point where it will interfere with the arrow. Conversely, if the hand is too low, it can be difficult to feel an anchor point for it.

The size of the aperture through the peepsight is entirely up to you; some people prefer a tiny hole that only permits a view of part of the front sight and others prefer a large hole that allows a far greater view but that may not be so precise in alignment.

Many sights cut down the light from the target. Using a peep exacerbates this problem; poorly lit targets, or dark targets concealed under dark undergrowth can be totally invisible. Sights should therefore be chosen carefully, with scopes, lenses and peeps that will give the maximum possible light. Shooting will often take place in poor light conditions, but manufacturers have realized that black-shrouded scope sights designed to keep all stray light out are actually extremely difficult to use and modern scope sights are nearly all made from light-gathering plastics, and their size has increased with the years as well. Many now also come equipped with fibre-optic pins that glow and can be seen easily in nearly all light conditions. If a scope sight is being used without a peepsight and the image is blurred, this is not necessarily due to a faulty lens; fitting a peepsight will clarify the picture.

Adjusting the Cable Guard

When a bow is purchased new, the cable guard, which is designed to keep the cables from interfering with the arrow, is usually locked in place and should be clear of the arrows. However, there is considerable vibration in compound bows and bits often work loose without the archer becoming aware of it until it is too late. Sometimes the cable guard can work loose and prevent the arrows from being laid on the arrow rest. It will need to be turned back and locked in place, so that there is a clearance of ³/₈ inch between it and the fletchings. This is usually done by tightening set screws or grub screws set in the guard mount. If it is any further out there will be too much side strain on the limbs and the bow will be distorted. Cable sliders or rollers can be fitted to reduce the friction of cables over the guard and if the cables are held inside the guard they will be fitted with a slider.

One idea for eliminating the need for a cable guard and balancing the pull of the cables on the limbs is to arrange four cables, two on each side of the string. There are some bows now being built which incorporate this concept.

Adjusting the Let-off

A few bows have provision for adjusting the let-off, the amount by which the weight drops off as the bow is drawn from the peak weight. This is usually inherent in the bow's design and is normally about 60 per cent, but in some this can be changed to 65 per cent or even up to 80 per cent or down to 50 per cent. The method is usually in the design of the wheels, but the best guide to this is the manufacturer's handbook. Most bows cannot be adjusted for let-off.

Adjusting the Wheel Rollover

After any work involving cables, wheels or string, it is essential to check that the wheel rollover is equal. If the bow is fitted with identical wheels at each end, they must be matched in their angular movement. This is simple to check by drawing the bow slowly and watching the movement of the wheels; if they start at the same angle and come to rest at full draw at the same angle, they are correctly adjusted. If not, the bow's performance may be affected and the movement of the nocking point as the string is drawn may be uneven. The wheel rollover can be adjusted on some bows by slackening off the bow tension, removing one of the cables and twisting or untwisting it to shorten or lengthen it as necessary, so that its length is equal to the other cable. Since bow cables are usually fitted as equal lengths, this problem is unlikely to occur.

Some bows are now single-cam models, with the working cam at the lower end and an idler wheel at the top. This eliminates the problem of unequal wheel rollover, and some of these are the fastest-shooting bows available. It may be necessary to check the movement of the nocking point on these, since one early problem with them was that the nocking point moved out of vertical alignment at full draw. This problem has virtually been eliminated by improvements in design, however.

Reducing Hysteresis

This sounds like a medical complaint, but it is simply the amount of energy lost by the bow in friction and other factors when the string is loosed. The amount of energy stored by the bow is less than it gives out. It is particularly evident in compound bows, where there is so much opportunity for friction to have adverse effects. It can be found by drawing the bow up with a spring balance to full draw and noting the rise in draw weight to the peak, then the drop down to full draw. When the bow is slowly let down, as the peak is passed, the poundage does not rise to the peak it reached previously. This difference is hysteresis. Thus it can be seen that the bow will push the arrow out with rather less energy than was thought. This factor can never be entirely eliminated, since some of the friction is within the structure of the limbs, but it can be reduced by measures such as lubricating the wheel bearings, removing as much weight as possible from the string, waxing the string, etc. Anything added to the string reduces the energy put into the arrow. At one well-known archery dealer's, I was once told that it was surprising how many compound bows came in for servicing or repairs with rusty wheel pivot pins. It pays to oil them occasionally.

Overdraws

An overdraw is an arrow rest extension which fits on the bow handle riser in order to allow the use of shorter and lighter arrows. This can also have the effect of making the bow less stable and more difficult to shoot because of added sensitivity, a lower bracing height and a faster arrow. If taken too far, however, it is possible to damage the bow if the arrow becomes too light to absorb the energy put into it, so selection of correct arrow weight and size becomes crucial. Overdraws do not seem to have become very popular in Britain, and are not often seen.

Going for Speed

In recent years, particularly with the rise of 3D shooting, bow speed has become more important. It has been calculated that the trajectory of a light arrow is flatter than that of a heavier one, but the lighter arrow will also travel faster, of course. The amount of drop can become critical on 3D targets, so that if an arrow is dropping 4 inches over, say 25 yards, where a faster and lighter arrow might only drop 2 inches, this could make a considerable difference to scores.

Various measures can be taken to make a bow shoot faster for the same weight. One of these is to use cams instead of wheels. They give a different feel to the bow, since when it is drawn, the weight rises rapidly to the peak, stays there for some distance, then drops down to the valley very quickly. This means that the bow is pushing the arrow out with more power for longer, with a longer power stroke. This also makes these bows difficult to shoot, since they can be hard to draw up the rapid rise in weight from rest, and any relaxation of the drawing hand can result in the string being snatched out of the hand. There have been injuries to archers who were unaware of these factors, when the most extreme cams are fitted. These cams are often fitted to bows with rearward curving risers to make the bracing height even lower. Some American field archery organizations are now limiting arrow speeds, since they have found that these extremely fast bows can create problems of safety.

The quest for higher speeds has resulted in bow manufacturers boasting that their bow is the fastest in the world, and it is possible to find the arrow speed stated in two scales, from two different organizations, measured in two different ways. It is evident that compromises must be made in design, as with everything, and the laws of physics and mechanics often dictate that trade-offs must be made. Arrow speed is increased at the cost of an easily handled bow.

Drawing one of these fast bows is quite different from drawing one with round wheels, which is built for stability and smoothness. The latter draws steadily and easily with less effort for the same poundage and is more comfortable to use, with less of the feeling that it is going to suddenly take control and jerk itself out of the archer's hands. The passion for fast bows has not taken over entirely in Britain and many archers still prefer something more moderate in action.

Some archers are also concerned about arrow weight, the weight of points, the weight per inch of shafts, the weight of nocks, and so on. The weight per inch of arrow shafts can be calculated in grains, so that if an inch of shaft is cut off the reduction in weight can be known precisely. Piles can be obtained in a range of weights, and those archers concerned with very high levels of performance and the precise calculation of all aspects of their equipment can become obsessed, but as in many other areas, most people are forced to compromise. Light arrows are less stable, inherently less accurate and more sensitive to errors in technique. Heavier arrows are more forgiving, and it may be noticeable that many top archers are not overly concerned with the weight of the arrow, but prefer to shoot an arrow that falls in the middle of the range suitable for their bow.

There can be differences in the performance of arrows, even though they may appear to be perfectly matched. It is possible for slight variations in performance to appear after a set has been shot for a while, so it is useful to find out if any in a particular set are not shooting as straight as they should, and either attempt to find out why and rectify the fault or discard them. It is possible for a shaft to appear straight and yet not shoot consistently straight. Usually the most obvious measure to take with such arrows is to replace the fletchings, even if they appear to be perfectly acceptable. Then the nock may be changed. This should cure the problem, but beware of the rogue arrow which seems to be exactly right in every respect, but will not fly correctly or accurately. It may be worth carefully checking your arrows after every period of shooting. Certainly field arrows get far more punishment than target arrows, and can sometimes be found to be bent even when it is known that they have never missed the target and should therefore be in perfect condition.

It seems that very few field archers in Britain are very concerned with the details of finely weighed arrows beyond a concern that they should shoot straight.

Bow Care and Maintenance

All machines fail, and the more complex they are, the more often they will fail.

Good design and workmanship can reduce failure, but it takes time for this to take effect and to design out the points where failure can occur. Sometimes, of course, it can never be entirely eliminated, so bows will fail, however well they are made. Care in use and regular checks of the equipment can reduce the chances of failure, since it is possible sometimes to see where problems may be occurring before they get too bad. And, as I have said, compound bows are subject to far more vibration and shock than any other type and therefore need checking more often.

Get into the habit of examining your bow before shooting. Check the state of the string and cables, looking for fraying and wear and making sure that serving is in place and not too worn. Check for cracks anywhere, for tightness, and for mud or sand in the cable grooves of the wheels, since this will wear cables through quickly. Wax the string regularly, with the special waxes devised for the new string materials. This helps to prevent fraying. Traditional beeswax works well on Dacron, preventing it from becoming too dry. It keeps in essential moisture. Check the serving regularly – it wears and needs replacing occasionally.

Things One Should Never Do to a Bow

1 Leave a strung bow in the back of a car on a hot day. Recurve bows can twist alarmingly.
2 Dry fire a bow (i.e. firing without an arrow). The bow is not designed to absorb the energy that should go into the arrow, and

it is possible to break the bow or the string, although one American bow company said that they dry fired a bow 3,000 times without adverse effect. They also found that they could test bow handles to destruction using Fastflight string, which is six times stronger than steel. Bows fitted with steel cables could not be tested since the steel cables always broke first.

3 Attempt to draw a bow beyond its designed draw length.
4 Shoot with worn cables or strings. They should be replaced as soon as signs of wear appear. If you are replacing serving, replace the string beneath as well if it is worn. Certain string materials have a limited life, although one type, S4, a mixture of Fastflight, Kevlar and Vectran is said to have a life of 25,000 shots, which must be adequate for most bow strings.
5 Leave a compound bow unused for some time without letting off some of the tension in the cables and string by unscrewing the limb bolts. Strings can break even when a bow is not in use. Not only that, but it is also possible for bows to break.

Curing Problems

Fault	1st fix	2nd fix	Compound
Arrows fly left.	Screw sight to left.	Screw arrow rest plunger in.	Adjust arrow rest to right.
Arrows fly right.	Screw sight to right.	Screw arrow rest plunger out.	Adjust arrow rest to left.
Arrows drop low.	Screw sight down.	Check nocking point – it may be too high.	Adjust arrow rest up.
Arrows fly too high.	Screw sight up.	Nocking point may be too low.	Adjust arrow rest down.
Arrows curve left.	Check that the arrow size fits the bow draw weight. Arrows too stiff?		
Arrows curve right.	As above but the arrow may not be stiff enough.		
Strange noises from the bow.	Check everything!		

Arrow will not stay on rest.	Check rest.	Check that your fingers are not squeezing the arrow nock.	
Stabiliser mount loose.	Workshop job – see chapter 15.		
Arrows fishtail.	Arrow rest not aligned with string.	Try bare shaft planing test.	
Arrows porpoise.	Check nocking point height.	Try bare shaft planing test.	
One arrow deviates from others.	Faulty arrow – replace.		
Arrows fly high right.	Screw sight up and right.	Screw arrow rest down and left.	Move nocking point up and arrow rest left.
Arrows fly low right.	Screw sight down and right.	Screw arrow rest up and left.	Move nocking point down and arrow rest left.
Arrows flying high left.	Screw sight up and left.	Screw arrow rest down and right.	Move nocking point up and arrow rest right.
Arrows flying low left.	Screw sight down and left.	Screw arrow rest up and right.	Move nocking point down and arrow rest right.
String bruising arm.	Arm locked – relax elbow.		

7 Field Archery Rounds

Target archers shoot at the same target all day, or even for two days. Field archers shoot at a wide variety of targets in a wide variety of circumstances and conditions and this is the basic differences between the two forms of archery.

Field archery is conducted in rounds, with a round consisting of any number of targets as decided by the shoot organizers or laid down in the rules of the national ruling body concerned. Since there are three ruling bodies, each of which has its own rounds, there are many options to choose from, but in practice, only one or two are in common use.

The major differences between the rounds laid down by the various bodies are simple to explain. GNAS and EFAA rounds are based on or are laid down by international bodies such as FITA and most of the targets used by them are black and white ringed faces. Both bodies support international contests and send teams to participate in them. However, NFAS, does not shoot to international rules, does not have international teams and has expressed in its major policy document that it has no interest in international shooting. It also does not use black and white ringed target faces.

EFAA Rounds

Unmarked Distance Rounds

The **Big Game Round** is in standard units of fourteen targets, with a maximum distance of 60 yards, on animal faces, as outlined in the IFAA rules. The **3D Animal round** is also in standard units of fourteen targets, with a maximum distance of 60 yards, on 3D animal figures. The scoring and number of shots is the same as the Big Game round.

Marked Distance Rounds

The **3D Animal Round** is also exactly the same as the Unmarked 3D Animal round except that target distances are measured and stated near the shooting markers.

IFAA Rounds

EFAA also uses IFAA rounds as follows (other organizations do not use IFAA rounds). IFAA rounds are both marked and unmarked distances. Archers normally shoot in pairs. The rules of shooting and more details of the rounds can be found in the appendix. As with the other organizations, this brief outline is only for rough guidance.

Field Round

Four face sizes of 20 cm, 35 cm, 50 cm, and 65 cm diameter are used, each being a black spot with a white inner ring and black outer ring. Four shots are taken at each target. The scoring is five for the spot, four for the inner ring and three for the outer ring, so that the maximum possible on each target is twenty points. The distances are up to 80 yards with a minimum of 20 feet. Rounds are shot in standard units of fourteen targets or multiples of fourteen.

Hunter Round

Face sizes are similar to the Field round, but the faces are all black with a white spot. The scoring is also the same as the Field round, as is the number of shots at each target. Distances are to a maximum of 70 yards. The number of targets is the same as for the Field round. Interestingly, there is no indication in the rule book of which of these rounds is marked distance and which unmarked.

Animal Round

Animal faces are grouped into four sizes from group 1, the largest, down to group 4, the smallest. Group 1 is shot between 40 and 60 yards, group 2 between 30 and 45 yards, group 3 between 20 and 35 yards and group 4 between 10 and 20 yards.

There are three shots at each target, but only until a score is made. Scoring is: first arrow kill, twenty points; first arrow wound, eighteen points; second arrow kill, sixteen points; second arrow wound, fourteen points; third arrow kill, twelve points; third arrow wound, ten points. Shooting positions can be walk-up (i.e. markers decreasing distance to target) or all arrows shot from one position. There will be markers indicating the distance of each target from the shooting pegs. Animal rounds can be marked or unmarked.

Other Rounds

The **International** round is a twenty-target round on standard Hunter round faces (black with white spot), with three arrows shot at each target. Scoring is the same as the Hunter round. Distances range up to a maximum of 65 yards, but again there is no indication of whether this is intended to be shot as a marked or unmarked round.

The **Expert Field** round is the same as the Field round except that subdividing lines are used on the target faces in the spot, for tie breakers. The scoring is: five points for a spot, four for the second circle, three for the third circle, two for the fourth circle and one for the fifth circle.

NFAS Rounds

All shooting is at unmarked distances. Archers shoot one at a time on all rounds.

Big Game Round

This uses animal faces of a wide range of sizes from the stoat, about 8 inches long, to the Swedish bear, of about 4 feet wide. Even larger ones can be used if the organizers of a shoot wish to paint their own, which is quite common. Front views of elephants are not unknown. The number of targets can be decided by the shoot organizers, and is often dependent on the amount of space available, but it is often forty targets, or thirty-six in winter because of the shorter hours of daylight. If the ground is small, shoots may involve going round twice, for example, twice eighteen targets to reach the total of thirty-six.

Shots are taken from three marker pegs in the ground, usually coloured red, white and blue. There is also usually a yellow peg for the use of archers under twelve. The first shot is from the red. If the archer hits the target and scores, he stands aside for the next person to shoot. If he misses, he moves on to the next peg and shoots again. If he scores, it will be a lower score, but if he misses this second shot, he moves on to the last peg for the last shot. This will be a lower score still. The marker pegs usually decrease in distance from the target, but the rules permit them to be reversed – although that is rare. Or they can all be in the same place, which is not uncommon on very short shots. Young archers between fourteen and fifteen shoot white-blue-blue pegs, while those twelve and thirteen years shoot blue-yellow-yellow pegs, so they are not shooting the longer distances. This is intended to accommodate the lower power of their bows.

Scoring is done when all those in the group have shot. They move down to the target and take their scores before touching the arrows and withdrawing them. An arrow which breaks into the line between two scoring areas is considered to have scored in the higher area, since the line is part of that area. Arrows must not be touched since their position maybe critical and a touch might move one into a higher scoring area.

A first arrow in the 'kill' area scores a maximum of twenty points. Anywhere in the outer scoring area is sixteen points. A second arrow score is fourteen or ten, while the third arrow scores eight or four. The best archers can get round a course with mainly first-arrow kills and no second arrows at all, and it is not unusual for some of the best compound unlimited archers to score nearly all kills with only one or two wounds (without hitting the animal, since the scoring rings can run outside its outline). Perfect rounds have been made in recent years.

Foresters Round

The NFAS has used Foresters faces as part of their National Championships ever since the first event, but in recent years the old ones have been discarded and replaced by Swedish Big Game faces with coloured spots stuck on for scoring spots, as well as to indicate the number of arrows to be shot at each face. A yellow spot indicates two shots, while a red spot indicates three. These target faces have worked well for many years, since the faces are larger than the traditional Foresters ones, with a wider range of sizes and animals. They also have circular kill areas printed on them, while the outer scoring area is entirely within the outline of the animal. In addition, their blank white backgrounds, although not very realistic, make them easy to see in woodland. It is probable that the growth of 3D shoots in the USA made the Foresters faces obsolete, especially after an American archer said that having animals with black spots on them was not very realistic.

It was once common to have mixed Big Game and Foresters rounds, but these seem to have died out with the phasing out of Foresters faces, and they were generally not as popular as purely Big Game rounds.

3D Targets

3D targets are slowly growing in use. The slow growth is due entirely to the expense, since most target figures now cost over £100 each, and most clubs can only buy a few each year, if any. They do last a long time, however, and are worth purchasing on that basis. They are said to last about 1,000 shots, and on the size of the attendance at the average shoot, this would mean that one should last for about ten shoots, which for most clubs holding open shoots twice a year, would be about five years or more.

A few clubs are now able to hold shoots consisting entirely of

3D targets, or at least a high proportion of them, mixed with Big Game faces. 3Ds are generally shot to Big Game scoring, rather than the American scoring and rules, which would involve two arrows shot at each target and the use of an extra scoring zone.

There is now an annual 3D Championship held by the NFAS, consisting of two courses shot on two days of forty targets each. Archers shoot two arrows and score ten for an inner kill, eight for an outer and five for anywhere on the remainder of the figure. This means that the maximum possible remains the same as for Big Game targets, but is more difficult to achieve. The demand for places in this championship is so great that entries have been limited to first come, first entered. This keeps the size of shooting groups at five people.

There has recently been a complaint by a competitor in the 3D Championships about shooting to American rules, since this required two shots at each target and he lost and broke some arrows on the second shot. Surely most field archers experienced in shooting unmarked distance courses will know that the chances of losing or damaging arrows are greater with the first shot, since with the second shot one always has a better idea of the distance. Many who have shot the two-shot 3D rules enjoy them simply because they get more shooting in. The requirement for greater skill to achieve a higher score is also an attraction. In Big Game rounds, one arrow can get a maximum score, and this may be an attraction for some who can get this with a bit of luck now and again, but there can be no doubt that only shooting skill can get a maximum score requiring two arrows.

Other Rounds

The **Woodsman** round differs from the Big Game round in that the archer shoots until he has a kill from three pegs, and the number of points scored is different. This round is very rarely shot. The **Poachers** round is also very rare and consists of Foresters targets, with three shots at each. The **East Midland** round consists of Big Game faces with three scoring shots at each, with ten points for a kill, and five for a wound, regardless of marker peg distances. This round is so rare that I have only ever known it to be shot once. The majority of NFAS members are happy to shoot Big Game most of the time and there is very little demand for other rounds. The essence of the Big Game round is that it is possible to shoot round a forty-target course, with a large variety of targets, by shooting only one arrow at most of the targets, and by doing so keep on the move, maintaining a rhythm of shooting, covering a reasonable amount of ground and, all being well, finishing in a reasonable time. The NFAS maintains that its policy is field archery for the fun of it, without getting involved in the high-performance stresses of international archery, and thus it perhaps appeals to a different sort of archer from the other organizations. Of course, there are a few who shoot NFAS rules most of the time, but are free to attend international shoots under other rules when they wish.

GNAS Rounds

Stamp Rounds

There are several rounds shot under GNAS field archery rules, the most popular being the Stamp marked, unmarked and combination rounds. These are named after the influential Don Stamp, author of *Field Archery*, and have taken the place of the previous Hunter and Field rounds.

On these rounds, archers shoot two at a time from pairs of markers. They are shot on black ringed FITA targets, with a yellow ('gold') centre spot and five scoring zones on each face, from five to one, and the target sizes are 20 cm, 40 cm, 60 cm, and 80 cm diameter. The round consists of twenty-four or twenty-eight targets, with one arrow shot at each target from four positions, so a total of 112 arrows are shot. The Unmarked Distance round has the maximum distance of the largest target at 50 metres. The Marked distance round is more difficult in that, because the distances are given, the shots are longer at the same sized faces. So for an archer accustomed to shooting unmarked distances, the Unmarked round is relatively easier than the Marked round. The maximum possible score is 560 points. The number of arrows shot means that these rounds can last longer than forty-target Big Game rounds shot in NFAS, despite having fewer targets and also despite archers shooting in pairs. The combination round comprises a unit of unmarked distance targets, in number equal to another unit of marked distance targets.

More detailed information on these rounds can be found in the appendix.

Other Rounds

GNAS shoots may also take the form of the **FITA Arrowhead** round. This is an International round that uses the same sized target faces as the Stamp rounds, but the distances are greater in some of the classes. Different classes shoot different distances, the Compound Unlimited class shooting the furthest, while the Barebow shoot the shortest. There is no doubt that the Arrowhead Round is more difficult than the Stamp rounds, since distances can be up to 70 metres. The Arrowhead can be shot marked or unmarked, and usually has twenty-four targets, although it can be twenty-six, twenty-eight, thirty-two or thirty-six targets. The **Arrowhead** round is identical to the FITA round, except that all arrows in a target have to be ringed with pencil so that ' pass-throughs' can be determined where it is suspected that one or more arrows have gone right through the target.

GNAS rules of shooting also permit a **Foresters** round on Foresters faces, with the usual fifteen, ten or five scoring, at distances up to 70 metres. This round can be shot marked or unmarked. The number of arrows shot at each target is the same as for NFAS Foresters rules. There is also a **Four-Shot Foresters** round, shot unmarked, with four shots at each target, as the name suggests. There is a **Big Game** round of twenty-eight faces, shot marked or unmarked, using the same scoring and arrow sequence as the NFAS Big Game round.

The **National Animal** round is shot on animal faces over thirty-two targets at unmarked distances. The scoring is ten points for a kill, and five for a wound, with two arrows at each target. Local or club rounds are also permitted. However, since the few GNAS field shoots are often attended by national team members and virtually all these shoots are on white ringed targets, it is likely that very few GNAS shoots are based on these latter rounds and, like some of the NFAS rounds, they are hardly ever used.

8 What to Shoot At

Target Faces

The variety of target faces used in field archery is one of the aspects that gives the sport its interest. Target faces are the bit at which the archer aims, while the butt is the support. Both are a constant problem to field archery clubs; they wear out or, to be more accurate, they get shot to pieces and have to be replaced.

Target faces come in a huge variety. Black and white ringed targets are used by GNAS field archers for Hunter and Field rounds at both unmarked and marked distance. These faces are marked with three scoring areas – five points for the centre ring, four for the inner ring and three for the outer. There are four sizes – 20 cm, 35 cm, 50 cm, 65 cm. The Field round face is black with a white centre while the Hunter one is the opposite, white with a black centre. There is also an Arrowhead round face which is divided into five scoring rings, with the scoring running five, four, three, two and one point from the centre outwards. These are much the same size as the Hunter and Field targets. International FITA faces can have a yellow centre spot and are 20 cm, 40 cm, 60 cm and 80 cm in diameter. IFAA faces follow the same pattern, but some have a black centre spot, a white inner ring and a black outer ring.

Probably the most interesting aspect of field archery is the Animal round target faces. These normally have only two scoring areas, a central area known as the 'kill' area and the rest of the body, which has a lower score. Legs, tails, antlers, ears, wings and other add-on parts do not usually score. It pays to know the target faces, since some can have their outer or 'wound' line well inside the apparent outline of the body, which can make scoring deceptive.

Animal faces come in a considerable variety, and are produced by several manufacturers. Swedish faces are available in several sizes, from the jay up to the wild boar and the big bear which is about 4 feet across and can be used at distances of 60 or 70 yards. There are twenty different animals in this range, all printed from excellent paintings with circular 'kill' areas in the centres. Their great advantage when shooting is that all the animals are on blank white backgrounds, which does not make them very realistic but does make them very easy to see. These faces are made of laminated paper with a mesh to strengthen them, which means that they are slightly more expensive than normal paper faces.

Other ranges come mainly from the USA and are almost entirely North American game animals. Many are photographed and are on natural backgrounds, which often makes them more realistic, more interesting and more difficult to shoot. Several depict dark-coloured animals on dark backgrounds, so on the field course they are often positioned beneath dark bushes to make them even more difficult. Since there are several ranges of these faces available from archery dealers, it pays to shop around and see who has what. It is entirely possible to lay a forty-target big-game course with a different target face on each. This gives tremendous interest to a shoot, since all the targets can be different sizes, different colours, and different distances. Some will be dark in tone and some light, and they will also vary in shape so that some will be upright and some horizontal, while a few will be diagonal. Some are thin and long, while others are round. Each one presents a different challenge to shooting, and since they are nearly always shot as unmarked distance targets, that factor adds to the interest.

These target faces always need to be pasted onto sheets of cardboard (the thicker the better) to give them strength, and they then have to be fastened onto a target butt to stop the arrows.

Clubs which have a resident artist can also produce their own target faces, and some have been doing so for many years. This can result in new and unknown faces appearing at a shoot, adding even more interest. There have been paintings of dinosaurs, African game, Native North Americans, American Western characters, medieval figures, armoured knights, and a huge variety of others, according to the imagination of the artists. One of the characteristics of some of these, however, is that the kill areas are sometimes not very generous.

3D Targets

A revolution in field archery occurred some years ago when a manufacturer in the USA produced something new – three-dimensional animal figures. These are made from a fairly hard plastic foam material that takes arrows easily and is long-lasting. The legs have steel tubes inside, which are slid over long steel stakes hammered into the ground to support the figure and help create a lifelike effect. Some figures, such as the bears and wild pigs, are black and are often positioned in a dark environment. They thus sometimes become invisible, and the archer is shooting into total darkness. All the figures have three scoring zones with an inner kill area, an outer kill area and the whole of the remainder of the animal counts as a wound area. American 3D rules give the two inner rings as different scores, but when shot under British Big Game rules, the innermost area is usually ignored.

These figures are great fun to shoot. The scoring rings are often difficult to see since they are merely rings moulded into the surface and cannot be altered easily, but they are of generous size so they are not impossibly difficult. It is possible to purchase a set of plastic cards with photographs of all these targets printed on them, so archers can carry a pocket guide to show where the scoring rings are. Under some rules no reference to targets can be carried, however, so if you intend to do this, check the rules first.

Most of these figures come in sections, making them easier to transport, and they are easily fitted together in the shooting area. Their major disadvantage is their price – they are hugely expensive, mainly of course because of transport costs; they are only about half the British price in the USA. The range is being extended steadily so that at the time of writing there are thirty-one different figures available, with four African animals recently added to the list. Some are huge, like the large elk, the caribou and the bison, which is over 6 feet long. Figures this size are very rarely encountered, partly because the prices run into hundreds of pounds, but also because the space required to shoot them – each of these could be shot at 80 yards, an unusually long distance for a field course. Consideration also has to be given to transport and storage, for they take up far more space than conventional targets. For the sheer pleasure of shooting them, however, they are well worthwhile.

It should also be mentioned that the costs can be compensated for by the length of time they last, since the larger ones can have a life of several years, and they have centre sections that can be replaced. Most are reckoned to last about a thousand shots.

One of the characteristics of 3D shooting is that one always knows when an arrow has hit, since a sound will denote a score somewhere on the figure, while silence will usually mean a miss.

This leads us on to one of the problems inherent in 3D targets – how does one find the arrows that have missed? There are several answers. One is try to position every target with a bank behind it so that missed arrows cannot go far and are easily found. Another is to place target butts or other backstops behind at a reasonable distance, but if this is not done carefully and the backstops are not draped with foliage or otherwise camouflaged, they can defeat the whole purpose of using 3D targets. A third method is used in a club that has a totally flat shooting ground. They merely engage a couple of club members to spend the day finding arrows with metal detectors, and so expertly is this done that most lost arrows are recovered by their owners from buckets back at the adminis-tration area at the end of the day.

One factor that does tend to detract from the appearance of some of the imported 3D figures is the finish. They are sprayed with an appropriate colour scheme, but often this is slightly shiny and when the sun is on them it somewhat spoils the realistic effect. If someone were able to develop a matt finish for these targets, it would be a considerable improvement.

In the USA, 3D field archery has developed almost into a sepa-rate sport, with its own rules and scoring system, and annual national championships attract thousands of competitors. One well-known British field archer and bow manufacturer said that 3D had raised the standard of archery in the USA to new heights. In Britain, some clubs are slowly building up their stocks of 3D targets so that at their open shoots the numbers are increasing. Few are able to put on entirely 3D shoots yet, but my own home club has been doing them for many years; the targets were entirely home-made until the American ones were purchased. These home-made targets were always very popular, and the use of various synthetic fur fabrics to cover them added to the realism.

At the time of writing, there is news of a German company producing 3D targets but I have no more information. If it is true, they will hopefully be cheaper than the American targets since transport costs will be lower, but it is likely that this will be counteracted by higher production costs.

Making 3Ds is not difficult, but it does demand some sculptural ability and some skill at drawing animals. Once the main principle is grasped that most mammals are basically pretty much the same with minor differences such as length of leg, thickness of body, length of neck and so on, they are fairly easy to make – see chapter 16.

Target Butts

The ideal archery target material has yet to be found. It is a simple requirement – what is needed is a cheap, easily obtained substance which will withstand being shot full of holes for years without any deterioration. It should also be light and easy to store and carry, weatherproof and capable of being left outside for years without any attention.

Target archers use straw bosses. These consist of 'ropes' of tightly bound straw coiled into a disc, which is sewn and bound together. These bosses are large and heavy, and although they are available in smaller sizes, they do not seem to be suitable for field archery since the shape is not ideal, nor are the size and weight or their ability to withstand the climate. So field archery has looked at several other choices. For many years cardboard was the material which offered most advantages in that it was cheap (even free very often if one knew where to get it), it would take a fair amount of pounding with arrows and it was fairly easy to deal with. Large amounts of discarded cardboard boxes were obtained, flattened out and bound or taped together in a layer several inches thick. They were then transported to the shooting ground, staked into place by hammering a long wooden stake into the ground at each end, attaching the cardboard with string with large rubber bands tied in to give some room for movement.

This was very labour-intensive, since it took time to gather sufficient cardboard, time to make it into butts, time to transport it to the ground, and when they were shot out a few months later, time to take them away and dispose of them. And by then they were often wet and soggy, were being used as residential quarters by slugs and were falling to bits so that they were generally not easy to carry. Those clubs which put on regular open shoots were obliged to make a whole new set of butts for every shoot, which could mean making eighty or so every year, an arduous and boring commitment.

Field archers put up with all this in order to keep the sport going but there was always the nagging feeling that, somehow, modern technology ought to have come up with something useable. Various plastics and rubber sheet mixtures were tried, and old carpet tiles sandwiched between the layers of cardboard were thought to lengthen the life of the butts, but neither was really the answer. One club tried a plastic foam mixture which produced oddly shaped blocks which could be cut into a shape suitable for mounting a target face on, but this only worked for a short time, for it was found that arrows sometimes went through holes previously made which had not closed. In addition, there was another problem: carbon arrows became welded into the stuff and were a terrible job to remove. Archers shooting carbons were exhausted at the end of the day from the sheer effort required to withdraw their arrows, and then they had to clean all the stuff off the shaft before it could be shot again.

One useful material was building insulation board. This is cheap, light and easily cut. When cut into strips about 9 inches wide and packed tightly into a strong wooden frame, edge on, it made very long-lasting target butts. It was found that soaking them with gallons of used engine oil worked wonderfully well to make them absorb the arrows and the holes closed well after withdrawal. However, there was one drawback: they were so heavy that anything over a couple of square feet was almost impossible to move and there was no question of moving them into different positions occasionally – they just stayed where they were until they gradually became absorbed into the ground and the undergrowth and were forgotten.

Another answer was a type of thick rubber foam, of which I have no knowledge or experience since I have never encountered it. It may be that this is so expensive that no field club could afford to use it, but butts made from it are available from the archery dealers.

Now, however, there is a very long-lasting material, which is cheap and easily obtained. It comes in thin sheets of foam rubber or plastic and when cut into strips 1 foot wide and strapped or lashed tightly together it makes wonderfully effective target butts which will last for years. It relies for its effectiveness on being only about ¼ inch thick and having fairly smooth surfaces on both sides. It is positioned edge on to the arrows, with the result that many of them slide between the layers, doing little or no damage to the material. The tightness of the binding or clamping causes the friction that stops the arrows. These butts are so durable that one club has had thirty or so positioned in its wood for several years, being regularly shot. They were recently taken apart and examined, and any damaged layers were removed and the butt restrapped. Many were found to be still in shootable condition after years of use.

These butts can be made cheaply and fairly easily, especially if a large bandsaw is available, or they can now be purchased ready made from some of the archery dealers considerably more cheaply than any other target butt. They are also light and easy to carry as well as being so broad-based that on flat ground they require very little support. A 2 inch by 2 inch stake at each end and a length of string is sufficient to hold them upright. Target faces can be pinned to them with plastic pins or held in place with a couple of pieces of string running vertically round the butt. The only drawback so far discovered after years of heavy use is that carbon shafts, when wet, pass through them rather easily. In every other way, these are ideal butts.

9 Finding a Ground

Most field archery clubs will feel the need to find a ground on which they can shoot, and, if possible, hold open competition shoots. This is not easy, but the degree of difficulty depends on which area of the country one is situated in, or, indeed, which country. Some areas have an abundance of woodland while others, even rural areas, have little. If you are fortunate enough to live in one of the well-wooded counties, you may well find a suitable ground with little difficulty.

What You Need

What do you need? Probably more than you would imagine at first. Any old bit of woodland will not do, as you will soon discover when the search begins. You will need:

- Easy access
- somewhere nearby to park
- a wood big enough to accommodate at least 14 targets
- a wood that can be shot in
- security from vandals
- no public footpaths
- a wood that can fairly easily be walked round
- a sympathetic and generous landowner
- a wood in which shooting can take place without endangering anyone outside
- a wood where no one will make complaints about your activity

All the above will need to be considered. Some factors will be obvious, others may only become apparent after a while.

Let us deal with each point in detail.

Access

This may seem obvious, until the search begins, and then it may be found that some excellent pieces of woodland have no easy access. You will need one with a good all-weather track at least nearby, and you may, of course, need permission to use it, possibly from a different landowner. Many good potential courses have foundered on this point. You will need to transport target butts and other equipment, so this access track really is essential. Lugging heavy target bosses across ploughed fields is not an option.

Parking

At least you should be able to park in a neighbouring field, again with permission from the landowner. If your club wishes to hold regular open competition shoots, as many do, there will need to be somewhere large enough to accommodate all competitors' vehicles. Resorting to using the nearest road, is not a satisfactory solution, obviously, but it may be necessary and informing the local police of your intentions may help.

A Big Enough Wood

It could be any sort of land, but Britain being as it is, it is likely to be a wood. In Arizona, for example, a field archery club can use almost any bit of desert. There are vast numbers of bits of woodland dotted about the English landscape, many called 'copses' or 'coverts', but these are generally far too small to be considered; about 10 acres is the minimum you will need, but the bigger the better, since a big wood will give the opportunity to change the course plan regularly. One Midlands club had a wood of 160 acres and was easily able to put on three open shoots per year with forty targets each, in different parts of the wood so that each shoot was completely different. Twenty acres is not a lot but it will be found that it is big enough to get forty targets in without too much difficulty.

A Wood That Can Be Shot In

Some woodland is so thickly grown that it is impossible to shoot in it, or the undergrowth is so thick that walking it is difficult. If it is a sea of brambles, as some are, try somewhere else. Woodland which consists of large mature trees, whether deciduous or coniferous, is usually the best. Beech wood is rare, and is often open to the public, but it does have almost no undergrowth whatsoever – although this can make it somewhat boring to shoot in.

Extremely soft and muddy ground can be difficult to use, as can ground that is so steep that it becomes a constant climbing exercise. After looking at a few bits of woodland, it becomes obvious at times why they are not being used as farmland. Survey your prospective ground with care, trying to assess all its possible advantages and disadvantages. Try walking it with a group of club members to get differing views and opinions. I have several times had a piece of wood suggested to me but on viewing or walking it discovered a major problem. One wood had the unusual feature of being very dark and depressing because of a high steep bank right along one side. It would not have been a pleasant experience to shoot in there.

Streams should be viewed with caution. If they are too deep to cross easily they will perhaps need bridging. This will provide the more energetic and creative club members with some interesting work, but the bridges will require upkeep. Streams can make shots more interesting, but they can also create muddy areas.

Security from Vandalism

This is a major problem for many clubs whose grounds lie anywhere near houses. Vandals are unable to stop themselves from destroying any target butt they come across, or ripping off target faces, or generally making life difficult for archers. Many clubs are unable to leave target butts out overnight, or to build a shed to keep them in without the danger of it being burnt down. If you are fortunate enough to find a wood well away from possible vandals, you may be able to build a permanent field course where butts can be left out for years without interference, enabling club members to go and shoot whenever they wish – although it is desirable to be able to move them around occasionally.

Public Footpaths

If your prospective wood has public right of way across it or a path used by the public, take care that you do not site any shots near it.

Dog walkers can be extremely aggressive if they have been walking a route every day for years and suddenly find it blocked in some way. Local councils can also be very uncooperative in this matter and may object to any shooting near public footpaths, although they seem to be curiously reluctant to send any officials to view the situation or to discuss it. You should put up warning notices to the effect that archery may be taking place, but do not say that it is dangerous, for that leaves the club open to legal problems.

A Wood That Can Easily Be Walked Round

It should not be too easy. Flat woodland is less interesting to shoot round, and has the disadvantage that club members can easily become so used to it that when they shoot elsewhere, on hilly grounds, they feel at a disadvantage. But it should not be too difficult either. Do not imagine that undergrowth can soon be cleared – it can't! Woodland which varies in terrain and in type of growth can be the most interesting to shoot.

A Sympathetic and Generous Landowner

Dealing with landowners can be a minefield. Some can be surprisingly helpful and will allow access to and use of their woodland, with parking and everything else, without charge. If you find any of this sort, treasure them.

Approach your landowner with caution and consideration, politely and diplomatically, explaining what you do and what you need clearly and concisely. You may meet with a flat refusal, in which case go away and try elsewhere. But you are more likely to meet someone who will treat your request with sympathy, although you will also come up against the problem of the pheasant shooting syndicate who rent the shooting rights over the land and who can afford to spend several hundred pounds per year to shoot a few birds. These groups wield considerable financial clout, and have been known to get a field archery club ejected from their ground with no recourse.

If you do get permission to use a piece of woodland, assure your landowner that you will do your best to look after the land, light no fires, leave no litter, care for the wildlife, cut no trees down, shoot no livestock and generally ensure that arrows never land outside your chosen area.

Your landowner may ask you to pay some rent. This is another minefield. He may suggest a nominal or reasonable fee if you are lucky. He may ask you to suggest what the club is able or willing to pay, in which case, of course, the club members must decide for themselves. If you are unlucky, he may think he has suddenly struck gold and will ask an unreasonably high rent, plus a fee for every car parking on the land, plus a cut from shoot entry fees, as well as some from any catering profits. In this case, I would leave well alone. It is not uncommon for greedy landowners to end up with nothing, having priced themselves out of the market. If your landowner is one of the more generous types, be prepared to make a gift at Christmas, invite him to the club annual dinner, invite him or his wife to present the prizes at an open shoot and generally show your appreciation of his generosity.

If the landowner is a company, it becomes more difficult, and you may be asked to pay for the services of a solicitor to draw up a legal agreement for your use of the ground; again, the club members must decide if that is a viable option. A company may also suggest some form of insurance and it may be necessary to ask your national ruling body whether their insurance covers you while practice shooting on your new ground. If you are lucky, it will, but if not, you may have to make your own arrangements for insurance. The problem of insurance can destroy any hope of getting the use of a ground if the landowner feels that he may be liable in some way, so approach this subject with care.

A Wood in Which No One Outside is Endangered

This may seem an obvious requirement, but small and narrow woods in particular can be a nightmare for course planners, as every target must be sited with safety in mind, with an adequate area for overshoots behind the target, but without encroaching in any way on any other target, and without shooting on to any ground outside the wood. Overshoots should always be planned so that they are well within the confines of the ground. Do not forget that a mis-shot arrow, or one which bounces off the edge of a butt, can travel 70 or 80 yards. An arrow found in a neighbouring field creates a difficult situation. If you are fortunate and have a big wood, there should be no problem, but it is wise to have a course officer whose job includes checking the siting of every target on the course since it is entirely possible for a club member to site one in a dangerous position. I was once totally horrified, on checking a course for an open shoot, to find a 3D turkey placed on top of a mound overlooking a field with cattle in, so that any arrows that missed would go downhill into the cattle.

Complaints

This is something you will have to cope with if it occurs, but be aware of the possibility of complaints from neighbours when choosing your ground, who will be certain, without ever seeing it happen, that you are spraying arrows indiscriminately all over the landscape, including his bit. There is no advice on how to handle this situation, but be aware that it could arise.

How to locate a Ground

Having considered what difficulties may be encountered, let us look at how to go about locating a ground. First, if you do not actually know of any woodland locally, buy an Ordnance Survey Landranger map covering your chosen area. Better still, if you can find one in a local bookshop, might be one of the Ordnance Survey Pathfinder series, which are on a scale of 1:25,000, which will give you even more detail and has the advantage of being small, so easy to handle out of doors. The new Explorer series is also 1:25,000, and each sheet covers a wider area than the Pathfinders. You may even, if you go to your local planning department, be able to get a map of even larger scale which might show one piece of land. All these maps will show all the woodland and even whether it is mixed, deciduous or coniferous. They will also show a great deal more of use, such as access tracks, nearby buildings and contours. Read the contours carefully; if the lines are close together you may be looking at land which is too steep to shoot on.

The old inch to the mile Ordnance Survey maps showed a red line round all Forestry Commission land. This is useful, because under the new name of Forestry Management Services, its woodland is available for public use. If you approach your local office, they may tell you whether there is a piece of woodland that you can use, providing that no one else is using it. This may seem a good thing at first, but beware that even the most remote forests are now open to walkers, ramblers, birdwatchers and mountain bikers, and you may have to make some arrangement to cope with this problem.

When you have found what looks like a promising piece of ground, go out and look at it from the nearest road, then go to the nearest houses and ask who the landowner is. They will usually have some idea. Approach the owner and put your case, politely and diplomatically. If he is agreeable, ask if you can have a walk through the wood. This is the way it *should* be done.

Sometimes you will be told of a piece of woodland that might be suitable. Go and check it; it may be a good thing, but far more often your informant will not really have understood what you want or why. If the land is unfenced, for example, as much woodland is, you will have no means of keeping people out.

When you have acquired your piece of woodland and gone through all the necessary processes, you can at last start moving in all the butts and other little necessities that make a field course home. In the course of time you may even be able to acquire a shed or some other form of store, or even clubhouse.

You may soon find that it is a good idea to move the butts a couple of times a year but it is worth considering having two or three large butts near your shed or base area, if you have the space, for simple practice purposes, for teaching beginners or for setting-up bows, calibrating sights or whatever. A couple of butts with measured distances along a range up to perhaps 80 yards can be very useful, not only for calibrating sights but for practising the judging of distances.

If you have the space, it is a good idea to have the measured distance range set apart from the beginners' range since the two often do not mix, especially when experienced archers are doing their own thing on the range while beginners need to be shooting at shorter distances.

If you are fortunate enough to be able to leave butts out at all times and there is the space, a permanent field course is a huge asset, since it may mean that club members can shoot whenever they feel like it, or that several club sessions can be held every week. Few clubs are this fortunate, but it can be done. To keep boredom at bay, it may be possible to move one or two target butts every month or so, if there is an energetic course officer in the club. Or twice a year, gather together as many club members as possible and move all the butts. The course officer should be able to plan all the new positions beforehand and put out markers, but all will need to be checked after any such move.

If you have the space and security for a permanent course, the number of targets put out may vary, but a dozen to eighteen can provide sufficient for a couple of hours' shooting, or even enough for a summer evening. You may also find that you can get permission from your landowner to put up a clubhouse or at least a target store. It may be worth trying to get permission to bring a large caravan or mobile home to the area. These can be surprisingly easy to buy, and are not expensive. If you are in an area where sites of mobile homes or holiday caravans are common, you may discover something that will suit your requirements being sold off very cheaply. These sites recycle their mobile homes after they become rather old, and are only too glad to get rid of them for a couple of hundred pounds. Specialist caravan-moving experts will charge a reasonable fee for moving one to your chosen site. All the internal fittings are flimsy and easily ripped out, so conversion to a meeting room and/or target store is simple. The kitchen area could even be converted for use as a catering area for open shoots.

10 Laying a Field Course

Designing or planning a field course requires knowledge of the ground. No one can walk into a wood and decide immediately where targets should be placed. For this reason, a thorough reconnaissance of a ground is necessary before you plan the layout. Course planners may need to walk a new piece of ground several times before they know it sufficiently to start planning target positions. It is necessary to know the boundaries, where the hills and hollows are, where the bogs, streams, swamps and lakes are, where the traps and hazards lie, how one part relates to others, and how the available space can be divided if more than one course or course unit is required. This prior knowledge should enable you to devise a circuit and to work out where the long shots are to go, since these are the most difficult to place. Shorter shots can often be fitted in between. In addition, a circuit should be just that – it must have no end, so that when the last target is shot, it should lead easily back to the first.

As you become familiar with the ground, you will hopefully see more possibilities for target positions and scope for more imaginative use of the ground. Use your imagination to see shots that might be interesting, challenging or spectacular. Look for places where dead ground might make the distances difficult to judge, where the trees provide shadows over targets, or where the rise or fall of ground makes shots more testing. Also bear in mind that long shots tend to be more interesting and dramatic than short ones.

When planning a course, it is useful to do it in a group of at least four people, which gives a wider range of ideas for shots and target positions, and also means that if there is doubt about the safety of a shot, one person can stand by the proposed shooting position and indicate the direction of shot while another goes to the proposed target position to check the overshoot area for safety. Perhaps it may be necessary for a third to go to the last target position, to show how that fits in. A map of the ground, even if only a rough sketch map, will be very useful, so that target positions can be plotted on it and distances marked. Even if it is to be an unmarked distance course, a rough idea of the distances is necessary in order to plan what size of target to place in each position. It can also give a useful overall view of the course layout, and, in addition, it can be useful for planning course changes.

It is possible, with sufficient familiarity of a piece of land, and a sketch map of it, to plan target positions and even whole courses without setting foot on the ground. The sketch map should show the direction of shots, the target numbers and the estimated distances. It is useful to see the relationship of one target to all the others and to see where some are badly placed and may need to be moved. Number 6 on the sample sketch map on page 188, for example, is not well placed since it is pointing out of the wood towards a field containing cattle. It might have to be moved to be parallel to the fence, which may mean moving number 7 in some way.

Note, too, that target 34 is pointing towards the main road, but you would know from your reconnaissance that there is a 4-foot high bank several yards behind it, with the target low down in a gully, and the shot taken off a high mound, so it should be safe.

The method used by my home club for course laying prior to an open shoot for many years was as follows. Several weeks before the shoot a group of club members would work round the wood, one carrying a sketch map, two others carrying bags of number boards and red pegs. The number boards were about 6 inches square and painted white, with the numbers in black, from 1 to 36 or 40, the usual maximum numbers of targets for NFAS rounds. These boards were drilled on each side so that they could be threaded with string and tied to trees about head high and seen above the ferns. There was also a set of number boards with the numbers in red.

The group would begin where the first target was to be placed, since this is usually easy to determine. A red number board marked the target position and a black board and a red peg marked the first shooting position. The group would move slowly round the wood, each member suggesting target and peg positions and the whole group examining each suggestion until distance, target size, angle of shot, relationship to other targets and, most of all, safety were decided to the satisfaction of all. Each target position and direction of shot was noted on the sketch map.

Sometimes one position would not be satisfactory in relation to a previous target and would need to be altered – perhaps only the angle of the peg position by a few feet. The whole process was lengthy and sometimes tedious, taking several hours, but when done properly it could speed up the placing of the targets enormously. Shooting peg positions have to be chosen so that both right-handed and left-handed archers can shoot properly. Sometimes pegs are behind trees and left-handers are often heard complaining that no one thought of them when the pegs were positioned.

The day before the shoot, every available club member was asked to come and help put targets out. They were divided into four teams, hopefully of at least four each. Each team was allocated a block of targets, usually ten, and given a list of targets, and a copy of the sketch map, showing target positions and numbers. Carrying marker pegs, stakes, string, target faces, mallets and anything else they might need, they plunged into the wood and set to work. Many butts might have to be moved or even carried into the wood to their designated positions. Stakes were hammered in and butts strung to them. Shooting pegs were placed and views taken of each shot. Any faults such as poor shooting positions for left-handed archers, or difficulties in seeing targets, were examined and rectified.

With enough willing hands, this course-laying can be done in a couple of hours and afterwards the whole course walked by at least two club officials to check for feasibility of shoot and safety. Part of this process might involve moving targets or pegs which are found to be unsafe – if, for example, the overshoot area of one target overlapped another shot.

This method was found to work well over many years, but it relied on a sufficient number of club members being willing and able to take part. It can be done with eight people, but more is better. It seems preferable to me to the method used in some clubs, where two members spend a week laying a course on their own. It also has the advantage of making members feel that their presence is needed and valued, and that they are making a contribution to a major club activity.

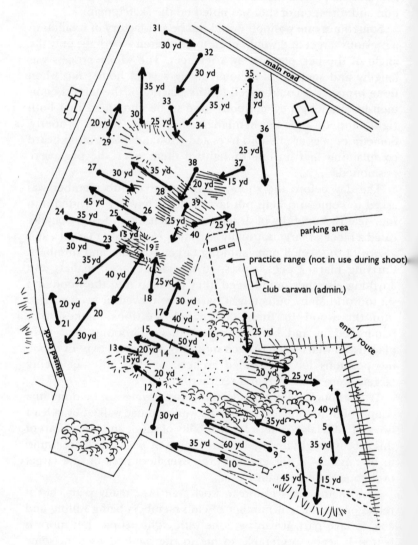

Fig. 23 Typical course layout

The process requires care and intelligence as well as experience. Any doubts expressed by anyone concerning the safety of targets or shots must be examined and laid to rest. There are few things more embarrassing at a shoot than being told by competitors that a shot is unsafe, and this should never be allowed to happen.

It will be seen from the sketch map that some targets have shots that appear to be pointing towards each other in a highly dangerous manner. These may in fact be perfectly safe because of differences in angle of shot, the terrain, the density of growth and other factors. Never believe that very dense undergrowth or anything of that sort will stop an arrow, however. Arrows are capable of shooting right through incredibly dense masses of growth.

It was the policy in this club to reverse the course for each open shoot, to make a change not only for competitors who attended regularly but also for club members. This ground had no children living nearby, which meant a lack of young vandals eager to spoil anything they could lay hands on, so targets could be left out after a shoot for club members to shoot – a wonderful advantage, since it meant that they could shoot the ground whenever they wished.

11 Organizing an Open Shoot

Organizing an open shoot is not difficult. It is helpful if you have sufficient club members willing to give their time and energy to it, and it can be a rewarding process. It can bring income to a club, but mainly it contributes towards maintaining field archery as a sport, for without clubs willing to stage open shoots, there would be little else to interest people. Some clubs do put on the occasional invitation shoot, especially if they have limited space and cannot accommodate the sort of numbers that attend open shoots. Much depends on the area in which the club is situated. In some areas field archers are thin on the ground and an open shoot might only attract fifty or so competitors, while in other areas a shoot at a club with a reputation for good shoots could attract 200 or more, though this would be quite rare. If your club is in an area where there are several clubs within 80 miles, for example, a first shoot could pull in a substantial number eager to try out a new ground.

Good organization is essential. All shoots follow the same pattern, but since I am familiar with the organization of NFAS shoots, I will look at the step-by-step procedure for those.

1 The club meets to decide on the date of the shoot, the format, how many targets there will be and which type – big game, foresters or 3D, or a combination.
2 Notify the date to the national controlling body. Get approval for the date, or alter it as necessary. (In the NFAS, the large number of shoots, particularly in summer, means juggling dates so that another club does not have a shoot on the same day within 60 miles.)

3 At least two months ahead, check the availability of the course.
4 Check the number of butts and 3D targets available. Will more be required?
5 Order target faces.
6 Paste target faces to cardboard.
7 The club meets to decide who is to do what, and who is available at the weekend of the shoot. Allocate the following areas: course planning, course laying, catering, supply of trophies, car parking, booking in, scorecard supply, toilet provision, safety.
8 Two or three weeks ahead, plan the course and make a map of the course. Inform or remind club members of the event.
9 Check availability of target number boards and marker pegs for the course.
10 Check availability, cleanliness etc., of accommodation for catering and administration (tents, caravan, buildings, etc.)
11 Whoever is responsible for booking in makes up a target sheet. This is a large sheet of card with all the target numbers arranged on it and space below each for writing in the names of the competitors who will be starting there, usually four to a target. Many people phone their entries in days or even weeks beforehand, some requesting to shoot with particular people. Accommodate such requests as far as possible, especially parents wanting to shoot with children. Indeed, there is a requirement that parents of children under 12 should shoot with them. This sheet is vital for knowing who is shooting where, how many are shooting, how many turn up, how many there are in each class, etc. Make out score-cards.
12 On the day before the shoot, set out targets. This involves as many club members as can be gathered together. Divide them into teams, each to deal with a set number of targets, usually ten each if there are to be forty targets. Each team puts out shooting pegs, target numbers where they can be seen, usually on trees, applies target faces to butts, moves and stakes butts where necessary, places 3D targets in position if they are being used, puts out direction indicators to show the way to the next target, and generally completes their area of the course. Sometimes each team is given a map showing where all the targets are to go and a list of targets. Targets should have numbers stuck on them to indicate their position on the course.

The author's equipment:
(i) Martin Sceptre compound bow, 45–60 lb draw weight, set on 50 lb. 30 in. draw, carbon limbs, fitted with Chek-it 2000 sight, Arten stabilizer, Martin arrow rest, peep sight
(ii) Arrows – Easton ACC carbon aluminium 3-28, 30 in. long for practice shooting
(iii) Arrows – Easton X7 2114 aluminium alloy, 30 in. for practice shooting
(iv) Quiver – Neet leather, with useful pouches and raccoon-tail decoration. Also with sheath knife for cutting arrows out of wood
(v) Two release aids, one a Skorten forefinger release with wrist strap, the other a Fletchmatic TR thumb-operated release

The archer in front is shooting hunting tackle, with hunting bow and wooden arrows, at a McKenzie deer. The shot is uphill and about 40 yards from the archer. The archer nearest the camera is waiting to take his first shot with his Browning compound bow. This is typical of most of this wood, open pine plantation, with dense fern in summer, dying down in winter. The summer growth obscures many of the targets and has to be cut back to make them visible

The car parking/assembly area at an open shoot

A proud archer, after having shot the only spot of the day on the big foot target at an open shoot

Shooting with a Classic Hunter oriental-style bow. This archer usually shoots compound unlimited, but brings the Classic Hunter out for fun shooting

Demonstrating the use of the take-down hunting bow with wooden arrows. Note the typical corner-of-the-mouth anchor point. The class is usually known as 'H/T'

Showing the use of the compound bow shot unlimited. This archer started shooting at the age of 58 and progressed rapidly, competing regularly at open shoots in England and Scotland. His compound bow is set at 60 lb draw weight and he shoots ACC carbon/alloy arrows. Note the position of the release aid, about to be triggered

Typical freestyle technique and equipment but using a two-finger draw. Note the open bow hand, usually shot with the aid of a wrist sling supporting the bow. The kisser is in the corner of the mouth rather than in the centre of the lips. This means a longer draw length is possible

Shooting compound unlimited

Taking aim at one deer in a group. They look close but the first shot was at 55 yards

English longbow men shooting in a 'herce' at Agincourt, 1988

A hand-tooled back quiver – a fine example of the leather worker's art

A typical homemade big-game target face, hand-painted

13 When the course is complete, the safety officer and three others walk round it checking for the safety of shots, overshoot areas, the visibility of targets, the security of target butts and 3D animals, correct shooting pegs and distances (on an unmarked course, it is vital that targets are placed at distances reasonable for their size, not too close or too far. A deer at 20 yards is silly, as is an 18-inch forester's face at 50 yards.)

14 Tape off any areas that require taping for various reasons – parking area, toilet areas, hazardous areas, etc.

15 Put up signs where necessary – road signs to indicate the route to course, the entrance, parking areas, toilets, catering, administration, booking in, etc.

16 On shoot day, arrive early – the first competitors will be arriving just after 9 o'clock, even if the shoot, as is usual, is not due to start until 10.30.

17 Set up toilets – this needs to be done before all else, since some competitors will need them as soon as they arrive. Set up hand washing facilities.

18 Car park attendants take their place.

19 Set up the catering facility, and bring in food and water supplies. Start cooking and selling the traditional bacon butties, tea, coffee, etc.

20 Set up administration and booking-in table, using the target sheet to check off competitors as they book in. Hand each a score-card, with their name, club, shooting class and starting target number on it. Collect entry fees.

21 The course officer checks course, seeing that all is in place and that no mysterious alterations have been made by local vandals overnight.

22 When all competitors have booked in, at the appointed start time, call them together for a briefing, and to make any changes in starting targets. Changes may need to be made if booked-in archers have not arrived, some competitors may be on targets on their own, or only two to a target, in which case they will be reallocated to make up numbers. Competitors should be welcomed to the shoot, informed of its content, the number and type of targets, any course hazards to watch for, the time of the lunch break, if any, the start time after lunch break, the scoring system (if it is thought to be necessary), the shooting peg arrangements, the starting signal, etc.

23 Groups of archers are led out to their starting targets by club members allocated to particular areas of the course, starting with those who have the furthest to go.

24 When all the archers are in place, give the starting signal in whatever way has been decided.

25 The course officer and assistants patrol the course, checking that targets withstand the onslaught of arrows, changing target faces during the day if any are shot out, etc.

26 While shoot is in progress, club members can usually relax, with the catering crew preparing for the lunch break and the administration team checking entry numbers and the treasurer counting the takings.

27 At lunchtime, club members, usually the children, go round selling raffle tickets to competitors.

28 The administration team set up table for trophies and raffle prizes.

29 As competitors return from the course, they hand in their score-cards.

30 When all groups are in and shooting is finished, the administration team collates the scores for each class and lists the winners. This was once done by listing all competitors, arduously writing their names in a book, then writing in their scores as they came in, and choosing the highest scores. It has now been replaced by a simpler system of collecting all the cards for one class and riffling through them for the three highest numbers, then noting these for the prizes. With two or three people doing this, working out winners became much faster.

31 Call competitors together for the prize-giving.

32 Give out raffle prizes first.

33 Call out the names of the prize-winners. Each comes forward to collect their trophy and shake hands with the Lady Paramount, who is usually a lady club member or the landowner's wife.

34 Present flowers to the Lady Paramount, if she is landowner's wife.

35 Proceedings end. Clear up, collect litter, store away any targets brought off the course, marker pegs, stakes, numbers, tape, etc. Clear away the catering. Collect all signs. Remove the toilets and empty the containers in deep hole dug for the purpose. Fill them in, covering with turf if necessary.

36 Go home – the best part of putting on a shoot, knowing that all went well.

37 Lie in the bath, feet tingling, having walked miles during the course of the day. Review the day in your mind.

38 Send shoot report to the national organization newsletter.

39 Treasurer takes money to the bank.

40 Start to think about organizing the next shoot . . .

12 National Championships

All three national ruling bodies hold national championship shoots.

GNAS Championships

The All British Championships used to be held at the Pentref club in South Wales, where the facilities are perhaps the best in the country for a field archery club, including a concert hall where the prize-giving can be held. The course is hillside with scattered clumps of trees and bushes, looking down into the Rhondda Valley, and is an excellent shooting ground that provides room for sufficient targets without cramping them too closely, and also for moving them into different positions when required. But they are now held at various venues round the country. The GNAS has adopted the same principle as the other organizations in order not to make the same entrants travel long distances to the event every year.

The championships are shot over two days, always at the May bank holiday weekend, and are shot as two courses, both with FITA targets of black, five rings with a yellow spot, or gold. One round is shot at marked distances, while the other is an unmarked round. Some archers from other European countries attend.

NFAS Championships

The NFAS Championships have been held on the third weekend of September every year, for two days, and have become the biggest archery contest in Britain. Numbers of contestants have risen year by year until it is now hovering around 650–700. This has proved to be a huge headache for the organizers and a large area of woodland is required to accommodate them. It has been customary for many years to have four courses, once of thirty-six targets but now of forty. Attempts are made to keep groups on each target down to four, thus only 160 people can shoot on each course, making a total of 640, and since this number is now being exceeded, groups sometimes consist of five archers.

The basic structure is that each archer will shoot two of the four courses over the two days. Normally, longbow and other wooden arrow classes shoot courses A and B, while all others, especially those with sights, will shoot X and Y courses. There is no difference in degree of difficulty between the two pairs of courses, but there is a considerable difference in the time taken to shoot them; it is customary for competitors on A and B to finish at least two hours before those on X and Y.

Scoring is on double score-cards; no one is permitted to score their own card, so frequent cross-checks are carried out to ensure that both sets of cards are correct, and that any discrepancies can be ironed out before things go too far.

The NFAS created a major problem for itself at its foundation when it was decided that the championships would be held at a different venue every year. This has meant that there is a constant search for a suitable venue, as they attempt to rotate it round the country so that each region has its turn. The other thought behind changing the venue regularly was that no one would have the advantage of knowing the ground beforehand, and it would be new to all competitors.

The search for a venue occupies several of the society's officers for some time every year. The ground must be big enough to accommodate the four courses, it must have an area for parking and preferably for camping and caravans, it must have easy access and it must not be too expensive. Many potential shooting grounds have been turned down after discovering that the landowners have become too demanding and asked for too high a rent. Sometimes arrangements have fallen through late in the day and another ground has had to be found at very short notice.

Notices are sent out to all NFAS members, with entry forms,

directions on how to find the ground, the rules of the contest in basic form, the classes, and lists of accommodation.

At one time, it was customary to permit every member of the society to enter the championships, but after several years it became apparent that people were entering who had very little shooting experience – often virtual beginners – and they were causing a great deal of difficulty to the more experienced archers who were there to compete on a serious championship basis. Often these archers found themselves shooting for a day with people who had no idea of the scoring systems, who had little shooting ability or experience, who lost a lot of arrows and held up the groups behind them while they searched for them, and who were generally a liability. It was therefore decreed that all competitors would be required to have been members for a certain length of time, on the assumption that this would cure the problem. However, it did not quite work as planned. The length of the membership period was arbitrary – what was considered sufficient for all concerned to have had enough experience. It was soon found, however, that there were people who were eligible to shoot under the new rule, but who still had had no experience of a competitive shoot. The problem was exemplified by one elderly competitor who said he had been a member for years, but he had never seen a Saunders Foresters face before and did not know the scoring system for them – this is at a time when half the targets were Saunders Foresters. He then admitted that he very rarely shot and had not been to a competition shoot for years.

A new scheme was devised. If they had never shot in a championship before, all entrants would produce score-cards for six shoots they had competed in. These were to be signed by a responsible official at each shoot. This system seems to have worked well, and the problem of inexperienced competitors has been resolved, with no drop in attendances. Some discretion is permitted for newcomers who have made exceptional progress, but such people usually try to ensure that they have completed the necessary qualifying six shoots.

One of the difficulties encountered by the organizers is finding sufficient people to lay the targets, act as stewards, and generally do all the hard work. At times, willing workers may have travelled hundreds of miles to help with the multitude of arrangements. Very often, members of local clubs are asked to volunteer their labour and some do so very readily, but it is a huge task and few are willing to do it on an annual basis. It has sometimes resulted in two hard workers laying each course on their own.

On the first day of the championships, eager archers arrive at the ground in their hundreds. The wise and lucky will have arrived in local accommodation the day before, or pitched their tents on the campsite. If all has gone well, this will be adjacent to the courses. This is a time of suppressed excitement and anticipation. Fully accoutred archers mill about the parking areas, practice areas, administration caravans, refreshment tents and dealers' tents, or some just stroll about meeting and greeting old friends and familiar faces. Some are wandering about eating the traditional bacon butties – the smell of frying bacon is common at field shoots.

The practice target area is crowded. There are about eight targets, at differing distances and of different animal faces, and about 200 people trying to get a few shots at them, queuing up for the privilege of stretching their arms and seeing whether they are on form.

Score-cards are collected from a marquee where long rows of tables have hundreds of them arranged in alphabetical order, with attendants handing them out. All the competitors will have pre-booked and their score-cards are all made out in advance, with their names, clubs, shooting style, which course they are designated to shoot on the first day, and their starting target number. Some people may not have arrived, so there will be adjustments to some of the groups in order to balance them. After this is done, the competitors are asked to assemble for the briefing. This is usually given over a loudspeaker system by the society's secretary, and outlines simple rules such as no changing of groups, score-cards to be done by two members of each group, no one to do their own score-cards, cards to be handed in at the end of the shoot, etc. The competitors are then instructed to follow marshals out to the courses.

Once out on the designated course, which may take some time to reach, since all four courses cannot be adjacent to the administration field, the archers are gathered together and briefed about rules of conduct – that any infringement of the rules should be reported to a marshal and any offenders will be asked to leave the course. After this, the competitors are led out to their first targets and, when all are in position, a previously arranged audible signal is given to start them shooting – a whistle, a hooter or a shotgun blast.

At one time, it was customary to shoot a Big Game course on one day and a Foresters course on the other, but it was found after a few years that this was not always fair in that some would shoot the Foresters course on a good day, and get high scores, while others in the same class might be forced to shoot it in rain on the other day and thus were at a disadvantage. The Foresters' targets had possible scores far higher than the Big Game ones, thirty and forty-five points against only twenty. Some archers therefore proposed that to iron out this inconsistency it would be a good idea to shoot an equal number of each type of target on each course, and eventually this method was adopted, so that it was possible to attain the same score on both days. In fact this did not happen very often due to differences in the courses; one might have longer targets than the other.

Quite recently, it has been suggested that, since Foresters faces are no longer being produced in the USA, and fewer clubs were putting on open shoots using them, they should be dropped from the national championships. In their place, it has been proposed that there should now be a higher scoring spot within the kill area of the Big Game targets, for an extra five points. This would mean that the top archers would still win by hitting these more difficult smaller areas, but the scoring anomalies of mixing Foresters and Big Game targets would be eliminated and all targets would now carry the same scores. It has yet to be seen how popular this will be and whether it will be accepted by the majority of archers.

There is normally no lunch break at championship shoots, simply because of the distance of the courses from the parking area, but there are one or two tea tents or caravans placed at strategic locations round. The competitors are able to stop at these for refreshments on their way round. Some people fear that they will start on a target near the tea tent and not see it again until they have finished shooting, but this does not happen often.

On completion of the day's shooting, the score-cards are handed in to the administration caravan or tent, where the scores for each archer are noted on his cards for the next day. Groups are changed for the following day so that no one shoots with the same archers on both days.

During the course of the shoot, there are marshals available on the course to deal with any problems such as target faces being shot out, butts which have become loose, or marker pegs which have been dislodged. There is also the possibility of a marker peg needing to be moved for some reason, perhaps because the target is totally invisible from it. This happens sometimes as heavy rain weighs down branches so that they obscure the target. On rare occasions, targets have had to be moved the night before the shoot because rain has created swamps round them.

A great deal of the success of a championship shoot lies in the skill of the course builders. If a course has been laid by an inexperienced group, targets can often be far too long for their size, or too close to be much of a challenge. It is common for there to be many complaints about the length of targets. They usually only apply to one course, the other having been built by another group who have judged target distances better. Too many long and very difficult targets can lead to a great deal of complaining. The view of many people is that they came to enjoy themselves, not to be presented with targets no one could hit. The philosophy adopted by some course builders is that, if it is a championship shoot, it ought to be more difficult than a normal one, but this is not the view of most competitors. The problem is compounded by the fact that no parameters are laid down for distances for each size of target. This has resulted in targets being set at previously unknown distances, horrendously far away. Some course builders adopt the approach, 'We always do our courses like this.' They do not realize that people have long since given up going to their club open shoots because the targets are always ridiculously distant.

Today, championship courses are inspected the day prior to the shoot, to check for safety, etc. However, in the past some very strange target positions have been created. On my first championship shoot, many targets were totally invisible. One, which must take the prize as the daftest I've ever seen, was an 18-inch wide Foresters face a yard behind a tree at least 1 foot in diameter, making it totally impossible to hit the centre of the target. There were a few holes down each side of the face, and an angry competitor had planted a row of broken wooden arrows along the top of the butt. The competitors' reaction to this course was such that the club responsible was obliged to make considerable alterations before the next day's shooting. To add insult to injury, the campsite had been ploughed the day before the shoot by a thoughtful farmer!

The championships should be a pleasure to shoot, since many archers look forward to them as the greatest event in the shoot calendar, and perhaps more care should be taken to ensure that they *are* a pleasure, rather than a chore. When complaints are made about the distances that targets have been set at, the usual response is: 'Well, *you* try doing it. You probably never have.' But some of us have done it, several times, and have not had any complaints about unreasonably long targets.

This results, of course, from courses being set for unmarked distances. With marked-distance courses, this problem does not arise since all the parameters are laid down for each size of target face. Since the NFAS is strongly in favour of unmarked distance at all times, there is room for improvement in the level of control over some of the distances. Rabbits at 40 yards may be challenging for some, but impossible for many.

At the end of the second day's shooting, score-cards are handed in and the administration team begins the huge task of collating the scores and working out the top scores and winners. The method used for working out the top scores is simple. All the cards for one class are given to one person who can quickly go through them and pick out the top three scores. Other cards are then put aside but not discarded. Even with nearly 700 people shooting, few classes contain more than fifty archers. One that can contain more than that is the Hunting Tackle,(H/T) class.

First place in every class receives a trophy and a medal. The trophies are returnable, the medals are kept. Second and third places also receive a medal. These medals are substantial chunks of metal specially designed with the NFAS owl embossed on them, in the traditional gold, silver and bronze. The prize-giving takes quite a while, since there are more classes than at most open shoots, and nearly all go to a third place. There are also team prizes and family prizes.

In a few weeks' time, the full results will be published and sent to every member of the NFAS. Now everyone will be able to see not only how well or how badly they shot, but how everyone else did, too. The results are published in descending order of scores with every entrant listed. So one can not only see where one came in the order, but also the scores of everyone else one was competing against.

Some interesting aspects of these lists are the statistics it is possible to compile from them. For example, it can be found that members from over seventy clubs attended, plus the annual average of forty-five independents, belonging to no club. It can be found that there were only one or two people from some clubs, while two or three had over twenty attending. Thus it can be discovered which are the biggest and most active clubs in the country, and where they are. It is also easy to see which are the most popular classes, and exactly how many archers shot in each class. It is also sometimes very clear that the scores were lower on the second day, on all the courses, among many of the competitors. The reason for this is not hard to find, since the whole championships is regarded by many people as a huge social event rather than a competition.

The calendar position of the NFAS Championships has been the subject of discussion for many years. Only once has it been held at any other time than mid-September, and that was once at the Whitsun weekend. Unfortunately, probably because it was a bank holiday weekend, the second day's shooting, on the Monday, was done in a downpour that lasted until shooting was over. It was later found that Nottingham, the nearest large town to the venue, was the wettest place in Britain on that day, with over 1 inch of rain. The usual date was reverted to for all subsequent years. The weather at that time is usually very good, and it is out of the holiday season but still in summer. It was once suggested that the championships should be held in winter, out of the target archery shooting season, in order to allow those who shoot both field and target to do their target shoots. This was rejected, since the number of people affected was minuscule, while those affected by having to camp out in winter was far higher.

There is now an annual 3D National Championship shoot under NFAS rules. When this was first suggested, there was some doubt that it would ever be possible due to the high cost of the targets and the difficulties of storing and transporting them. These problems have been overcome, but at the time of writing, there is a limit on the number of entrants due to the number of targets available and the size of courses. Thus far, it has only been possible to organize two courses, of forty targets each, so the number of entries has been limited to 400, which means five competitors per target. It has been a matter of first come first served for entries. The demand has certainly outstripped the places available, and the shoots so far have been very successful.

EFAA National Championships

The EFAA Championships are also held annually over two days, usually in early September. The venue is in a different area every year. Two courses are shot, with two rounds, Hunter and Field. Both are shot as marked distance rounds. The space required for these is somewhat less than the NFAS requirements, since the number of competitors is fewer.

The EFAA also holds a Bowhunter Championship, shot as unmarked rounds and usually with animal faces and 3D targets, also over two days.

In addition, it holds an Indoor Championship that is shot at 20 yards, 60 arrows being shot.

13 A Selection of Courses

As we have seen, clubs that have enough space often hold open shoots, sometimes, but not primarily, to boost their funds. Anyone who has held an open shoot or been involved in the huge amount of hard work it demands is often moved to wonder why they do it. The answer really is that, if they did not, the sport courses would cease to exist. It takes a lot of organization and physical labour to put on a shoot and yet some clubs have been doing it regularly for years; and once it is started, it becomes expected. Clubs shooting NFAS rules expect to put on shoots; it becomes part of the pattern of life, the reason for their existence. Without it, a club has no central aim or purpose.

Some grounds are superb, some are pretty good and a few – not many – not very good. If they are not particularly good, archers will still come and shoot at their open shoots, because many field archers will shoot anywhere, even though a course may be poor, and the shoots badly organized. Examples of club shoots being boycotted are few and far between, but there was one club which ceased holding open shoots because their ground was poor, the targets were badly positioned, and none of their members ever attended anyone else's open shoots. For these reasons the attendance at their shoots gradually fell to the point where it was no longer worth holding any. Many grounds are a pleasure to shoot on and many shoots are well organized. A few are described below, but they are only a selection of those I have had personal experience of shooting on. The information is correct at time of writing, but it must be borne in mind that clubs sometimes have to move grounds, so anyone contemplating visiting any of the clubs listed would be wise to check with the club secretaries before doing so.

- **Castle Field Archers, near Biddulph, Staffs.** Narrow deciduous woodland, following two streams. Can be difficult underfoot, many steep muddy banks. One shoot per year, some 3Ds, mainly Big Game. Parking in adjacent field. A good ground, very testing. (NFAS rules are used but the organization is not directly affiliated to the NFAS.)
- **Clayton Woodsmen, Newcastle-Under-Lyme, Staffs. NFAS.** Mixed deciduous woodland, approximately 20 acres. Club usually puts on two or three shoots per year. Ground slopes downhill, small valley down each side. Interesting to shoot, course changed for every shoot. Large clubhouse. Popular shoots, well organized. Animal rounds, some 3Ds. Ample parking, mainly on road. Good refreshments.
- **Cledford Field Archers, near Holmes Chapel, Cheshire. NFAS.** Small mixed deciduous wood, approximately 15 acres. Club usually puts on two or three shoots per year. Flat ground, closely grown. Tight course, well organized, well planned. Big Game rounds, some 3D targets. Ample parking in field near wood. Refreshments.
- **Lyme Valley Field Archers, near Audley, Staffs. NFAS.** Small narrow course on each side of a stream, very little flat, mainly banks. Mixed deciduous woodland. Quite beautiful ground, especially in spring. Tight course, targets close together. Usually puts on two or three open shoots per year. Popular. Courses can be difficult sometimes. Big Game rounds, some 3Ds. Small clubhouse. Ample parking, usually in adjacent field. Refreshments. Well organized.
- **Foxhill, Pendle Hill, Lancashire. NFAS, GNAS.** Thick pinewood plantation on north slope of Pendle Hill, famous for its witches. Fairly steep, not for the unfit. One or two shoots per year, sometimes NFAS, sometimes GNAS rules. Parking difficult. Refreshments. Big Game rounds, GNAS rounds.
- **Lawton Field Bowmen, near Newcastle-under-Lyme, Staffs. NFAS.** Fairly large ground, unusual undulating grassland with clumps and individual birch trees, areas of bushes, small valley down one end. Ample parking, big clubhouse. Near M6 motorway. Can be muddy at times. Big Game targets, some 3Ds, two or three shoots per year. Been on this ground for many years. Well organized, but some shoots have very long shots. Can be difficult.

- **Severn Valley Yeoman Foresters, (SVYF), near Ombersley, Worcestershire. NFAS.** A beautiful ground, an island of trees surrounded by fields. Deciduous woodland, fairly large. Parking tricky, some distance from wood. Two or three shoots per year. Big Game. Well organized. Small clubhouse. Refreshments.
- **Frankley, near Hagley, West Midlands. NFAS.** A beautiful ground, fairly large very ancient deciduous woodland on top of small hill. Parking adequate, outside wood. One or two shoots per year, but tend to use very long distances for size of targets. Big Game and 3D. Also have used Kinver Scout ground at times, which is quite spectacular on a small scale.
- **Rough Park, near Melbourne, Derbyshire. NFAS.** A large ground. Deciduous woodland, some very open. Two or three shoots per year on different parts of the wood. Big Game and 3D. Ample parking along woodland track. Sometimes difficult shoots, long distances for size of targets. Some courses are quite flat, others hilly. Refreshments.
- **Derwynd, near Darwin, Lancs. NFAS.** A beautiful ground, small and narrow, following a stream with small waterfalls. Parking some distance away, in a field. Few shoots, some years without any, usually shot round twice. Big Game. Clubhouse. Refreshments.
- **Warcock, near Salmesbury, Lancs. NFAS.** A long, narrow tapering course, 5 yards wide at one end, much wider at other. Deciduous wood, following a stream. Long walk from parking area. Undulating ground, many banks, few flat areas. One or two shoots per year, Big Game, 3Ds – mostly home-made. Refreshments.
- **Black Knight, near Brinscall, Lancashire. NFAS.** A small course, mainly grassy hillside with clumps of trees and old railway track, with deciduous trees. Easy parking on the same field. A strange course, with permanent butts, animal targets, often very small for the distances. Non-standard target faces. Catering van.
- **South Cheshire Field Archers, near Winsford, Cheshire. NFAS.** Fairly large 18-acre pinewood. Fairly flat. Dry ground. Parking on adjacent field. Big Game, sometimes home-made, 3Ds, some also home-made. Two shoots per year. Refreshments.
- **Charnwood, near Ashby-de-la-Zouche. Leicestershire. NFAS.** A large ground, mainly deciduous woodland. One shoot per year,

parking difficult. Very popular due to unusual use of ground with shots across open water, with crocodile at 60 yards, etc.

- **Cheshire County Bowmen, near Delamere Forest, Cheshire. GNAS** Target and Field. A large ground, not woodland but mainly round a small lake with belts of trees between fields. One open shoot, record status, per year. Parking in adjacent field. Shooting every other Sunday.
- **Ashcombe Valley, near Dawlish, Devon. NFAS.** A huge ground, part of a vast area of forest. Mixed woodland, some hilly, some flat, Large deciduous, some coniferous woodland. Open shoots, some 3D, part of the eight-day Devon Challenge. Parking not difficult. One of the best courses.
- **Duvelle Bowmen, near Derby. NFAS.** Deciduous woodland. Large, varied course, varied shoots, usually about twice per year. Parking on adjacent field. Well-organized courses, sometimes more difficult than average.
- **Liberty Archers, near RAF Lakenheath, Suffolk. NFAS.** Two shooting areas, both very flat, as befits the landscape of the area. One area is mainly oak wood, the other is open pinewood, birch and oak, very beautiful, grassy, like a huge garden. Have done a two-day 3D shoot for several years, at which the attendance is in the hundreds, archers travelling long distances. Lots of American influence here, as might be expected.

14 International Field Archery

There are several organizations which hold international field archery championships. FITA has a championship shoot every two years, the International Field Archery Association holds a biennial shoot and there are also European championship shoots. These contests are often held on far more difficult ground than British archers may be accustomed to.

The IFAA 1997 championships were held in South Africa, and the courses were on rocky scrubland, quite different from any ground in Britain. The rounds shot were the Unmarked Distance Animal Round, the Precision Round, the Game Trail and 3D rounds and most of the competitors were shooting in the compound bow classes. The shoot was held on a privately owned game ranch over a period of a week and the programme followed the pattern of: registration, practice range open, bow inspection, and the opening of the club field/hunter range, on days one to three. Day four: opening ceremony, registration, practice range open and bow inspection. Days five and six: tournament. On the final day the award ceremony and buffet were held.

There was an extensive programme of entertainments for the competitors which included game viewing, music and dance, nature videos, darts, double-handed broad axe throwing, an African night, and much more. The entry fees were all in Australian dollars and appeared to be quite high.

There is now a 'Champion of Nations' team contest in the World Field Archery Championships, inaugurated in 1996. The selection for this is a complex process involving competitors of several different classes, but all team members have to be in adult classes, not including Veterans or Professionals. Each national team contains seven members.

By way of contrast, the XVth World Field Championships, held under the FITA rules, were quite different and were held in the spectacular mountains of Slovenia, less than five miles from the Austrian and Italian borders. Snow-capped mountains could be seen from parts of the course, even though this was in June. Temperatures were in the 65-70°F range, so were quite comfortable. About 215 archers from twenty-three countries shot. There were qualification rounds to be shot, before the actual Championship shooting started, on Marked and Unmarked distance courses. There were some challenging shots on the courses, since the hilly terrain allowed several steeply angled shots, one being about seventy degrees downhill. This makes the holding of the bow difficult, as well as actual aiming. Body position makes the actual shot more difficult at this sort of angle.

The elimination rounds were shot on flatter ground, but still with some difficult shots – and this gave those archers who had been eliminated the chance to see the best shooting against each other. This arrangement now creates a tense finale situation rather than the previous system in which those with the highest scores won. The problem previously was that no one knew who these were until the prize giving.

The finals took place on level ground, down from the mountains, with all the previous competitors now watching the final contestants shoot off against each other. This meant a single arrow each at the last target between the last two competitors in each class. This new scheme, modelled on the new rules for Olympic Target archery, now creates far more dramatic shooting situations and breathtaking finals.

The USA

Field Archery is strongest in the USA, where it was invented after the Second World War as a means for out-of-season bowhunters to practise their skills. Bowhunting is legal in every state, and each has a different season, so that animals are not permitted to be shot at all times of the year. There is also a difference between the bowhunting and rifle hunting seasons so that there is an opportunity for bowhunters to shoot without competing against those with rifles.

The ethos of hunting live animals is different from the UK and many bowhunters claiming that they eat what they shoot. Moreover, they actually shoot very few animals since stalking skills are also necessary. One archer once declared that he knew a man who had been hunting for twelve years and had never yet managed to shoot an animal.

The US has the space, the climate, the facilities, the enthusiasm and the technology to develop field archery. The sport is divided, however, between several organizations, each with different rules and methods. The main ones are the National Field Archery Association, the International Bowhunters Association and the International Field Archery Association, but there are others.

The scale of the sport is also quite different and requires different organization for shoots. Where a major shoot will involve thousands of competitors, as well as spectators, there must be the organization to cope with such numbers. One American archer informed me that, when he attended the National Bowhunter Championships one year, there were 4,000 competitors. This is a staggering number to have to deal with, compared with the biggest archery competition in the UK, which has about 600–700 entries, and those from a far smaller area. How is that number accommodated? With no less than twenty courses, with eighteen targets on each course. Shooting groups are huge, compared to UK numbers. Normally, there would be sixteen archers in a group, with two scorers. They start out on the course at different times, each group being given a start time that must be adhered to. The administration staff must be extremely efficient at processing the scores. I was once told that at a major shoot, all the scores were processed and the winners – and there were many, in many different classes – announced in half an hour.

The following is an account by Mike Williams, a member of my home club, who travelled to the USA to try their version of field archery. The shoot was the Great Western Classic Trail Shoot at Redding, California, under the rules of the National Field Archery Association, with about 1,500 archers and the same number of spectators.

This shoot started a number of years ago and now attracts both amateur and professional archers from all over the world. Entry charges are dependent on class, for example, amateur or professional, child or adult, starting at $15 for a child and going up to $150 for the professionals.

The course consists of seventy 3D targets, all at marked distances, the shortest being 4 yards and the longest 101 yards. The size of the targets was well matched to the distances, the bigfoot or yeti, at 12 feet high, being the 101-yard shot, and the 4-yard shot being a butterfly with four spots on the wings.

The shoot was situated in beautiful wooded surroundings but the shooting areas were clear from any overhanging obstacles or heavy undergrowth, which meant that no one lost any arrows, so no time needed to be spent looking for them. This is important when up to twenty-five archers are shooting from any one peg. All archers shoot two arrows from the same position, with both arrows scoring, and up to ten archers may be shooting at the same time. The scoring system is eleven points for the spot, or centre kill, ten for the outer kill area and eight for anywhere else on the animal. On the smaller targets, this changes to eleven for a kill and ten anywhere else, as these targets are too small to have an inner ring in the kill.

When the course was laid, a lot of time obviously went into creating a scene, rather than just putting up a single target, so that from the shooting peg there were occasions when as many as twenty animal figures could be seen, although only two were to be shot at. The others were placed there just for the effect, and it was very effective.

Competitors were expected to book in on the practice day and be ready to start shooting at 8 o'clock on the first day; if they were not there in time, they were not allowed to shoot. Forty-five targets were shot on the first day, leaving twenty-five to be shot on the second. Shooting was completed by 1 o'clock, which allowed time for the administration to sort out the score-cards, to carry out any shoot-offs in case of ties in the scores, and to do the actual medal awards.

Having travelled 6,000 miles, I expected that the weather would be rather better than in England, but I was disappointed. On the first day, the practice day, the weather was beautiful, the sun was shining and there was no breeze, but this did not last long and by evening it was raining quite heavily. Day two was not bad, a little overcast but no rain until the evening, when it really did rain heavily. Day three started with a typical British drizzle with occasional heavier downpours, which made our contingent feel very much at home. This cleared by lunchtime and the weather returned to sunshine, although the rain returned in the evening.

Everyone was very friendly; they were fascinated by a group of British people travelling 6,000 miles to their shoot, some of whom shot with unsighted bows, including a traditional longbow and a young archer shooting barebow. Others in the group were shooting with compounds with pins or sights. Most of the American archers – perhaps over 95 percent – were shooting in what is classed in the UK as Compound Unlimited, although they have their own classifications which can be numerous and complex.

The major archery equipment suppliers, who also sponsor some of the professionals and very accomplished amateurs, donate most of the raffle prizes, consisting of high-quality bows and accessories and many more highly prized items.

The food was typical of most American food outlets, being of a high standard, in great quantities and very affordable. There were food and drink stalls well spaced around the course.

Car parking was similar to the UK, with drivers parking where possible, but there was so much space that there was always room to park, even though it was sometimes away from the main registration area.

The event was well organized and the standard of archery was impressive, not only the level of scoring, but the numbers of archers who achieved high levels. Americans tend to put a great deal of enthusiasm into everything, and the number of helpers at this shoot, many of whom had travelled great distances to be there, was impressive. Each target shooting area had an area reserved for spectators, something else quite different from current practice in the UK.

The bigfoot target is down a steep hillside, which makes the shooting more difficult, and in some years there is a $50,000 dollar prize for any archer getting two arrows in the centre spot.

The International Scene

The following is an account of Tony Weston's international archery experiences. Tony has been several times NFAS National Compound Unlimited Champion.

My whole international shooting experience has been based on IFAA World and European Bowhunter Championships in South Africa, Portugal, Australia, Germany, Italy (three times) and France (twice). The most noticeable feature of all these tournaments was the friendliness, and how accommodating all these countries have been towards the tournaments. It is also an honour for archers to compete for their countries. For example, in South Africa, team members have to compete strongly for their team colours and are awarded them at the same time as their cricket and rugby teams, each sport being given equal status.

Partly because of this and also because of their training facilities and significant sponsorship, all the archers from other nations are of a very high standard indeed. When travelling to these events, everyone knows that they have to be on top form to get a place anywhere in the top ten or twenty. Everyone is highly competitive, and yet still finds the time to look after other competitors, help with equipment, etc., even if they do not speak the same language. Everyone respects each other and makes a real effort to be considerate to each other.

The standard of organization at these events is fantastic. Most tournaments consist of between 500 and 1,300 competitors, and the organizers make it look easy to cope with numbers such as these. Tournaments are normally held over four or five shooting days. Bow inspections and practice ranges are open two or three days prior to the start of the tournament. The start is usually after some form of opening ceremony. Double scoring is done on every target (each archer has two score-cards, scored by other members of the group and cross-checked at intervals) and, since all the tournaments I have attended are held under IFAA rules, certain rounds can be guaranteed and the courses are planned and laid out to a high level of consistency and quality. The maximum distance on any round is 60 yards and the minimum is 10 yards. Starts are made on time, and all scores and positions are posted two hours after the close of the courses for each day.

The host nation can choose to use various rounds and it is often difficult to compete on a level platform with the host nation on some of those rounds. For example, Australians and Italians seem to love speed shooting – five targets at five distances in forty seconds. A pop-up target appears for five seconds then disappears and two seconds later another appears at a different distance for another five seconds. This is particularly difficult for compound unlimited archers. Normally the week consists of two animal rounds with paper faces, one 3D animal round – normally one shot at each target, so there is no second chance – plus a two-shot 3D round (the same as the 3D round used in the NFAS National 3D Championships) and the special animal round, which is whatever the host country prefers.

After shooting each evening there is normally some sort of entertainment laid on, sometimes consisting of a fun shoot such as an elk at 120 yards to win a bow, or a shoot-out at the OK Corral. There are often invitations to see various local traditions such as tribal dancing in South Africa, or a barbecue.

Weather and terrain play a large part in these tournaments. Quite apart from the spiders, snakes, crocodiles and other wildlife in Australia. (The Australians tried to convince some of the Germans that an animal called a 'drop-dead bear', a cross between a koala and a European brown bear, drops from trees and attacks as anyone goes under them. They seemed convinced, since they spent most of the day walking about looking upwards.) It was so hot in Australia that I carried three litres of Power Aid drink for each half of each course. After the first day I was followed by a marshal for most of the course, checking that I was all right, since I was going red. By the end of the week I was followed by a marshal carrying an umbrella.

Everything hurts in South Africa – again, a lot of spiders, snakes and other such animals with big pointy teeth. On the last day of the shoot I bent down to pull arrows and was bitten on my back, which really hurt. Fearing the worst – a spider from the web above my head – we removed my shirt to find an ant! Two targets later I fell into some nasty grass which shot lots of little needles into my side. I picked them out of my side and chest, causing a large red rash, changed my shirt and we continued. Apart from that, the size of the thorns on the bushes is worth seeing; 4–5 inches is not uncommon.

On one trip to Italy, where I thought it would be hot and sunny as we flew into Venice, it soon turned out to be really cold, wet and miserable as we travelled a lot further north than we had anticipated, into the mountains. We spent the week in T-shirts shooting among the ski lifts and on the ski slopes. I always take waterproofs and a couple of fleeces with me now.

Most courses around the world are physically demanding as the distances between targets are quite long, for safety reasons and to get the most out of the terrain. It is not uncommon to walk a mountain twice in a day, and four courses over four days equals four mountains each walked twice. This tends to be a little exhausting.

Having been competing internationally for a while now, I have made some really good friends from all over the world, and have been treated to some amazing hospitality, even to the extent of being put up in South Africa for a few weeks and attending the engagement of one of the French international archers to the sister of one of the South African archers.

Equipment set-ups are very similar throughout the world, except that the UK has fallen behind a long way, especially when it comes to speed set-ups. At the World Championships in Germany the Italians had the fastest bows, with arrows travelling at over 400 feet per second (300 is considered fast), and most other countries' teams were shooting bows set to shoot at between 360 and 390 fps, while the English were shooting at about 300 to 330 fps and the poor Dutch at around the 280 fps mark. This gives the country with the fastest set-up a big advantage on unmarked distances, since speed makes a significant difference to sight marks, with the Italians having a sight range of 4–6 mm. over a distance range of 10–60 yards and the English with a sight mark range of 28 mm for the same distances.

However, the fairly good news is that IFAA have voted in a speed limit of 300 fps for arrows, to be brought into use in January 2001, which should put everyone on a more level footing and make it a lot safer, as quite a few bows were breaking during the tournaments because of the shock going through them.

Agincourt 1986-8

Now and again, some bold individual or organization will put on a really unusual shoot. These are worth keeping an eye open for, since they can be immensely enjoyable. In 1986, the Plantaganet Society, which specialized in demonstrating medieval archery, organized a weekend shoot at Agincourt, scene of the English bowmen's greatest victory in 1415. Those who attended had a superb weekend, packed with well-organized events in addition to the actual shooting.

A coach was laid on to take entrants from Nottingham to France. This gradually filled up as it made its way towards Dover and the ferry. Some of the passengers were strangely attired in oddments of pseudo-medieval dress, like steel helmets and chain mail, and although this was not a requirement for the weekend, there was some emphasis on the use of longbows and the wearing of period costume.

On arrival in the Agincourt area, it was found that the village itself was too small to support even a small hotel, so many of the visitors were accommodated in hotels in nearby French towns, where they were pleased to discover that French hotels, unlike those in Britain, charge only for a room, so if five people share a room, it is rather cheaper than at home, although breakfast consists only of croissants and jam.

Booking in the next day was done outside the battle museum, which seemed to be remarkably empty. Local dignitaries arrived, the chairman of the Syndicat d'Initiative (a sort of combined tourist and chamber of commerce organization) which was supporting the event, made a speech, several others made speeches, few of which were understandable by the English audience, and eventually the archers made their way up a lane and out on to the battlefield. The fields now, as then, are of rolling wheat, with small meadows on each side of the actual battleground site. The shoot was to take place in these meadows, twenty targets on the first day, twenty the next. Twenty per day is not many, and can normally be shot in a couple of hours, but for some reason, these took far longer.

Before the shooting started, all the longbow archers lined up in a 'herce', a long curving line of several ranks, for the benefit of French Television cameramen. This was to demonstrate how it was thought the archers actually operated during the battle. On a signal, all drew back their strings, and loosed a hail of arrows across the field. This was mighty impressive, even with only a hundred or so archers. It took little imagination to feel how it might have been on a larger scale – quite terrifying to be on the receiving end. Anyone who has seen the 1943 film of Henry V will have some idea.

The actual targets for the shoot were unusual. They were all at considerable distances, many at about 60 yards, and all were figures of soldiers, crossbowmen, knights, lackeys, men-at-arms etc. There was, however, some doubt about the wisdom of shooting some of them, since it was soon discovered that each target had upon it an envelope containing a note. This made plain what the target was, or who, and how many points could be scored by hitting it. Some archers were dismayed to discover that their first shots on the first target scored them minus points, since they had shot someone on the English side! After the first shots, more care was taken in assessing each target. Did the knight have a red cross on his shield? If so, it was better not to shoot at him, just at his sword. On reaching the target, however, one might receive a nasty shock: he was a French knight who had picked up an English shield on the field, and he should have been shot at, so no score on this target. Shots at a rather fancily dressed young man were discounted, since he was a herald, responsible for transmitting messages between the opposing armies, and he was inviolable, not to be shot. On the other hand, anyone who put the required three arrows into a certain Genoese crossbowman got treble points, since he was the chief crossbowman. Those three shots were then worth 120 points, and boosted one's score considerably. One target appeared to be a figure furtively making its way across the field with a large sack on its back. The scoring on this was more than usually complex – plus scores for striking the figure, but minus scores for his sack, since he was a thief making off with the English crown jewels!

The targets were spread wide apart round the meadows and

required considerable walking throughout the day. The well-painted faces were supported by straw bales from local farms, and it soon became evident that French straw bales are packed somewhat more loosely than English ones and often allowed arrows to pass right through. This meant considerable time spent searching the long grass for lost arrows.

After twenty targets had been shot, the archers made their way back to the assembly area at the crossroads which now lies in the middle of where the battle was fought. Here a solitary bar-restaurant did its best trade for many years as thirsty archers stood about in the roads drinking and joking, some being photographed in their costumes while others marvelled at the vast dump of empty bottles across the road from the bar – there were truckloads of them.

In the evening, visits were made to the local bars in the nearby town of Hesdin. As with most French towns in the evenings, the population seemed to have deserted the place, the streets were empty, with no traffic. Where do the French go in the evenings? The town was like the average English town used to be fifty years ago, before the coming of mass car ownership. Bars were discovered, of course, and the strong French beer soon took its toll. It may look and taste innocuous, but it is quite a lot more alcoholic than stronger-flavoured English beers.

On the following day, the shoot continued, on another set of twenty targets, in the same style as on the previous day. The challenge of shooting at many longer targets than usual was considerable, and some arrows fell to the side of the tall and narrow man-sized targets. After shooting was finished, score cards were handed in, and the prize-giving took place. However, there was a special event in the evening, when the coach took the competitors to a nearby town for a dinner. The party's arrival in the town square surprised the locals who were sitting outside the bars and restaurants, since the vehicles unloaded fancily dressed English visitors, many of the ladies looking especially graceful in long medieval-style gowns and headdresses.

The dinner took place in a stone-built hall, complete with animal heads and ancient weapons hung on the walls. When the meal was over, another prize-giving took place. This took the form of speeches, photographs signed by the local mayor – French mayors have far wider powers than those in British towns – and scrolls commemorating the event presented individually to each archer, called out in turn. Each archer was also paid the going rate for medieval archers – threepence a day, unless they were from Cheshire, in which case, Cheshire archers being reckoned to be the best, they received sixpence.

The coach home the next day was an anticlimax after a great weekend, well supported by the local French people. HM Customs were somewhat surprised to see, in the coach's cargo bay, a collection of steel-edged weapons with several helmets. They hurriedly shut the hatches and tried to ignore what they had seen.

There was a certain thrill in shooting on this ancient battlefield, but it was sobering to visit the small memorial stone, about ½ a mile east of the café. It marked the French grave pits, and there was a sombre group of dark conifers, as well as a panel pointing out the various points of interest of the battle. The woodlands where the English archers stood flanking the open ground no longer exist, but it took little imagination to recall that deadly day.

Two years later, the Plantaganet Society staged the same event again, but it was rather spoiled by a strike at Dover and the coaches sat on the harbour for hours until they boarded the ferry and eventually arrived at their destination at six in the morning, when shooting was supposed to start at 10.30. This meant a quite a lot of sleep-deprived English archers shot the field of Agincourt that day, but this time there were more French archers joining in, and they proved themselves no mean hands with the bows.

Two years later still, another shoot brought even more French archers, and they took most of the prizes.

Equipment

As might be expected, not all countries have archery dealers, and archers in some countries may have considerable difficulty in obtaining equipment. One international archer described the equipment of one team at an international shoot as outdated and inadequate, which, it must be assumed, was not the fault of the archers concerned, but it was heartening that members of other national teams loaned them – or gave them, in some instances – the equipment they needed. The problems of obtaining equipment solely by mail order at a long distance must be considerable, compounded by not having contacts with archers who are up to date with currents trends in equipment design and use.

Countries Affiliated to the IFAA

- **Europe**: Austria, Belgium, Denmark, England, Finland, France, Germany, Ireland, Italy, Portugal, San Marino, Scotland, Sweden, Switzerland, Wales.
- **Americas**: Argentina, Canada, USA.
- **Asia and Pacific**: Australia, Hong Kong, Malaysia, New Zealand, Singapore.
- **Africa**: Botswana, Mauritius, Namibia, South Africa, Zambia, Zimbabwe.

International Tournaments

The programme of international shoots is not extensive, and is organized by at least three different organizations: FITA, IFAA and the European Field Archery Association.

FITA field tournaments include the International Championships held every two years at a different venue. The European Field Championships are held in the years between the International Championship, according to FITA rules. FITA also organizes the World Games.

IFAA International Bowhunter Championships are also held at different venues on each occasion, using animal targets and unmarked distances.

The European Field Archery Association also organizes international tournaments.

15 Do-It-Yourself

The archer must be a home handyman, at least to a small extent, whether he likes it or not, since there are always jobs to do, such as refletching shafts, reserving bowstrings, etc., which one cannot really ask fellow archers or the nearest archery dealer to do. Many archers take a pride in their ability to make and straighten their own arrows, make quivers and even bows. In the early days of recurve bows, before metal handles were dreamed of, a few archers even used to make their own recurve laminate bows.

Bows

Making a bow is not difficult, but there are certain tools that are virtually essential if it is not to become very arduous. One is a bandsaw, another a belt sander. Cutting out the formers round which the limb is glued is very difficult without a bandsaw. It used to be said by those who attempted the art that it was necessary to make at least ten bows before getting one that was even satisfactory. My own two attempts resulted in two broken bows before I had even shot them – it is astonishing how fragile fibreglass laminate bow limbs are when stressed in the wrong way. If a limb is held in a vice, for example, any attempt to bend it will snap it quite easily, since the material is designed for bending gradually over a considerable length, not over one point. Both bows broke because the stress on the limbs was very uneven. The stress must therefore be balanced evenly over both limbs, which explains why compound limbs must be adjusted gradually and evenly, and the tiller checked after any adjustment.

Longbows may be easier to make than laminate bows, once the

correct materials have been acquired, and there are more longbow makers in Britain today than makers of laminate bows. Making a longbow, of course, is a highly skilled task, taking considerable experience, but it is possible because it does not require a great deal of modern machinery and can be done with simple tools. I do not intend to delve into the art of making longbows, however, since this is beyond the skills or ambitions of most field archers.

Compounds are more complex and there are currently only two compound manufacturers in the country. I have known only two archers who made their own compound bows, one of which the maker shot very successfully for many years. The other, curiously, had a bow he claimed to have designed and made himself, but the steel parts were covered with rust!

Wooden Arrows

Most arrows can be made at home from parts purchased from archery shops. The shafts can be selected to the correct size, and fletchings and piles can be chosen in the shop or from mail-order catalogues. You can get the shafts cut to the correct length by the dealer, or you can cut them quite easily yourself; there is no mysterious black art involved. A razor saw, obtainable at model shops, serves very well. It is a miniature tenon saw with a rigid blade and very fine teeth, and can even be used to cut carbon/alloy shafts.

Shafts

To make wooden arrows, first select your shafts. If at all possible, this should be done in the shop, where boxes of shafts should be available to choose from. There are several woods available for arrows, but the best is Port Orford cedar, from the west coast of the USA. Some years ago, this became unavailable due to the protection of a species of owl, and wooden arrow archers were dismayed, but other sources were found and supplies of shafts resumed. Port Orford cedar is chosen not only for the straightness of its grain but also for its lightness and shock resistance.

Wooden shafts are sold in 32-inch lengths and two diameters, $5/16$ and $11/32$ inch. The smaller diameter is suitable for shorter arrows – 26 inches or less – and bows of less than 40 pounds draw, while the larger is more suitable for longer draw lengths and higher draw weights. Shafts are produced in a range of spines, or degrees of flexibility, so that they can be chosen for specific bow draw weights. They are colour coded on the cut ends to simplify selection for a draw weight. It has sometimes been known for very keen wooden arrow archers to 'barrel' their shafts by sanding them down from the centre towards each end and carefully matching the spine, but this is probably more trouble than it is worth for most people.

Wooden shaft sizes

$^5/_{16}$ inch diameter: 20/30, 30/35, 35/40, 40/45 lb bow weight

$^{11}/_{32}$ inch diameter: 45/50, 50/55, 55/60, 60/65, 65/70, 70/75 and 75+ lb bow weight

Draw Length

Longbow Bow weight	24 in	26 in	28 in	30 in	32 in	Recurve Bow weight
30/38 lb	N/A	20/25	25/30	30/35	35/40	20/25 lb
38/45 lb	20/25	25/30	30/35	35/40	40/45	25/30 lb
45/53 lb	25/30	30/35	35/40	40/45	45/50	30/35 lb
53/60 lb	30/35	35/40	40/45	45/50	50/55	35/40 lb
60/68 lb	35/40	40/45	45/50	50/55	55/60	40/45 lb
68/75 lb	40/45	45/50	50/55	55/60	60/65	45/50 lb
75/83 lb	45/50	50/55	55/60	60/65	65/70	50/55 lb

This chart is based on experience of which spines fit which bow weights. (thanks to D.G. Quicks for permission to include this chart)

Select shafts by stiffness first, whichever is most suitable for your bow weight, then for straightness. Roll each shaft on a flat surface, such as a glass shop counter, and select those that rattle least as they roll. Check the grain on each very carefully. If any appear to have grain that will cause them to bend later, or to develop weak-

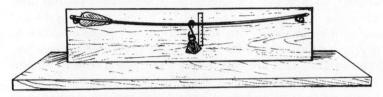

Fig. 24 Simple spine measuring device

nesses, reject them. If the grain appears to be straight and runs for the whole length of the shaft, then that should be suitable.

Nocks

Arrow nocks come in a wide range of colours and sizes. There are some that are designed primarily for use on wooden arrows, and these fit over the shaft with a conical hollow, when the shaft has been tapered with a taper tenon tool. Make sure you choose the correct size for the shaft, it being expressed in fractions of an inch diameter. Incorrectly sized nocks can be fitted but they will soon be seen to be unsuitable. Bright colours are preferable for field archery, since they will show up more easily in the target, and also when they have missed. They can be chosen to match the colour of the fletchings. It should be borne in mind that field targets are not always situated in good light conditions.

Fit the nocks first by tapering one end of the shaft with the taper tenon tool, which is like a pencil sharpener, and which forms the end into a cone. Glue the nocks on with fletching cement, so that the layers of the grain run at right angles to the slot of the nock. This makes the arrow stiffer and more resistant to the force of the bow. Turn the nocks before the glue sets, and then turn them back to their original position, to ensure that they are on straight. This should be quite easy if you have used the taper tenon tool correctly. A slight deviation in the angle of the nock will cause the arrow to fly strangely differently from others. It is possible to buy a precision instrument to check nocks, but this is little superfluous with wooden shafts. Some nocks are made especially for wooden arrows and have a ridge moulded on them which can be used to indicate the cock feather position if the nock is fitted correctly, with the slot at a right angle to the cock feather.

Piles

Fit the piles by again tapering the end of the shaft, after cutting it to the correct length. There is a tendency for wooden arrow experts to make their shafts too long, and this affects their performance. The theory seems to be that if they are too long and the pile breaks off, there is still enough shaft left to glue another pile on and thus still have a shootable arrow. Unfortunately, this rarely works very well since it results in arrows of odd lengths with different spine values, since changing the length changes the spine of the shaft. Taper piles come in two sizes, and the correct size will fit flush on the shaft. Some piles are designed to fit over the shaft with a parallel fit, but if they have a larger diameter than the shaft they will have a tendency to punch into the butt, making a larger hole than the shaft diameter, which will mean that the shaft is not retained by any friction and will pass through the butt too easily. They can also have a tendency to pull off when being removed from a butt. To prevent this, it is possible to drill through the pile and shaft and fit a panel pin or brass wire into the hole, cutting it off almost flush and hammering the ends flat, thus riveting the pile to the shaft. Few wooden arrow archers do this, but many lose piles inside butts.

An alternative method of fitting parallel piles is to cut the shaft down so that the pile fits flush onto the shaft. This method, however, often makes the shaft very weak at the point where the step has been cut in the wood and it will break easily on impact.

Clean the piles internally by soaking them in acetone, which should remove any remnants of grease. Fitting the pile is best if you are able to hold the shaft in a vice, using a clothes peg between the shaft and the vice jaws. Heat hot melt glue with a candle and smear it over the open end of the pile, then quickly fit it, rotating it as you push it into place. If you have applied sufficient glue, it will ooze out and can be wiped off while it is still hot. For wooden shafts, apply plenty, since the tapered structure enables piles to come off inside the butts quite frequently otherwise. They are often impossible to retrieve from the interior of the butts, so secure fitting is important.

For wooden shafts, several types of pile are available. Some are the common bullet piles, made from coated steel; brass piles are more expensive. Field piles have a stepped shape that is designed to reduce penetration of butts or trees. Heavyweight piles, up to 125 grains, are sometimes chosen in order to gain greater stability in flight.

Fletchings

Fletchings are available in a wide variety. The rules insist that wooden arrows shot with longbows are fletched with feathers and most wooden arrow enthusiasts prefer them; plastic fletchings on wooden shafts do not seem to be appropriate. Feathers can be bought ready cut to shape in several sizes; for wooden shafts the usual choice is for the larger sizes. Bright colours are preferable, simply so that the arrows will show better in the target, or when they miss and disappear. Dark or dull colours will be difficult to see both in the target and in the ground.

Fletchings are available in several sizes, plastic ones in more than feathers. Choose a size appropriate to the size of the arrow, so that long feathers, for example, fit long shafts. Traditionally, longbow arrows are fitted with long feathers, and the true enthusiasts can buy uncut feathers and cut them to their preferred shape with a feather-burning device. This will need to be home-made, since as far as I am aware, they are not available in the UK.

Fletchings are, of course, made to stabilize the arrow but they also contribute to the wind resistance, so it is desirable to fit the smallest fletchings consistent with the size of the shaft. Carbon shafts will be stable with surprisingly small fletches. There are fashions in fletchings; at one time slotted ones were popular, but they disappeared after a while. Curly plastic fletchings are now popular for target archery but are subject to damage in the butts used for field archery, since it is common for arrows to penetrate to the point where the fletchings are affected. Flexible plastic fletchings resist this, but it will be found that some recover their shape quickly while others will be permanently distorted. Only trial and error will establish which are best. If you have chosen the wrong ones, you will have to resort to the fletching jig.

This is an item every archer needs sooner or later. Make sure that the feathers all curve in the same direction. Packs of well-chosen feathers should all be curved similarly, the point being that feathers from one wing of the bird curve in the opposite direction from the other, and mixing them on one shaft will cause undesir-

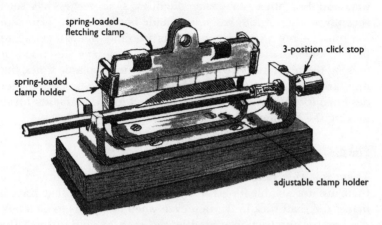

spring-loaded
fletching clamp

3-position click stop

spring-loaded
clamp holder

adjustable clamp holder

Fig. 25 A simple fletching jig

able flight characteristics. A fletching jig is essential for fletching with feathers, since they have to be held in the clamp until the cement dries sufficiently to prevent the curve reappearing.

Place the shaft in the jig with the nock firmly in place. Fit the feather into the clamp so that it will fit the shaft about an inch below the slot of the nock. Apply a thin string of fletching cement to the base of the feather, and slide the clamp into place. There is no need to push it down too hard on the shaft. Make sure you have the shaft at the correct angle to get the cock feather at right angles to the slot of the nock. Wipe off excess adhesive before it sets. Patience is required before removing the clamp from each feather. If it is removed before the glue is properly set, the feather will recover its natural curve, whereas if it is left long enough, it will sit straight on the shaft. Remove the clamp carefully and slowly, since if too much adhesive has been applied, it may well also have glued the feather to the clamp and will tear off the shaft, causing much frustration. Applying wax to the edges of the clamp sometimes helps to prevent this. Make sure to space the fletch about 1–1¼ inches below the slot of the nock to allow space for the fingers to grip the arrow above the fletching when necessary. Turn the shaft to fit the other feathers; your fletching jig will give you the correct angles on the shaft.

Weather proofing feather fletchings has always been a problem.

231

Those colourful feathers soon flatten onto the shaft when they get wet, and lose their stabilizing qualities. One archer was seen recently at a shoot with half a lemonade bottle over the arrows in her quiver – not a bad idea, but waterproofing the feathers seems better. One method is spray varnish, which was described as making the feathers more like the consistency of plastic vanes, but one archer has experimented with a silicon-based powder designed for lubricating bicycle chains and found that it was ideal, making the feathers fully waterproof.

Finishes

There is a wide range of finishes available for wood, but some of them are not suitable for arrows. Varnish is not appropriate since it makes the shaft stick in the butt even when it appears to be totally dry because the friction caused by the shaft moving through the material heats up the surface. Some archers prefer to use wax-based furniture polish, the idea being not only to give the shaft an aesthetically pleasing appearance but also to seal the natural moisture into the shaft, since if it is allowed to dry out the shaft will be substantially weakened. Rubbing down with fine wire wool or fine glass paper before applying the final coat will aid both appearance and feel.

It is important to test wooden arrows to discover their individual flight characteristics. They can be numbered to keep track of the best performers. Test shoot them at various distances, of course, to see which are the most consistently accurate, and nurture the best.

One can make wooden arrows, or even repair broken shafts, by splicing the shaft into a long square of hardwood, gluing it in place, then rounding off the square. This used to be done by Victorian arrow makers, and footed arrows, as they are known, are still available from specialist makers, but the average archer will not be prepared to go to such lengths. Such arrows are expensive and rarely shot on field courses.

Alloy Arrows

Most alloy arrows can be purchased as bare shafts so that you can still make up arrows to your own specification in the same way as with wooden shafts, but alloys are easier to deal with. It is possible to save by doing so, but not as much as might be hoped! It is possible to purchase shafts with nocks and piles fitted, so only the fletching has to be done, but fitting piles and nocks is so simple that it might as well be done at home.

Shafts

Cut the shafts to the required length with a razor saw, check that the end is square and use a smooth file to square it off if it is not. Ensure that all shafts are cut to the same length before proceeding any further – how often does the obvious get forgotten! This is especially important if you are shooting freestyle with a clicker on the bow, since if the arrow length is not consistent, nor will your shooting be.

Piles

Fitting piles is the same as for wooden arrows, except that they now fit inside the shaft, so ensure that they are all the same diameter and fit before attempting to glue them in. It is easy to get one that is made for a slightly different diameter shaft, which will not quite go into the shaft or rattles slightly inside. If it rattles, do not attempt to make it fit by lashing loads of hot melt cement round it – it will still come out eventually.

Use only the hot melt cement sold for the purpose by the archery dealers. Many archers have found to their cost that many other adhesives do not work. Sometimes this is because they either break down under shock, or never truly set hard, and in both cases the piles are likely to be left somewhere inside a butt. Care should also be taken not to overheat the alloy tube, since this may destroy the heat treatment and weaken it. A candle works well enough. This can also be used for removing piles from shafts when required, such as from broken shafts. The shaft will need gentle heating for about 2 inches of its length so that the pile can be withdrawn with a pair of pliers.

Some piles can help to lengthen a shaft – within limits. If a shaft is too short, another length can be slid onto the pile before it is inserted into the shaft. This can lengthen a shaft by ½ inch but I would hesitate to recommend any more than that. I have shot lengthened shafts in this manner without any adverse effect.

The weight of the pile can be critical. Some piles are available in several different weights and it is a matter of trial and error to find the weight preferred. Light piles will allow the arrow to fly higher but will possibly make it stiffer so that it will also fly slightly to the left, although this can easily be adjusted for on most bows. Some archers are of the opinion that heavier piles will make an arrow more stable in flight, but this again must be a matter of compromise to find maximum performance.

Fletchings

Most fletching jigs allow for adjustment so that the vane, or fletch, can be glued *on* the shaft parallel to its axis, or can be set at a slight angle to cause the arrow to spin in flight, much as the rifling of a gun barrel adds spin to a bullet, and this aids stability and accuracy. There is an optimum angle of 2 degrees of offset; more is no better; it will cause drag and therefore loss of velocity. The direction of rotation is not important, but some fletching jigs will only permit adjustment in one direction. It is important to clean shafts and fletchings before gluing, since any residual surface contamination will make the adhesion less efficient. Cleaning is best done with acetone.

Nocks

Broken nocks sometimes have to be removed from shafts. With the old type of shafts with conical nock ends and overfitted nocks this was a simple matter of cutting the broken plastic away, cleaning the rubbish off the shaft and gluing on a new nock. However, the newer insert nocks can be trickier since they can break off inside the tube without leaving anything to grip. Drilling out sometimes works, or a wire bent at the end to form a small hook can be inserted to pull it out. Another method suggested is to insert a hot nail, held in pliers, to soften the plastic before withdrawing it.

Damaged Arrows

Bent arrows are a major problem for field archers, and virtually everyone who has shot alloy arrows has suffered it. The worst thing to do is to attempt to straighten them by hand rather than using a straightening jig. It will be almost as if all the fingers have left bends in the shaft. Tempting though it may be to attempt to reduce the drastic appearance, it is best left to the straightening jig if you are fortunate enough to possess one or know a club member who does. It is quite surprising how the most alarmingly bent arrows can be made straight again. However, if they are dented, it will create a weak point that may well break when you attempt to straighten it. Often the bend is just below the fletching or just above the pile, in which case it may be necessary to remove them and refit them afterwards. Constantly bending and straightening shafts does not do them any good, since they will eventually be rippled for almost all their length, and it will be better to replace them.

If dents are not too deep, they can sometimes be removed by ramming a steel rod of the same diameter as the internal measurement of the shaft, down it. This process is not highly recommended, since it can cause cracks in some shafts; any cracked shafts should be discarded immediately. Indeed an arrow shaft of any material which is faulty should never be shot again. I once saw an archer whose shaft broke as he loosed it in a compound bow and the broken end drove deep into his bow hand.

Carbon Arrows

There are now several varieties of carbon-aluminium alloy or pure carbon arrows available and these have the advantage over alloy arrows of being far more resistant to bending so that they hardly ever need to be checked for bends. If one does become bent, it is best simply to discard it, since it will be virtually impossible to straighten it. Carbon arrows are very durable and even when lost in the undergrowth for a couple of years they can be reconstituted and used again, since the carbon does not deteriorate. Carbon alloy arrows must be treated with caution, however, since it is possible for the alloy to corrode internally.

Some forms of damage to carbon shafts can be treated successfully with superglue. Broken fibres can be glued down by applying the glue then wrapping the shaft tightly with tape. The tape should come off without pulling any fibres with it.

A problem has occurred with some carbon shafts with internally fitted piles in that they are not strong enough to resist the shock of impact with surfaces harder than target butts. When they are accidentally shot into trees, for example, it is quite common to find the pile driven into the shaft for some distance, thus reducing the shaft to less than the required length. There is little that can be done to repair this sort of damage.

Carbon shafts can shatter when they strike an object at the wrong angle, or they can split, but some of the newer models with fibres wrapped round the shaft may be more resistant to that type of damage.

Bowstrings

There are a number of new materials available for making bowstrings, most of them more expensive than the good old reliable B60 Dacron. Most can be bought from the archery dealers in reels sufficient to make several bowstrings, and it is relatively simple to make strings for both recurve and compound bows, once the correct length is established. Most compounds have the length of the string inscribed on their specification labels, as do some recurve bows. The art of getting the string to come out the correct length is a little tricky, since much depends on the string material and its degree of stretch. B60 Dacron has some stretch so that after making up a string it needs to be stretched with a weight hung on it for a couple of days or put on the bow for a while before being shot. If this is not done, it may stretch after being shot, which will upset the bow performance and any new sight marks. The newer string materials are less elastic so this problem should not occur, but the string needs to be made carefully to get the correct length.

A bowstring jig is easily made, and will enable strings of varying lengths to be made by adjusting the position of the cross piece at one end. I would recommend using only black string if Dacron is the choice, since white gets dirty easily, and can also dazzle you when shooting with the sun behind you. Some of the new string materials are available in a variety of colours, and are even striped.

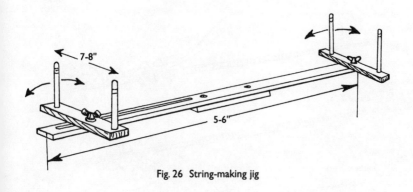

Fig. 26 String-making jig

The number of strands in the string is important. Dacron can be made into twelve-strand strings for recurve bows and sixteen strands is normal for compounds, but the latter gives a rather thick string. The newer Fastflight and Dyneema strings are very strong and strings can be made from them with fewer strands, but the best check is to count the strands in the string you intend to replace. The bowstring is an 'endless' string, which means that it is a continuous loop. The ends are not tied together, but simply twisted. This may seem to become shorter. And, as I have said, Dacron will stretch. About ½ inch should be allowed for shortening, so set the posts about ½ inch too long, but if it is a Dacron string, do not do this, since its stretch will cancel out the shortening effect.

Wind the thread round the posts until you have the required number of strands, then allow an extra 6 inches or so. Tie it to the opposite post at the same end as the start and cut the thread reel off. Now turn the posts at that end through 90 degrees and serve across the thread from one post to the other. You will now find that you will need to turn the posts again in line in order to bind the served section into a loop. Be careful to adjust the string to get a loop of the required size. If it is a compound string, the loops will be quite small, just sufficient to fit onto their anchor points on the bow, but if it is a recurve string, the loop at the lower end of the bow will need to be about 1½ inches long, while the one at the upper end, usually the one that slides down the limb when unstringing the bow, will need to be slightly longer, about 2 inches. These end loops should be served with soft-twist nylon that will

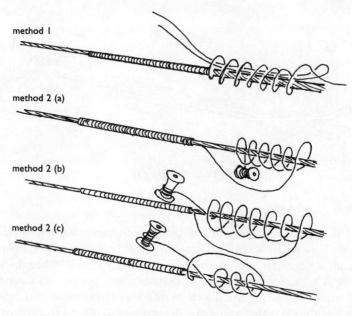

method 1

method 2 (a)

method 2 (b)

method 2 (c)

Fig. 27 Two methods of finishing off serving

protect the string without abrading it, although this is not the best material for centre serving. Bind the two sides together for about 6 inches, and finish off in one of the two methods shown. If any other method is used, it is almost certain to become loose. Good serving requires practice and an even tension on the serving thread. Patience is, perhaps, another necessity. A good serving tool is also a great help, and there is a variety available, some better than others. Try asking fellow archers for their recommendations before purchasing. Superglue can be used to set any loose ends after cutting off thread, but try not to get it on the bowstring itself, since it is a hard glue and may possibly damage the string, especially any of the non-stretch materials.

The centre serving is critical and needs to be done with care and the right material; Dacron strings can be served with nylon monofilament. It is necessary to work out just where it is required, since about 6 inches will be needed and it will need to be in such a position as to cover the arrow nocking point plus an inch or so above that, and extend down to cover the length where the bow

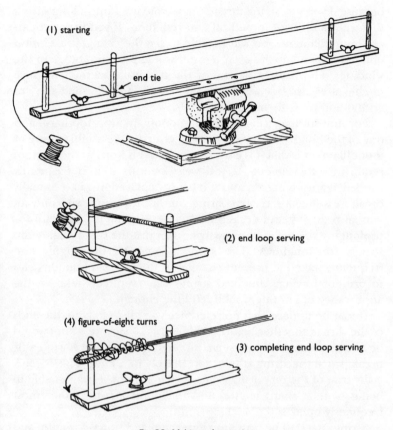

(1) starting

end tie

(2) end loop serving

(4) figure-of-eight turns

(3) completing end loop serving

Fig. 28 Making a bowstring

arm contacts the string (it should not contact, but it often will). At this stage it might be better to remove the string from the jig and – greatly daring – fit it to the bow. If you have made a half decent job of it, it will not break or pull apart when the tension of the bow comes on it, and you will be very pleased at your own skill. The position for the centre serving can now be marked, and the string removed from the bow and refitted to the string jig. The centre serving should be started at the upper end and continued down for about 6 inches, keeping an even tension on the thread all the time. If you are using nylon monofilament, this can be frustrating since the material is tricky. Keep a firm grip on the end at all times,

239

because if you lose it, the thread will vibrate itself into a long spring that will be difficult to pull off and retighten. If you use transparent monofilament, you will be able to see the changes in tension quite easily, and any uneven tension will appear as a bulge in the windings. Finish off with one of the two usual methods – clove hitches are easy but will not hold – and carefully melt the cut end(s) and press them onto the coils.

For non-stretch string material, monofilament is too hard, and one of the braided threads is recommended. One useful feature of monofilament is that it is easy to see when it is worn to the point of requiring replacement. It will wear smooth if it is frequently rubbed against a bracer, and if it is not replaced, it will eventually break. A well-made recurve string can last for years, with only an annual reserving and occasional waxing. Waxing is important for prolonging the life of any bowstring, not just the traditional hemp strings for longbows. The string should be thoroughly and frequently waxed to prevent changes in the internal humidity and to prevent fraying. Unwaxed strings can eventually take on the appearance of knitting wool if left long enough.

It may be noticed that no reference was made to tying the ends of the thread together before serving; this is because a knot would be a weak point. This may seem rather surprising, but it can easily break, since the string is bent too sharply in a knot. This is especially true of the newer materials, which are not very amenable to being bent at sharp angles, and the point at which they most frequently break is the nocking point.

Strings need to be twisted to give them additional strength, and also to prevent the fraying of individual threads, but twisting shortens them and, as I have said, will affect the bracing height of the bow. Twisting will increase the bracing height, while untwisting will, of course, have the opposite effect. This may be more critical for those who shoot barebow, since the changing effect can be taken up by changes in sight marks on bows fitted with sights. It is not a good idea to twist the string too much, since this will both weaken it and increase its elasticity. One and a half turns per inch is the recommended maximum.

Centre servings can be a problem when the turns start to separate, as they almost always will after prolonged use. They will start at the nocking point and, if left unattended, will gradually widen until the bowstring becomes visible and starts to wear. Remedial action should be taken before this stage by pushing the turns together and working gradually down the serving until the gaps disappear off the end. This can be done – very carefully, of course – by using the wire-cutting part of a pair of pliers without squeezing the jaws tight, but just using them to push sideways on the serving. This should close the gaps without any need to reserve the string. Bear in mind that non-stretch strings do not like being crushed and can easily be damaged, so take great care. For the same reason, monofilament serving should not be used.

Longbow strings can be made by this method, but the more traditional string has a permanent loop at the lower end and a timber hitch at the upper end, which enables the archer to adjust the string length and bracing height very quickly if necessary.

A new string will, of course, make a difference to the performance of any bow. If sights are fitted, they will also need to be recalibrated. You will need to discover how much difference the string has made. It is always a good idea to carry a spare string which has been shot in so that if a string breaks during a shoot, it can soon be replaced. Unfortunately, compound bows do not make this easy.

Stabilizer Bushes

Stabilizer mounts are sometimes subjected to considerable strain, especially when the archer falls and the bow hits the ground. The steel or brass bushes that hold the thread of the stabilizer are usually pushed into the magnesium alloy handle and held in place simply by friction. They are usually splined, i.e. grooves are cut into the surface of the bush parallel with the long axis, and these serve to form a better grip in the magnesium. Sometimes, however, they become loose and the stabilizers wobble about and cannot be used.

The most obvious fix for this problem is the well-known two-part epoxy resin adhesive. This will not usually last for very long, since it sets hard and brittle and will not accept any flexing. The best option may be to pay a visit to your nearest dealer and ask them to fix the problem. However, one method I have found to be effective is to refit the bush and drill a small hole through the side of the bow handle and into it. Take a small bolt about $1/8$ inch in diameter, slightly larger than the size of the hole, and screw it into the hole very carefully. If you have chosen the right size, the bolt will cut its own thread into the hole and will enter the bush and lock it in place. This has to be done with care, since any overtightening will strip the new thread and make it useless. If it is done carefully, it can prevent any further problems and will permit long stabilizers to be screwed in tightly.

Sight Mounts

Compound bows are subjected to considerable shock and vibration, and parts work loose quite easily. A loose sight mount that cannot be tightened can make a bow useless. The use of large scope sights often means that thick blocks have to be made and fitted under the sight mount and this exacerbates the problem, with a loose sight moving through a range of over ½ inch; accurate aiming becomes impossible. If the thread has become worn so that the mounting bolts cannot be tightened properly, there are two possible cures.

First a threaded coil insert could be screwed in to replace the worn thread. These can be obtained in a wide range of sizes, but they are not common everyday objects and may only be available from an engineering supplier. It may be possible to screw them into the existing holes, but this would mean fitting smaller screws, which would not fit the holes in the mounting blocks and would still allow too much movement. Therefore, it might be better to drill the holes out to a size that would permit the fitting of thread inserts for the size of the original mounting bolts.

These sight mounting bolts are not easy to obtain, and another visit to an engineering supplier might result in finding longer bolts. If so, try drilling the holes deeper and screwing these in. I have found this method to be effective, but unless you have no objection to the bolts going right through the bow handle, care will be needed in drilling the holes deeper. The choice of drill size is important, too, since if it is too large, it will be impossible for the bolts to cut a new thread. Using the right sized thread-cutting tap tool will be useful, but this may not be available – few people posses them. However, a new bolt with two deep grooves filed into the thread lengthways can make an improvized tap that will work well

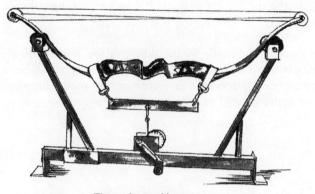

The professional bow press

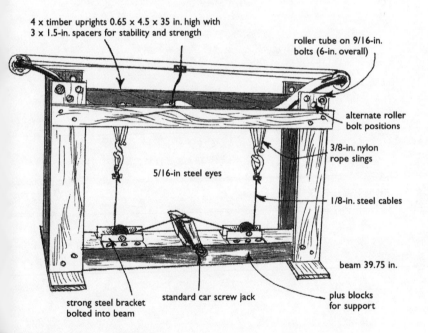

4 x timber uprights 0.65 x 4.5 x 35 in. high with
3 x 1.5-in. spacers for stability and strength

roller tube on 9/16-in.
bolts (6-in. overall)

alternate roller
bolt positions

3/8-in. nylon
rope slings

5/16-in steel eyes

1/8-in. steel cables

beam 39.75 in.

strong steel bracket
bolted into beam

standard car screw jack

plus blocks
for support

Home-built bow press (designed by Colin Beadon,
Barbados, with thanks to Bow Magazine)

Fig. 29 Compound bow presses

enough in the soft alloy. Longer bolts can be a lasting cure for this problem.

Other items can be made by the do-it-yourself enthusiast. Finger tabs are easily cut out of a suitable leather, bracers can be made from a variety of materials, and quivers can be made out of a wide variety of materials and to a variety of designs.

16 Making 3D Targets

Making your own 3D targets is not as difficult as might be imagined. There are several methods which can be used, and several useful materials available. The most obvious material is expanded polystyrene, but a few test shots will soon convince you of its unsuitability. Arrows penetrate quite easily, but when they come out the back, they can make huge holes, acting rather like dum-dum bullets, and creating many granules and lumps that are difficult to pick up and which show up only too easily on any background. The stuff is really not very long-lasting.

Two materials are worth considering. One is cardboard, which is cheap – often free – much longer lasting than one would imagine, and easy to work with. The other is a rather specialized plastic known as etherfoam. This is available from some of the archery dealers as target butts but is too expensive to cut up for 3D targets. If you can obtain some from plastic manufacturers, it is simple to work with, being easy to cut and shape. Its resilience is its main property, since arrows penetrate quite well and the holes close up when they are withdrawn. It will last a long time and resists a great number of arrows. However, it is not readily available and even when purchased from plastics manufacturers, it is still expensive, so cardboard will be the material of choice here.

The first thing is to find a suitable illustration of an animal, preferably a side view. Copy the outline onto a sheet of cardboard to the size intended. You do not have to be a brilliant artist to do this, but it helps. This outline is the basis for your figure; it helps fix the shape in your mind, as well as the scale. Use this as a guide while you are working. You may now realize, as never before, that animals' legs are not the same as humans, since the joints are in the wrong places; the elbows are high on the body, as are knees on

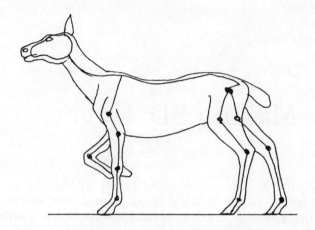

Basic skeletal structure of mammal, showing leg joint positions

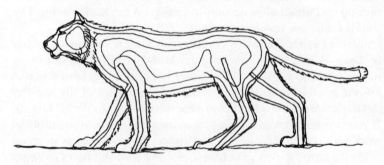

Steel rods or tubes in legs

Draw full outline of animal, full size required, on sheet of cardboard
This shape can be used for several big cats, lions, tigers, etc. Build out in layers

Fig. 30 Making 3D targets

the hind legs, and the most visible and obvious joint on the hind legs is really the heel. Many animals walk on what corresponds to human fingertips. Once this is realized, it becomes easier to construct 3D figures.

You can choose from two methods when making legs. If you can obtain a quantity of steel tubing, about ¾ inch in diameter, available at large DIY stores, you can build this into the legs as the American 3D figure manufacturers do, so that they can be slid down onto steel stakes driven into the ground. To do this the legs need to be parallel, otherwise it will be impossible to slide them down. The other method is to use wooden struts inside the legs and stake the completed figures in place by lashing the legs to stakes in the ground. The major disadvantage of this method is, of course, that arrows shot into them often break the struts, but they can be replaced. Probably the best compromise would be to use steel tubes but without sliding them over steel stakes.

Construction

If you have access to a large bandshaw, this job is far easier. However, an electric jigsaw can be used instead. This is how it is done:

1 Draw an outline for the head and body, tape several layers of thick card together, about 5 inches thick, and cut out the outline (fig. 30). The resultant figure will probably be rather thicker than you had originally planned and look rather clumsy. If this seems likely, then make the outline drawing thinner. There is always the temptation to slap on more layers in order to add strength and resist arrow wear, and no one can really anticipate how fat or bulky the end figure will be, but it is almost certain that it will be fatter than expected.

2 Draw the front legs (fig. 31a) and repeat the process. Both front legs can be the same, or if you can draw fairly well, they can be made in a fast walk position. (fig. 31a).

3 Repeat the process for the back legs. These are the awkward ones, since they have a prominent joint backwards.

4 Cut out wood strips, approximately 1 in × 2 in and tape the layers of card round them. Note that in nearly all hind legs, a joint will be necessary.

5 Tape or glue the body layers together after roughly rounding off the square corners.

6 Attach the legs to body, using woodworking glue and/or tape.

7 Fill in the gaps between the legs with layers of scrap card – by this time there will be plenty available (fig. 31b). Cover this with thin corrugated card, which is easy to tear and shape.

8 Cover the whole figure with any sort of strong tape, the more the better.

9 Paint or cover the figure with fur fabric. Fur fabric of various colours and lengths of hair can be found in markets, or old fur coats can sometimes be obtained from club members. Woodworking glue or fabric adhesive can be used for this, but costs start to rise at this point.

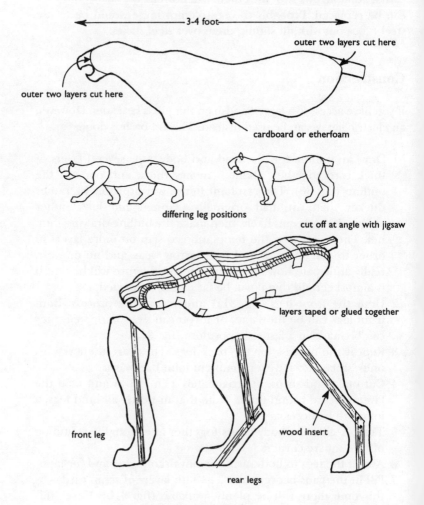

Fig. 31a Making a 3D big cat

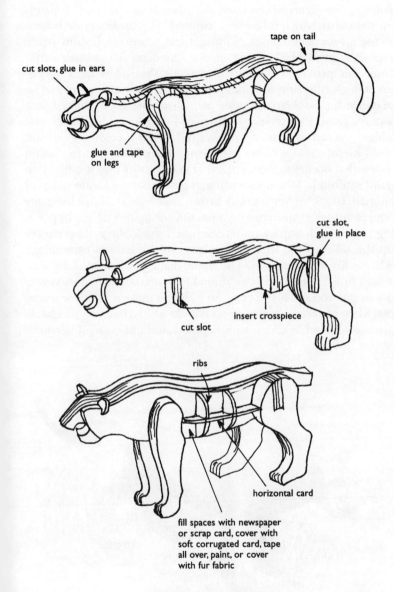

cut slots, glue in ears

tape on tail

glue and tape
on legs

cut slot,
glue in place

insert crosspiece

cut slot

ribs

horizontal card

fill spaces with newspaper
or scrap card, cover with
soft corrugated card, tape
all over, paint, or cover
with fur fabric

Fig. 31b Making a 3D big cat

249

Painting the figure is the crux (fig. 31c). It will be judged mainly on the way in which it has been painted. The cardinal rule is *never* to use gloss enamel paint. Nothing looks so unreal as shiny paint, especially gloss black. Some of the American 3D animals suffer from this problem; they are not really shiny, but there is just enough gloss to ruin the illusion of reality. A suitable paint can be made with school-type powder paint from art shops, mixed with watered-down PVA glue. With four or five colours, plus black and white, you can mix any colour desired, but two colours alone are really useful – yellow ochre and burnt umber. Yellow ochre is a dull yellow that occurs so frequently that many artists find it difficult to paint without it. Mixed with white, it is suitable for a wide range of animals. Burnt umber is a dark brown, and is also suitable for many figures. Added realism can be given to your figures simply by painting them much lighter underneath and gradually getting darker up the sides to the back. This is part of the natural camouflage scheme for many animals. The home-made paint should dry with a matt finish and make your animal look incredibly realistic when out in the woods – if you can find it! If you make a tiger, for example, when the black stripes go on it looks gaudy, but against a background of dead bracken, with dappled sunlight on it, it becomes almost invisible.

Fig. 31(c) A completed big cat figure before painting – add stripes or spots as preferred

Birds

Large birds are easy to make, the larger the better. In fact, it is hardly worth the effort of making small figures, simply because they take as long to make as larger ones but are soon shot to pieces. Draw a simple outline of body and head, cut out in several layers, tape them together and add progressively smaller teardrop-shaped layers until you have a rounded body. Tails can usually be added later, and legs can be rounded wood or steel tube

1 Cut four layers of thick card to profile
2 Cut slots for the tail
3 Cut slots for the legs
4 Add progressively smaller layers
5 Add legs, wood or steel tube
6 Tape all over and paint in dull non-gloss colours

Fig. 32 Construction of a 3D bird

hammered into the body, then taped in place. (See fig. 32) Again, good painting can make all the difference between ending up with a vulture or a turkey. Most of all, when making 3D targets, it is essential to get the basic shape and proportions right at the start; it can hardly ever be put right later.

The Standing Bear

This one is worth making simply because it can be so impressive. It can also last for years if it is not shot too much or too often. It can be made almost any size, the only limit really being its weight and your storage facilities; about 5 or 6 feet high will do very well – it is then suitable for shooting at the longer distances, such as 60 or 70 yards.

Get the head shape right – I once had to saw the head off a just-completed bear because the head came out badly, and had to be rebuilt. This is the process:

1 Draw the front view, without the front legs, but with the hind legs.
2 Cut out round the outline at least six layers of thick card and tape them together.
3 Cut a keel piece to fit down the front at right angles, including in it a profile of the head, and another for the back, with the back of the head.
4 Glue or tape it in place.
5 Cut quarter circles of card to fit in between on the third plane, the horizontal.
6 Fill spaces with balled newspaper or scrap card.
7 Cover with thin, corrugated card.
8 Add cut-outs of front legs, including claws.
9 Tape all over, since this adds tremendously to the overall strength of the figure.
10 Cover with black or brown fur fabric.
11 Paint the eyes, nose and mouth, include teeth made from wood, making sure the teeth are cream-coloured rather than white. The details add realism. Add a pink tongue, made from cardboard.
12 Transport to the club and wait for gasps of admiration.

1 Cut out core from six to seven layers of thick card, at least 5 ft high
2 Bend feet over
3 Cut out a centre 'keel', front and back, and glue or tape in place
4 Cut quarter round pieces, glue or tape in place, back and front
5 Fill spaces with balled paper or scrap card
6 Cover with corrugated card
7 Tape all over
8 Cover with fur fabric or paint (not gloss black!)

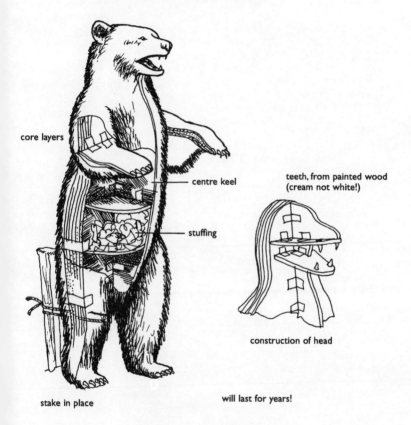

core layers

centre keel

stuffing

teeth, from painted wood
(cream not white!)

construction of head

stake in place

will last for years!

Fig. 33 Construction of a 3D bear

This bear is heavy and not very easy to carry. If it is over about 5
feet tall, it will be bulky to store as well, so be careful with the size.
It will last for years if it is shot at just once a year during a shoot.
The fur fabric may have a tendency to fall off here and there and

may need to be reglued every year or so, but that is all the maintenance required. Fur fabric can be sewn on, and the level of sewing skills need not be very high. Another covering material is sackcloth, which can be glued on and will provide tremendous strength.

17 Rules and Classifications

The full rules and regulations of the various field archery organizations are given in the relevant appendix, but here I want to give a brief outline of the principles behind them and the classifications the various organizations use.

Rules

Most rules are devised with a certain aim in mind. Many were originally formulated to prevent one archer from having an unfair advantage over others, but it is arguable whether any rules can ever do this without careful delineation of what constitutes an 'unfair' advantage. The NFAS has far fewer rules than the others because its policy has always been to keep rules to an absolute minimum and it has never adopted the 'unfair advantage' policy. This makes life simpler, and few members who shoot under its rules seem overly concerned with the possibility of another archer having such an advantage.

There have been attempts to rationalize some of the rules. Some were seen as increasingly unnecessary or even ludicrous, and were discarded. The rule that restricted the size of a kisser button seemed to be of this type. What did it matter how big a kisser was? There was a practical limit to what could be used, but the size was unlikely to give an archer an unfair advantage.

String walking is a technique used for aiming whereby the fingers are moved to differing positions on the string according to the distance of the target. Pre-determined positions are used, whereby the hand is moved up or down the string. Its associated technique, 'face-walking', means moving the hand down the face to different anchor points according to target distance. The hand will be moved further down for longer targets and further up for shorter shots. Both are difficult techniques to apply accurately, and both are suspect since they are methods of aiming without the use of sights. However, it would appear from the rules of shooting of the IFAA that both these techniques are permitted in the barebow class. Some rules are not applied very rigidly by common consent, but care must be taken that they are not safety rules.

Hold-ups can occur on some shoots, and they can be irritating. The most common cause is archers looking for their lost arrows. Since most of us have lost arrows at some time, especially when beginners, one can have some sympathy with an archer who has lost an arrow which might be costly to replace. However, it is irritating to be forced to wait frequently while the group in front searches for lost arrows on every other target. Huge hold-ups are often caused by archers losing arrows on long and difficult targets. The answer here lies with the shoot course planners in taking note and avoiding such targets on future shoots.

Some shoots progress very slowly, not because of hold-ups, but because of people who are naturally slow; one girl my group was stuck behind seemed to do everything in slow motion and made our shoot last far longer than it should. A lack of awareness of others often seems to be a problem and slow groups taking their time do not often seem to be aware of the fact that others are waiting for them to shoot on every target.

Another cause of slow shooting occurs when a target is being shot on walk-up pegs, if the archers are allowed to move forward to the target area after they have shot all the pegs. In some areas this may not matter but on difficult ground with elderly archers, it can cause the following archers to wait a considerable time. This does not happen often, but has been particularly noticeable on some shoots, where the archer should just step aside out of the line of shot rather than walking up to the target area to wait.

Some rules contain time limits for shooting. These were introduced in order to create a degree of control over the length of time shoots lasted. Before time limits, it was found that one or two archers could make a tournament last far longer than necessary by selfishly taking a very long time to shoot. This was also happening

RULES AND CLASSIFICATIONS

in target archery, where I noticed, at my first target tournament, that two archers made the contest last nearly an hour longer by keeping everyone waiting. The habit of drawing up, aiming, then coming down again – and again, and again – developed to an alarming degree until it was driving everyone else to distraction. The time limits were introduced in order to check this habit.

There is no time limit in NFAS shooting simply because it has never been found to be necessary. There is a limitation on the time that can be spent looking for lost arrows, but it is frequently ignored. A forty-target NFAS shoot can be completed in four or five hours without difficulty, partly because the habit of drawing up and coming down is not one that has ever developed amongst NFAS members, the majority of whom shoot without sights. It is a habit developed mainly in the Freestyle class, and in the NFAS this is a very small group. In addition, it is probable that anyone doing this would soon be made aware of the feelings of the other archers.

Cheating

Cheating is rare, as it is difficult without the knowledge and consent of other members of the shooting group. The general feeling is that the few who do cheat are only cheating themselves, since most archers are competing against themselves in order to improve their performances, rather than in the hope of winning.

The question of what to do if someone is found to be cheating rarely arises, but when it does, what is to be done? A quiet word to the person concerned will often work. Where there are no marshals or technical commission roving the course, fellow archers may have to pluck up the courage to advise the person concerned to stop. Waiting to report the matter to the shoot organizers after the event is over may be too late, and they may take little notice. The form of the cheating can be simple – sometimes it is someone drawing the arrows and calling out the scores before anyone can stop them, but advising them to leave the arrows untouched until they are scored can usually stop this. All the organizations have rules designed to prevent this, saying that the arrows should be left in the target, untouched, until they have been scored.

Sometimes someone might stand in the incorrect position. On an NFAS shoot I once saw a competitor in the group in front standing in front of the first peg, rather than behind it, in order to gain

FIELD ARCHERY: A COMPLETE GUIDE

2 yards, when the remainder of his group were were unable to see. A quiet query about whether he was aware of this caused him to move into the correct position.

There have been occasions at GNAS field shoots when I have had serious doubts about the qualifications of some officials. Many years ago, my bow was being inspected before the shoot by some- one I was later told was an international judge. He queried the patterns on my bow handle and informed me that, if this had been an international shoot, he would make me cover them, since I would be able to line my string up against them. I was somewhat stunned by this, as no rule exists, in any field archery organization, concerning lining up the string. Like most other archers with sights, I normally lined it up with the bow-sight.

At another shoot, the tackle inspection involved inspecting the layers of my finger tab. 'What are you looking for?' I asked. 'It has been known for people to write down the distances in there,' was the reply. This is total nonsense, since no one could know the distances beforehand, and anyway they could write them anywhere else: a tab is the most inconvenient place to write anything. At the next shoot, the tackle inspection again involved looking between the two layers of leather of my tab. Again I asked what the inspec- tor was looking for. This time, however, there was a different reply. 'It has been known for people to conceal hooks in there. You'd be surprised what some of them get up to!' This was, I thought, quite astonishing. How could anyone conceal a release aid – I presume that was what was meant – inside a finger tab? And any other sort of 'hook' would be utterly useless. I was forced to the conclusion that some of these officials were not really very well qualified for their jobs and should perhaps have gone away to read the rulebook more carefully. Other incidents have convinced me that there may be a need for these officials to be better trained or briefed. If they are quoting non-existent or incorrect rules, or if they are misinter- preting rules, they are doing their sport a disservice.

In recent years, improvements have been made by FITA to its rules and their interpretation. A major revision of rules took place, more notice was taken of what was wanted by the archers, and this is now the prevailing concept. A more common-sense interpretation of rules, with perhaps a little less rigidity, is now being applied to which no doubt, many people will say, 'And not before time'. Judges for field shoots now are required to be qualified to judge field archery.

For the determined cheat, there is plenty of opportunity to make changes after having gone through the tackle inspection. Items inspected could easily be put aside and others used on the shoot, but now roving technical commission members have the powers to inspect tackle anywhere on the course, so those who have changed items may be liable to be detected.

The NFAS has no technical commission and no pre-shoot tackle inspection, but this has hardly ever caused any difficulties. No one has ever suggested that the introduction of such procedures might be a good thing.

Bow Classes

This is an easy reference condensed guide to the rules for various classes. Full details are given in the relevant appendix.

GNAS and FITA

- **Olympic (Freestyle) Recurve**. Metal or wooden handle riser, metal or carbon arrows. Arrow rest, pressure button stabilizers of any length and number. One aiming mark allowed, finger release, string serving not to be above archer's nose. Overdraws limited to 4 cm from throat of bow handle.
- **Compound Unlimited**. Anything allowed. Peak weight may not exceed 60 pounds. No electrical aids to aiming or releasing allowed. Overdraw limited to 6 cm from throat of bow handle.
- **Compound Limited**. As Unlimited but no scope or release aid allowed.
- **Barebow Recurve**. Metal or wooden riser, metal or carbon arrows. Arrow rest and pressure button permitted. No stabilizer and no sights permitted. String walking is allowed (this is the only class that allows this). String serving must not be above archer's nose.
- **Traditional**. As Barebow, but wooden arrows with feather fletchings, no pressure button allowed.

EFAA and IFAA

- **Barebow, Recurve and Compound (BB)**. Bows, arrows, strings and accessories to be free from sights, marks, blemishes or laminations which could be used for aiming. An adjustable arrow rest may be used to control the space between the arrow and the face of the bow window. The use of stabilizers is permitted. One permanent nocking point only. No mechanical device other than one non-adjustable draw check and/or level mounted on the bow, neither of which may extend above the arrow. All arrows to be identical in length, weight, diameter, fletchings and nocks, with regard to colour, with allowance for wear and tear.

- **Freestyle Limited, Recurve and Compound (FS)**. Any type of sight permitted. Release aids are not permitted. Any type of bow, sight, or release aid recognized by the IFAA committee permitted.
- **Bowhunter, Recurve and Compound (BH)** Bows, arrows, strings, accessories to be free of sight marks, blemishes and/or laminations that could be used for aiming. A levelling device is not permitted. No device of any type that may be used for sighting may be used or attached to the archer's equipment. No draw check device or clicker. String to be of one colour only, but a serving of one other colour may be used. One consistent nocking point only is permitted (where the arrow touches the string). Nocking point may be held with one or two indicators. One consistent anchor point only is permitted. Archer to touch the arrow when nocked with the index finger against the nock. Finger position may not be changed during competition. In cases of physical disability or deformity special dispensation may be made. All arrows used to be identical in length, weight, diameter, fletchings and nocks, without regard for colour, with allowance for wear and tear. Brush buttons in their proper places at the recurve tip of the bow, string silencers no closer than 12 inches above or below the nocking point and bow quiver installed on the opposite side of the sight window with no part visible in the bow window is permitted. One straight stabilizer, coupling device included if used, not exceeding 12 inches as measured from the back of the bow may be used. No forked stabilizer or any counterbalance. The plunger (where the stabilizer is screwed in) is part of the stabilizer. Bow weight shall not be adjusted during any one round.
- **Bowhunter Unlimited (BU)**. Any type of bow and release aid recognized by the IFAA committee allowed. A sight with a maximum of five fixed reference points that must not be moved

during a round will be permitted. Pin sights to be of straight stock from point of anchor to sighting point with only one sighting reference possible from each pin or reference point. Hooded pins or scope sights not allowed. Release aids permitted. A kisser button or string peepsight permitted, but not both. All other rules for Bowhunter style will apply.

- **Bowhunter Limited (BL)** The same rules as for Bowhunter Unlimited except that release aids are not permitted.
- **Longbow**. A one-piece straight-ended bow of any material. The belly must be free of any marks or blemishes that can be used as sighting aids. The bow may contain a window and an arrow shelf. Only one nocking point allowed on the string. Arrows to be of wood, fletched with natural feather, and of the same length, fletch and pile, without regard for colour. Nocks may be of any material, and any weight of pile may be used. Bow must be shot with the Mediterranean loose. One consistent anchor point to be used.
- A new rule, just introduced, limits compound bow speeds to 300 fps(feet per second). There is no information as to how this will be checked.

NFAS

- **Freestyle**. As EFAA and GNAS.
- **Compound Unlimited**. Anything including overdraws and release aids allowed.
- **Compound Limited**. Five-pin sight allowed but no external guard or surround. Mediterranean loose. Stabilizer up to draw length allowed. Peep sight or kisser allowed, but not both. No draw check permitted. Only one nocking point allowed.
- **Bowhunter**. Compound. Mediterranean loose, any arrows. Stabilizers up to draw length allowed. No draw checks allowed, no weight restrictions. Overdraws up to 2 inches from throat of handle allowed.
- **Barebow**. Metal or wooden handle riser, recurve bow with metal or carbon arrows allowed. Three fingers under allowed. Stabilizers up to archer's draw length allowed (not arrow length). No draw checks.
- **Traditional Classes**. Longbow, American Flat Bow, Hunting Tackle. All three must be shot with wooden arrows with feather fletchings,

no stabilizers, no sights, and Mediterranean loose. Hunting Tackle bow can be recurve, one-piece or take-down, wood or metal riser. AFB bow must bend only one way when strung.

Classifications

Both GNAS and EFAA have had classification schemes for many years, which enable archers to attain different levels of shooting skill. Some archers place considerable importance on classifications and are constantly striving to get to the next level, and there can be no doubt that this encourages high levels of shooting ability and is a constant spur. The NFAS has no such classification schemes and the general view is that the organization does not support the introduction of any.

GNAS

The GNAS classifications are: 3rd class, 2nd class, 1st class, Master Bowman and Grand Master Bowman. The exalted rank of Grand Master was introduced some years ago when it was felt that too many people were becoming Master Bowmen without a higher rank to aim for. Qualifying scores for each level are sometimes revised. The qualifying scores for the Animal round are included here, but the tables for other rounds can be found in the GNAS rules of shooting.

National Animal Round Classification

Olympic and Compound Limited

	GMB	MB	B	1	2	3
Ladies	430	380	340	290	240	190
Gentlemen	470	430	375	320	265	210
Junior Ladies		330	280	230	265	210
Junior Gentlemen		380	330	280	230	180

Barebow and Compound Barebow

	GMB	MB	B	1	2	3
Ladies	370	320	270	220	175	130
Gentlemen	420	370	320	270	225	180
Junior Ladies		250	205	160	120	80
Junior Gentlemen		320	270	220	170	120

Traditional & Longbow

Ladies	310	240	195	150	110	70
Gentlemen	360	310	260	210	165	120
Junior Ladies		190	150	110	80	50
Junior Gentlemen		240	195	150	110	70

Compound Unlimited

Ladies	450	400	350	300	255	210
Gentlemen	490	450	400	350	295	230
Junior Ladies		350	300	250	200	150
Junior Gentlemen		400	350	300	250	200

It can easily be seen that the qualifying scores are different according to the inherent accuracy of the bows used, the Compound Unlimited being the most accurate to shoot and therefore having the highest scores, and also that ladies' scores are lower than men's. This is not always the case, however, since at one NFAS National Championship, the highest scorer was a young lady of about eighteen, who beat all the men in the Compound Unlimited class.

The GNAS lays down how many shoots must be done to qualify in each class. It is not merely a matter of going to one shoot, doing brilliantly well and therefore qualifying in a class. There are lists of rounds which may be shot to qualify for each class and these increase in number as the qualification rises. These are available from the GNAS in the GNAS Handicap and Qualification Tables, which also include the rules for operating the schemes. Clubs are not obliged to operate such schemes and may enter them voluntarily.

EFAA

The EFAA has the titles Field Master, Grand Field Master and Supreme Field Master when certain scores are attained in certain rounds, usually standard twenty-eight target rounds such as the Field, Hunter or combination rounds. The required score must be shot twice in any twelve-month period. Patches are awarded for these scores.

FM, GFM and SFM scores for HS, LB/AFB

	GENTS		LADIES		JUNIORS	
	HS	LB/AFB	HS	LB/AFB	HS	LB/AFB
FM	315	265	305	260	305	260
GFM	340	295	325	280	320	275
SFM	365	330	345	305	335	290

FM, GFM and SFM scores for recurves

	GENTS			LADIES			JUNIORS		
	FS	BB	BH	FS	BB	BH	FS	BB	BH
FM	455	410	385	455	405	380	455	405	380
GFM	465	425	405	460	415	395	460	410	390
SFM	480	440	420	470	430	405	465	420	400

FM, GFM and SFM scores for compounds

	FS	FU	BB	BL	BU	BH
GENTS						
FM	460	505	415	460	485	395
GFM	485	520	450	485	500	430
SFM	505	530	480	505	520	470
LADIES						
FM	455	505	410	455	480	385
GFM	470	510	430	470	490	410
SFM	490	520	455	490	505	440
JUNIORS						
FM	455	505	410	455	480	385
GFM	465	510	425	465	490	405
SFM	480	515	440	480	495	420

Further details of the award and administration of these classifications can be found in the EFAA Constitution Rules and Procedures.

Other Classifications in the EFAA

The classification system adopted by EFAA is that laid down by the IFAA. Based on a twenty-eight target round, there are the following classes:

Class	Freestyle Limited	Freestyle Unlimited	Barebow
A	450-plus	500-plus	400-plus
B	350-449	400-499	300-399
C	0-349	0-399	0-299

Class	Bowhunter Limited	Bowhunter Unlimited	Bowhunter
A	450-plus	475- plus	375-plus
B	300-449	325-474	225-374
C	0-299	0-324	0-224

Class	Longbow
A	250-plus
B	150-249
C	0-149

18 Instruction and Coaching

Each field archery organization in Great Britain has its own system for teaching beginners.

GNAS

The GNAS has a system of training courses for coaches at different levels. A club instructor may attend a coaching course that will last a weekend and undertake an examination that will also last a weekend. Aspiring coaches learn how to do the basic training of beginners and will be expected to demonstrate their skill. They will also be expected to have a considerable knowledge of archery and undertake a written and an oral examination to test the extent of their knowledge of the rules, procedures, customs, equipment, target face sizes, and scoring, etc. However, it must be said that they will not be tested on their knowledge of field archery. The most that might be expected there is simply the knowledge of what it is.

The next level is County Coach. This requires a much deeper knowledge of the techniques of shooting, the use of the body, the use of equipment, and the psychology of shooting the bow, as well as requiring a commitment to give up a considerable amount of time in travelling to different venues to coach, attend courses, run courses, etc.

The top level of coaching skill is the International Coach. At this level, coaching is for the national team for the Olympics and International Championships, and requires even more dedication and a very high degree of knowledge. Coaching at this stage is important since it can mean the difference between success or failure for both individuals and team.

EFAA

The EFAA has a coaching scheme that trains beginners' coaches. These coaches or instructors – the terms are interchangeable – are intended to teach beginners the basic techniques of shooting but the most important aspect is that they are able to teach how to shoot safely, without danger to other archers or onlookers. The trainee coaches are expected to demonstrate that they are capable of doing this.

There is no scheme of training for higher levels, but several members of EFAA have undergone advanced-level coaching courses run by the National Field Archery Association of the United States.

NFAS

The NFAS instituted a coaching system several years ago. The basic qualification for trainee coaches was that they should have been shooting for a minimum of three years. However, in situations where a qualified coach is desperately needed, sometimes that requirement can become a little elastic. There are instances, for example, where a club wishes to hire an indoor venue for winter use from a local authority and that might require a qualified coach before permission will be given.

The NFAS course is carried out over two weekends, with an examination at the end that requires both a demonstration of practical teaching – giving a ten-minute lecture – and a written examination. Aspects covered included the psychology of shooting and how to deal with beginners. There is no requirement for an extensive knowledge of the rules, since a rule-book could always be consulted if necessary. A general knowledge of field archery is expected, however.

On successfully passing this course, the new coach is qualified only to teach beginners, since the NFAS does not shoot to international level. The qualification lasts for five years and is renewable on production of a logbook showing that coaching has been done regularly during the period.

Coaching in Clubs

Aspiring coaches need to be willing to give up their shooting time for others, and this is not very common, since archers are there to shoot, and giving up one's time to teach others is a considerable sacrifice. If, for example, the club has two beginners every couple of weeks, the coach will be employed with them almost all the time and get very little personal practice done. Therefore, it is a good idea if a club has two or more qualified coaches who can trade time with each other, or at least split the load when more than two beginners are present.

It is essential for a club to have people who are willing to undertake the teaching of beginners, because there is a constant turnover of club members and if new members are not forthcoming, the club can soon find itself dying of attrition. New blood is vital and must be encouraged. Anyone who expresses an interest in coming along to find out what it is all about must be encouraged to give it a try. At my first club, I was dismayed to see how often people stood and watched us shooting, and when anyone tentatively asked any questions or expressed an interest in learning, no one in the club wanted to give up their shooting time. The little core of eight never grew any larger, but they were quite happy shooting the same round every Sunday afternoon.

Some clubs organize beginners' courses at regular times of the year, and perhaps that works in gathering a number of beginners together at the same time and progressing them through the course at roughly the same rate, hoping to end with the whole batch joining the club. However, some people may be put off by having to wait until the club is ready to accommodate them. It could be said that if they are not prepared to wait, they could not be very interested anyway, but quite often some people cannot attend the course regularly or have a holiday booked in the middle of it. In my experience, it is better to take people when they are able to attend, except for those who can never come on Sundays, or on the club evening in the summer months.

An instructor should be aware of the loss rate amongst beginners and resign himself to the fact that most of those he trains, even the very promising and talented, will not last long. When they rush off to buy their equipment, do not imagine that they are hooked; it is quite common for beginners to go and buy all the gear, then give up the next day, as if all they wanted was to own the stuff, not use it. My home club tried the idea of charging a substantial starter fee in the hope that this would discourage the less serious and persuade people to go through the whole five sessions the fee was supposed to pay for. Even this was not wholly successful, however, as we found that quite a number would turn up, pay the fee, then never be seen again after the first lesson. The club instructor must also expect some people to phone for information, arrange to visit the club, then never be seen. In some areas, they are known as 'tyrekickers' or 'timewasters' or even 'dreamers'.

The proportion of beginners who complete the course of basic training, join the club, and stay for at least a year is about one in five. So do not expect too much. Something that you have found immensely enjoyable, fascinating and even beautiful at times may have a limited appeal for others for reasons which only they know. It is also a good idea to find out where they live first, so you do not waste a morning teaching someone who is only there for the weekend and lives in the Outer Hebrides. There will also sometimes be the mother of a very keen small boy who is only eight. The NFAS has a useful rule that says anyone of that age must be accompanied at all times by a parent, which often puts parents off, for some reason.

19 Safety and Etiquette

Safety

Many safety rules may seem to be obvious, but it should be borne in mind that even the most obvious have been broken by someone at some time, often by children but sometimes by adults as well. These are the safety rules for shooting:

- Never shoot an arrow so that you cannot see where it is likely to land.
- Never shoot an arrow straight up into the air. I once met a man who had lost one eye this way.
- Never shoot a cracked or bent arrow. A cracked wooden shaft can break when shot and be driven into the hand.
- Never point an arrow in a drawn bow at anyone and certainly never shoot at anyone, no matter how far away they appear to be.
- Never even pretend to shoot at anyone – some have weak hearts and nervous dispositions.
- When you have finished scoring a target and moved away from it, do not go back for another look – the next group may already have started shooting it.
- Never move in front of anyone who is about to shoot – they may not see you in time to prevent a mis-shot arrow.
- Remember at all times that you are using a lethal weapon. You may not be shooting with broadhead piles, but bullet piles will penetrate a body quite easily.
- While someone else is shooting, be aware of the surroundings and of others about you, and bear in mind that the person shoot-

ing has his whole attention on his shot and may not be aware of something outside his area of vision.

- If some kind of danger occurs when someone is about to shoot, shout 'fast'. This call should stop someone from shooting.
- When people are looking for lost arrows behind a target they may not be visible to anyone coming onto the shooting positions, so position someone standing in front of the target as a warning to them.
- Look out for members of the public who may have entered the wood, having not seen or even having ignored warning signs, and who may walk across the front of targets being shot.
- While others are shooting, do not wander about admiring the flora and fauna – you may wander into someone else's shooting lane.
- The area to the left and about three or four yards forward of an archer is a danger area, since that is where arrows will go if the nock splits when the arrow is loosed.

Safe Field Courses

Since most field archery grounds in Britain are woodland, archers are often not able to see other groups while shooting. The idea of being in a wood with an unknown number of unseen people shooting arrows in all directions is enough to make safety-conscious people tremble, so everything possible should be done to minimize the dangers. Although field archery has been labelled as a dangerous sport, the safety precautions, as well as the conduct of archers, makes it one of the safest, with a very low injury rate. Those injuries that do occur often arise from causes other than being shot by arrows. There has been no serious injury in field archery for many years, and the few arrows which have hit people have usually been on the legs, often glancing blows from arrows bouncing off trees, which cause virtually no injury.

Careful course design prevents accidents. Targets must be positioned so that there is a clear area behind each one of at least 40 yards, preferably more. No one should ever find themselves shooting towards anyone else, at whatever distance. It is extremely disconcerting for an archer to come on to the aim on a target and see someone moving behind it, even many yards away. It is usually possible to stagger target positions so that no one is shooting towards anyone on another target, or moving away from or towards a target. Overshoot areas should not intersect, so that anyone searching for lost arrows in an overshoot area is not in danger from another target. Bearing in mind the distance arrows can travel if they miss – over 100 yards is possible – all targets should be positioned to allow for this. Targets on steep uphill slopes are especially dangerous. An archer may be shooting up at 45 degrees, at maximum angle for distance, and if he misses, the arrow will travel well over 100 yards. In one incident, this happened and the arrow travelled right over to the far side of the course and landed vertically at the side of a target, just where someone withdrawing arrows may have been standing.

No targets should ever be in such a position that missed shots will go outside the ground, nor should arrows be pointed towards buildings, people or livestock.

Targets should never be positioned so that only sky can be seen round them.

All target positions on a course should be checked by at least two people responsible for safety.

It will often be found that moving shooting pegs a few feet will make a target safe by changing the angle of the shot, without the laborious task of moving the target itself.

The route to each target must be carefully considered so that it does not cross a shooting area and routes should be marked so that archers are not wandering about looking for the next target and getting into dangerous situations. Targets are often difficult to see from the rear, and woodland is often so thick that other groups are impossible to see, even though they may be heard. Sound does not travel as far as it seems in woodland, since trees seem to absorb it. All field archers should be alert to possible dangers while shooting is going on.

Courtesy and Etiquette

The observation of the courtesies on the field archery ground can make it a pleasant experience to shoot with strangers, a lack of courtesy can make a day memorable for the wrong reasons. When meeting at the start of a shoot, on the first target, it is customary for members of a group to introduce themselves, sometimes with handshakes.

Observing the following points can make a day go well.

- Do not let the same person draw all the arrows all day. This can become very tiring.
- If you are shooting at an NFAS shoot, there is no laid-down order of shooting, but it is regarded as bad manners to rush to the red peg in order to shoot first. It is usual for the male archers to shoot first, and any juniors last. Lady archers may shoot first if they wish. If someone wishes to shoot last on every target, there is no objection.
- If anyone in the group loses an arrow, everyone assists in the search, unless it is necessary for one person to stand in front of the target as a warning to the following group.
- Do not talk in a loud voice while someone in the group is shooting.
- Do not speak to the person shooting unless something hazardous occurs.
- Do not use bad language at any time – especially when you miss a shot.
- Do not laugh when someone makes a bad shot – it can happen to anyone.
- Do not act in a noisy and boisterous fashion so that it distracts and annoys others.
- Do not spend so much time talking that you slow down the shooting of others or prevent them from shooting.
- If a difficult fence has to be climbed, or a steep slope, offer to assist by holding other archers' bows if necessary.
- Some lady archers like to be offered assistance, but others prefer to be independent. It does no harm to offer.
- Never prevent someone from shooting by standing in their way or walking into their shooting area.
- At the end of shooting, it is customary to thank the scorers for their work and to shake hands, thanking others of the group for their company.
- It is usually regarded as discourteous to pick up anyone else's bow, but in some circumstances, when they may appear to have forgotten where they left it, it is a courtesy to do so.
- Never draw anyone else's bow without first asking permission.

- If there is someone in the group who is on their first shoot, or who admits to having very little experience, they should be assured that they will be treated exactly like everyone else.

20 Keeping Records

There is no need to keep personal records – indeed, I know of no one else who does, but it is a practice I have often recommended, since it has positive uses. I only regret that I did not start doing so until I had been shooting for several years.

My record book originally began with several columns drawn down two opposite pages, labelled 'Date, Venue, Round, Score, Maximum possible score, Percentage, Place and Comments.' These required different spacing, of course, so that the comment space was enough to get several words in. The method was to use two pages per year, and this was sufficient since it was possible to record one shoot per line and there was enough space on a page to get all the year's shoots in.

One of the most useful aspects was the working out of the percentage score. This is quite easy, since it only means dividing the actual score by the total possible score and multiplying the result by 100. Sometimes this was easy enough to do mentally, for example, a score of six hundred out of a possible eight hundred is simply three quarters, which translates easily into 75 per cent.

The point of this was that it was possible to compare performances over a period of time, such as a year, and see if there was an improvement. I could compare one year with another and see how much improvement there had been – or if there had been a decline. The variables of courses and shoots were not calculated, since this would be almost impossible on many shoots; some were easy, some far more difficult. This would, of course, be reflected in the scores. It was also necessary to take account of different rounds, since at one time Foresters rounds were more popular, and not only was the scoring on these more difficult, but the scores were higher than Big Game rounds. For example, the Big Game round has a maximum of twenty points on each target, but the maximum possible is easier to attain because of the size of the scoring area. However, the Foresters target face has a centre spot and one can gain a possible forty-five points from three arrows in it, but it is more difficult to achieve this. A percentage score of 85 per cent of the total possible is not too difficult for a Big Game round, but far more difficult for a Foresters round.

On looking back, my comments seem to have been mainly about the weather, and sometimes about the quality of the course. Some courses are superb, a real pleasure to shoot in, and some have been memorable in other ways, too, such as the bridge over a raging torrent which collapsed under me in pouring rain, resulting in a mad scramble for the bank while trying to save my bow. On another one a patch of very green grass turned out to be a deep bog and I found myself spread out over the surface, trying to haul my legs out after taking off my quiver and passing that and my bow to the appalled onlookers. There was also the most superb shoot in snow, when arrows were skipping off ice into the target at one point.

There are other records that can be kept or derived from these, such as separate records of national championships or records of different courses, where the total number of courses shot over the years reaches a staggering number. Your personal shoot record, if it is to be of any real interest and value, of course needs to be as accurate as possible, which is difficult if you attend a shoot where the rules are changed so that it is a problem to find out what the maximum possible score might be. With standard rounds, it is easy, but sometimes organizers throw in something unusual. For example, at one recent shoot, it was announced at the start that there were a number of targets that had optional pegs. One could shoot from the usual red, white or blue markers, but there was an option of choosing to shoot from a longer peg for double the score, but only with one arrow. What a wonderful idea! But out on the course, it turned out that some of the targets with this option were exceptionally long and difficult. It meant that a hit was doubled in value, but if one missed there was no second chance. This also meant that calculating the maximum possible score became somewhat tricky, since I had not noted how many such targets there were, nor were the organizers certain. Never mind, it was a good shoot on a difficult ground, very muddy and slippery. Recording such a shoot seemed worthwhile.

If you are in the habit of winning the occasional shoot, then it is worth recording the wins. In the years to come, it may be a reminder of the good days in field archery.

21 Target Panic, Freezing and Other Afflictions

There are several problems that sometimes affect archers and their shooting performance, which can be physical or mental in origin. The physical problems are often more quickly cured.

Physical Problems

Physical problems include damaged muscles or ligaments, which can cause difficulties in walking or shooting. Sometimes the damage will prevent shooting for a while until the injury heals, and it is, of course, wise not to shoot if you have a strained shoulder, neck or arm muscles. Elbows can also develop problems – tennis elbow can become 'archer's elbow'. This can usually be dealt with by a GP with a steroid injection.

Many field archers suffer damage to feet, legs, ankles, hips, etc., which are sometimes caused by overstressing the body on arduous courses. Fitness helps to prevent these and, of course, they become more likely with age. Again, most of these can be cured by time and rest. Elastic bandages can help support some parts such as wrists, elbows, ankles and knees.

Using a bow with a draw weight that is too heavy can cause injuries to arms, neck and shoulders. These can be cured by using lighter equipment, but this change can be quite drastic and requires a considerable outlay in new bows if it cannot be accommodated by adjusting the bow to a lower weight. Many archers shoot high weights simply to make their arrow trajectory as flat as possible, but the advent of highly stressed fast bows with exaggerated cams makes such a bow more difficult to draw and to control, and the possibility of overstressing the body becomes greater. A 70-pound bow with large cams is much more difficult to draw than the same weight with round wheels, since the cams increase the weight very rapidly.

In the days before compound bows, many American hunters used hunting bows that were short and powerful in order to drive an arrow with a broadhead through an animal. They would often strain wrists, fingers, elbows, arms or shoulders in the process. Particularly at risk were finger tendons, and some of these, after being damaged, never recovered. Some of this damage occurred as a result of people trying to be macho and boasting about shooting powerful bows.

Physical strains will often cure themselves, given time and the reduction of stress, and it can sometimes be beneficial to go to an osteopath for treatment.

Psychological Problems

There are shooting problems which are caused by the mind, and which can be extremely difficult to overcome, especially if the archer does not know how to cure them, as is often the case.

These problems are more common than is generally realized; one authority claims that nearly 90 per cent of archers suffer from them at some time, although few will admit it. There seems to be a feeling of shame at having one of these afflictions, as if they are signs of a terrible weakness, but admitting it is the first step to finding a cure. In all my shooting experience, only one archer I know has admitted to being target shy, and it affected him so badly that he was forced to give up shooting his recurve bow and found that a crossbow was the only answer that would allow him to carry on shooting. His arrow loss rate had shot up as he experienced more and more difficulty in getting the bow on to the target, and was eventually unable to hit a target at all. However, there are accounts of archers who are badly afflicted who were able to cure them with the simple treatments available, and have since become very successful archers. There is every possibility that anyone with one of these can cure themselves if only they can find out how. The inability to discover a cure is maddeningly frustrating and makes the problem worse. There are three types of psychological problems: freezing, target shyness and target panic.

Freezing is simply the inability to release the arrow when aiming at the target. It seems ludicrous when stated in bald terms like that. How can it be possible? The cause is in the mind, and is often the fear of missing the target. Most psychological problems in shooting are caused by fear of one type or another. The archer draws the string, comes on to the aim and – nothing happens. There is a long stillness while the mind struggles to control the body and make the hand move. Eventually it does, but the arrow often misses, and that compounds the problem. The fear of missing then increases.

Target shyness, target panic and flinching are all similar and have the same cause – the lack of confidence in being able to hit the target, even when one has been doing so successfully for years. Target shyness can manifest itself in several ways, but one is the inability to hold the sight on the target. The method adopted to deal with this is often not very effective, and sometimes results in the archer bringing the bow down onto the target and loosing in the hope that the sight will just be on the centre at the right moment. Sometimes it is, of course, but more often the resultant pattern of arrows will be a vertical line. The moving bow does not produce very accurate results, and the anguished frustration of the archer may cause even more problems. One archer tells how he very nearly shot someone 80 yards away when he flinched several yards off the target, but he has since cured the problem and now shoots very successfully.

Flinching results in an involuntary release or a twitching when attempting to release or loose. A release aid and a compound bow will not cure the problem, as it occurs with those as well. Sometimes it is even an inability to release by fumbling to find the trigger.

The mind barrier which causes this can be broken, that is certain. This knowledge alone will go some way towards a cure. If some can do it, so can anyone else. Several methods can be used, depending on the equipment being used.

A freestyle shooter may find that a clicker will help. A clicker is simple to fit on a recurve bow, and is intended as a draw check indicator, but in this case it can be used as a trigger. The bow is drawn to almost its full length, then an extra pull is required to pull the arrow point through the clicker. This pause enables the archer to aim on the target, with the knowledge that should he loose the arrow from under the clicker, it will usually throw the arrow off to the right (in a right-handed bow). All that is required is something to stop the arrow from being shot prematurely, and the clicker can do that. The aim can now be held on the target.

Compound shooters using releases have a problem which is not so easily cured, since a clicker is extremely difficult to use with a release. Here the difficulty is to pull the string back to a point where the arrow is still held under the clicker, but a little extra pull will bring it out, when the release can be triggered. This is not easy, mainly because the technique of drawing a compound bow usually means drawing it as far as possible in one movement, into the valley. There is no draw length left for any further movement, so the clicker cannot be operated.

Another answer therefore has to be found. Draw the bow without an arrow in it. Aim at anything. Hold the bow at full draw for a few seconds, counting if that will help. That will prove that you do not have to release the string. Indeed doing so with no arrow may damage the bow. Practise this for a few times. Now put an arrow in the bow and draw up, preferably with a butt or boss at eye level, about 5 yards away. Aim, but do not release. Do this again and again. (One experienced coach said that he made people do this with the boss behind a window, and no one ever released or loosed.) Use several points on the boss to aim at, hold, then come down, then draw up again on to another aiming point.

Do this exercise several times daily for several minutes or even half an hour. Do it for several days, then for a couple of weeks. It will help to reprogram the way the mind sees the target. You will probably soon discover that there is no difficulty in holding on your aim, and holding it on the target. I found it useful to do this on a butt hung at eye level in my garage, knowing that if I loosed I could possibly send an arrow through the butt, through the metal garage door and into my car behind it. This, I found, was quite effective in preventing me from loosing an arrow.

Further exercises can be used. Progress on to shooting at a blank target butt, by drawing up, aiming, then closing your eyes. Now go through a process of feeling whether your body is held straight, your shoulders are in their correct shooting positions, your feet are correctly placed, your arms are held correctly and your hands are right, with the bow hand properly on the handle, and your string hand straight with the wrist relaxed. With your eyes still closed, loose the arrow. Repeat this over and over again, until you can go out and hold on a target and loose without any sensation of panic. Your shooting should have improved tremendously, and you will now have greater confidence in your ability to hit the target – with every shot.

These same methods can be used to cure the freezing, but one additional method can also be also useful, and that is simply to shoot at a blank butt for several days, or even a couple of weeks. No one can freeze by shooting at a butt with no target face on it, so this may very well solve that problem and it can also be used for the others.

Appendix I
Rules of Organizations

EFAA

The EFAA does not support hunting of live animals.

The EFAA adopts the Bye-laws (Shooting Rules) of the IFAA (International Field Archery Association) articles VI to XI inclusive, with the following additions.

GENERAL RULES

1 SHOOTING RULES

A *American Flat Bow (AFB)*

   i   A one-piece straight-ended bow of any material.

   ii The belly must be free of any marks or blemishes that can be used as sighting aids.

   iii The bow may contain a window and an arrow shelf.

   iv Only one nocking point is allowed on the string.

   v   Arrows must be of wood, fletched with natural feather, and must be of the same length, fletch, and pile, without regard for colour.

   vi Nocks may be of any material, any weight of pile may be used.

   vii The bow must be shot with the 'Mediterranean' loose.

   viii One consistent anchor point must be used.

B *Hunting Style Division (HS)*

   i   No device of any type that may be used for sighting may be used, or attached to the archer's equipment.

   ii   There shall be no device, mechanical or otherwise, in the sight window, except the arrow rest and adjustable pressure button where used.

   iii   The following are NOT permitted: clickers, draw checks, levels, stabilizers and devices for lengthening or shortening the draw length of an archer.

   iv   Laminations, artificial marks or blemishes may not appear on the upper limb in the field of vision at full draw. A sight window that is altered from standard configuration and not offered as a standard option without charge by the manufacturer, is NOT acceptable.

   v   String shall be of ONE colour only, with a single nocking point. A serving of any ONE colour may be used. Any marks, ties or string attachments (except brush buttons properly located or silencers less than 12 inches from the nocking point) are NOT permitted.

   vi   One anchor point only is permitted (i.e. no face walking).

   vii   An archer shall hold the string when shooting in the traditional manner, i.e. index finger above the nock and middle finger below the nock, except in cases of physical deformity or handicap for which special dispensation may be given (apply to General Secretary).

   viii   Arrows shall be made of wood. Piles must be of such dimension as not to cause excessive damage to the target faces. Fletch must be feather. All arrows shall be identical in length, weight, diameter and fletching, with allowances for wear and tear. Arrows which do not conform to the permitted specification must not be included in or carried with the archer's equipment during competition; exceptions are arrows found during the shoot and damaged arrows accepted for convenience of carrying.

   ix   A bow quiver installed on the opposite side of the sight window, with no part of the quiver visible in the sight window, is permitted.

   x   There shall be no restrictions placed on the bow draw weight.

   xi   Compound bows shall not be permitted in this division.

C *Longbow Division (LB)*

   i   The bow shall be of 'D' section through its entire length, and shall be made entirely of wood or laminations of wood. Nocks may be made of any other material.

ii There shall be no sight window or arrow rest allowed. Arrows must be shot off the hand.

iii The length between nocks shall not be less than 5 feet for arrows up to 26 inches in length, and not less than 5 feet 6 inches for arrows over 26 inches in length.

iv The limb thickness from belly to back is at no point to be less than three-fifths of the overall width of the limb at any point.

v No device of any type that may be used for sighting shall be permitted, either on the bow or attached to the archer's equipment.

vi The following are NOT permitted: clickers, draw checks, levels, stabilizers and devices for lengthening or shortening the draw length of the archer.

vii Laminations, artificial marks or blemishes, may NOT appear on the upper limb in the field of vision at full draw.

viii String shall be of ONE colour only, with a single nocking point. A serving of any ONE colour may be used. Any marks, ties or string attachments (except brush buttons properly located or silencers less than 12 inches from the nocking point) are NOT permitted.

ix One anchor point only is permitted (i.e. no face walking).

x An archer shall hold the string when shooting in the traditional manner, i.e. index finger above the nock and middle finger below the nock, except in cases of physical deformity or handicap for which special dispensation may be made(apply to General Secretary).

ix Arrows shall be made of wood. Piles must be of such diameter as not to cause excessive damage to target faces. Fletch must be feather. All arrows shall be identical in length, weight, diameter and fletching, with allowance for wear and tear. Arrows which do not conform to the permitted specification must NOT be included in or carried with the archer's equipment during competition; exceptions are arrows found during the shoot and damaged arrows accepted for the convenience of carrying.

xi There shall be no restriction placed on the bow draw weight.

D *Bowhunter, Bowhunter Unlimited, Bowhunter Limited*

For EFAA domestic competition only the following IFAA Bye-Laws are amended as follows:

i Bye-Laws Vi, E   4 Bowhunter – Recurve and Compound (BH)
                   5 Bowhunter Unlimited (BU)
                   6 Bowhunter Limited (BL)

ii   That sub-paragraph 4b be altered to:

No device of any type that may be used for sighting may be attached to the archer's equipment. No clicker will be permitted.

2   TOURNAMENT RULES

The number of times an archer may draw an arrow before releasing the arrow is limited to FOUR. If the arrow is not then shot it will be scored as a miss. The only exception to this rule will be in a dangerous situation, at the discretion of the Target Captain (or the first scorer if it is the Target Captain in question).

In EFAA tournaments the EFAA does not have a Veteran class for archers aged 55 and above.

3   OFFICIAL ROUNDS

1 Unmarked Distance Round

A *Forester's Round*

i   The standard unit shall consist of the following fourteen shots:
three 24-inch diameter faces at distances from 40–60 yards
four 18-inch diameter faces at distances from 35–40 yards
four 12-inch diameter faces at distances from 15–30 yards
three 6-inch diameter faces at distances from 20–30 feet

ii   *Targets.* The target faces will be of animal or bird design in full colour and shall have inscribed on them an outer circle of fixed diameter, an inner circle of half that diameter, and a spot of one-sixth that diameter thus:

24-inch face	12-inch inner circle	4-inch spot
18-inch face	9-inch inner circle	3-inch spot
12-inch face	6-inch inner circle	3-inch spot
6-inch face	3-inch inner circle	1-inch spot

iii   It is strongly recommended that two 6-inch faces are used at each 6-inch target to minimize arrow damage.

iv   *Shooting Rules.* At 6-inch targets one arrow is shot from one marker. At 12-inch Targets two arrows are shot, one from each of two markers. At 18-inch targets three arrows are shot, one from each of three markers. At 24-inch targets four arrows are shot, one each from each of four markers. Multi-marker shots can be equidistant from the target or walk-up or walk-away shots. One arrow is to be shot from each marker.

v   Scoring
    Aiming spot – 15 points
    Inner circle – 10 points
    Outer circle – 5 points

vi *Cubs.* Special stakes may be used which should at no time be more than 30 yards from the target butt.

vii *Juniors.* As adult with the exception of the 24-inch face targets which are to be shot from the nearest adult peg. Juniors will shoot a maximum of 50 yards on the 24-inch face (a special peg may be set if necessary to achieve this).

viii It is strongly recommended that black markers are used for the Foresters round to distinguish them from those other rounds on the same course.

ix Although a personal record may be kept on the archer's membership card, the round is not recognized for classification purposes.

B *Big Game Round*

i   The standard round shall consist of the following fourteen shots;

Number of Target Faces	Number and Type of Shot	Maximum Distance	Minimum Distance
3 Group 1	3 × 5 yard walk up	60 yards	40 yards
3 Group 2	3 × 3 yard walk up	45 yards	30 yards
4 Group 3	4 × 1 distance	35 yards	20 yards
4 Group 4	4 × 1 distance	20 yards	10 yards

ii The targets, shooting rules, scoring and recording for the Big Game round are exactly the same as for the Marked Animal round, see Article VII, section C of the IFAA rules.

C *3D Animal Round*

i   The standard unit shall consist of the following fourteen shots:

Number of Target Faces	Number and Type of Shot	Maximum Distance	Minimum Distance
3 Group 1	3 × 5 yard walk up	60 yards	40 yards
3 group 2	3 × 3 yard walk up	45 yards	30 yards
4 Group 3	4 × 1 distance	35 yards	20 yards
3 Group 4	4 × 1 distance	20 yards	10 yards

ii *Examples*

    Group 1 3D animals: large deer, standing bear and dall ram

    Group 2 3D animals; small bear, cougar, boar and pronghorn

    Group 3 3D animals; strutting turkey, coyote, javelina and small deer

    Group 4 3D animals; turkey and rock rascals

Targets may be any IFAA recognized 3D targets.

iii The above groups correspond with the groups already outlined for shooting with paper target in the Big Game rounds.

iv *Scoring.* The outer kill line must be completely broken for the higher score, otherwise scoring shall be as for the paper round.

2 Marked Distance Rounds

A *Foresters Round*

  i The standard unit shall consist of the following shots:

      3 × 4 shot on a 24-inch diameter face with the first marker set between 40 and 60 yards. Markers to be no further than 5 yards apart.

      4 × 3 shot on an 18-inch target face with the first marker set between 30 and 40 yards. Markers to be no further than 4 yards apart.

      4 × 2 shot on a 12-inch diameter face with the first marker set between 15 and 30 yards. Markers to be no more than 3 yards apart.

      3 × 1 shot on a 6-inch diameter face with the first marker set between 20 and 30 feet.

  ii One arrow to be shot from each marker. Multi-marker shots can be walk-ups or fans with the width to be no more than 5 yards overall.

  ii It is recommended that the markers be coloured green.

  iv A round shall consist of two units and shall be recognized for record purposes, but cannot be used for classification purposes, although it may be recorded on the back of the archer's classification card.

  v Juniors shall shoot the adult markers except on the 4 shot 24-inch face, where they shall shoot from two special blue markers set between 40 and 50 yards. Two arrows shall be shot from each marker.

vi Cubs will shoot from black markers and the unit shall consist of the following shots:

Distance to be shot	Number of shots	Size of face
To be shot from adult pegs	1	6-inch
"	1	6-inch
"	1	6-inch
10 yd	2	12-inch
10 yd	2	12-inch
15 yd	2	12-inch
15 yd	2	12-inch
20 yd	3	18-inch
20 yd	3	18-inch
20 yd	3	18-inch
20 yd	3	18-inch
25 yd	4	24-inch
30 yd	4	24-inch
15, 20, 25 & 30 yd	4	24-inch

vii Targets shall be of animal or bird design in full colour and shall have inscribed upon them an outer circle of fixed diameter, an inner circle of half that diameter and a spot of one-sixth that diameter, thus:

24-inch face	12-inch inner circle	4-inch spot
18-inch face	9-inch inner circle	3-inch spot
12-inch face	6-inch inner circle	2-inch spot
6-inch face	3-inch inner circle	1-inch spot

It is strongly recommended that two 6-inch faces are used at each target to minimize arrow damage.

viii Scoring shall be:

aiming spot: 15 points
inner circle: 10 points
outer circle: 5 points

4 SHOOTING RULES FOR UNMARKED ROUNDS

The rules governing unmarked distance rounds are identical to those governing marked distance rounds, except in the following particulars:

a) *Equipment.* At no time, on any unmarked distance rounds, shall any device be allowed that would in any way be an aid in establishing the distance of the shot.

b) *Shooting Positions.* On unmarked distance rounds the order of the shooting positions shall be indicated on the markers. For cub archers special markers shall be used which shall at no time be more than 30 yards from the target butt.

c) *Course Layout.* On unmarked distance rounds lanes may be such that an archer can be required to modify his shooting position to obtain an uninterrupted flight path to the target, or to avoid obstruction to his bow or its action.

5 SAFETY

a) It is recommended that a first-aid kit be readily accessible, and that its whereabouts be made known by prominent signs.

b) No archer may draw or point an arrow in a dangerous manner.

The above rules are those for shooting and rounds for EFAA. They are not a complete set of rules. Those concerning the constitution, structure, classifications, policies, etc. can be found in the EFAA official rules handbook.

IFAA RULES

Extracts from International Field Archery Association Book of Rules

ARTICLE VI – GENERAL RULES FOR FIELD ARCHERY GAMES

A *Terms*

Unit   – a fourteen-target course including all official shots.
Round – shooting two such units or twice round one unit.
Marker – shooting position.
Face   – target face.
Butt   – any object against which a face is placed.
Target – this term in connection with a marker number, e.g. '4th target'.
Spot   – aiming centre.
Stop   – warning call to other archers.
Walk-up – a target at which shooting positions are at different distances and at which the longest distance is shot first and the other distances in sequence, walking up to the butt.

Fan — a target at which there are four shooting positions, all at equal distances from the butt.

Straight — a target at which there is a single shooting position from which all arrows are shot.

B *Targets*

1 Faces shall not be placed over other larger faces, nor shall there be any artificial marks on the butt or in the foreground that could be used as points of aim.

2 All butts must be positioned square to the centre of the shooting lane.

3 In all tournaments using official IFAA rounds, a minimum of eight faces must be used on all butts requiring 20 cm faces. Faces shall be arranged as follows: two blocks of four faces each (see diagram).

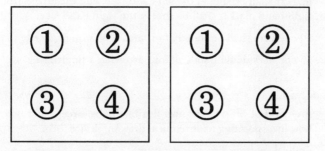

A minimum of two faces must be used where 35 cm. faces are specified, these shall be placed side by side on a horizontal level.

C *Shooting Positions*

1 Each target shall have an indicator board at the shooting position; each board shall be visible on approach to the shooting position; this board shall carry the following information:

Target number and distance.

2 The distance of each shot shall be clearly shown on each marker. At least one marker for each shooting position is mandatory. More markers may be used as preferred by the host nation.

3 Where equal distance markers are used, the minimum distance between any two adjacent markers shall be 3 feet, and the maximum distance between the extreme markers shall be 15 feet.

4   20 cm faces shall be shot in sequence: top left, top right, bottom left, bottom right (see diagram).

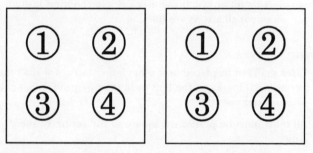

5   35 cm faces shall be shot all four arrows at a single face. Arrows shot from the left-hand side shall be shot at the left-hand face and vice versa, except on fan shots where two arrows from the left-hand marker shall be shot at the left-hand face, and the arrows from the right-hand marker shall be shot at the right-hand face.

6   50 cm faces shall be shot all four arrows at a single face.

7   65 cm faces shall be shot all four arrows at a single face.

D *Equipment*

1   Any kind of bow, having two flexible limbs, except a crossbow or bow incorporating a mechanical drawing device.

2   Optical spotting aids are permitted.

3   The archer shall support both the mass weight and the holding weight of the bow without any assistance from any external aid, other than those defined in the relevant styles.

E *Shooting Styles*

1 *Barebow – Recurve and Compound (BB)*

a   Bows, arrows, strings and accessories shall be free from sights, marks, blemishes or laminations which could be used for aiming.

b   An adjustable arrowrest may be used to control the space between the arrow and the face of the bow window.

c   The use of stabilizers shall be permitted.

d   One permanent nocking point only is permitted which may be marked by one or two nock locators e   No mechanical device will be permitted other than one non-adjustable draw check and/or level mounted on the bow, neither of which may extend above the arrow.

f   All arrows used shall be identical in length, weight, diameter, fletching and nocks without regard to colour, with allowance for wear and tear.

2 *Freestyle Limited – Recurve and Compound (FS)*

a   Any type of sight is permitted.

b   Release aids are not permitted.

3 *Freestyle Unlimited (FU)*

a   Any type of bow, sight, release aid recognised by the I.F.A.A. Committee is permitted.

4 *Bowhunter – Recurve and Compound (BH)*

a   Bows, arrows, strings and accessories shall be free from sight marks, blemishes and/or laminations which could be used for aiming. A levelling device is not permitted.

b   No device of any type that may be used for sighting may be attached to the archer's equipment. No clicker will be permitted.

c   One permanent nocking point only is allowed on the string. Nocking point may be marked by one or two nock locators.

d   One consistent anchor point only is permitted.

e   An archer shall touch the arrow when nocked with the index finger against the nock. Finger position may not be changed during competition. In cases of physical deformity or handicap special dispensation shall be made.

f   All arrows used shall be identical in length, weight, diameter, fletchings and nock without regard for colour, with allowance for wear and tear.

g   Brush buttons in their proper places at the recurve tip of the bow, string silencers no closer than 12 inches above or below the nocking point and bow quiver installed on the opposite side of the sight window with no part of the quiver visible in the bow window is permitted. One straight stabilizer, coupling device included, if used, not exceeding 12 inches as measured from the back of the bow may be used. No forked stabilizer or any counterbalance will be legal. The plunger (where the stabilizer is screwed in) is part of the stabilizer.

h   Bow weight shall not be adjusted during any one round.

5 *Bowhunter Unlimited (BU)*

a   Any type of bow and release aid recognised by the IFAA Committee is permitted.

b   A sight with a maximum of five fixed reference points that must not be moved during a round will be allowed.

c   Pin sights are to be of straight stock from point of anchor to sighting points with only one sighting reference possible from each pin or reference point. Hooded pins or scopes are not permitted.

d   Release aids are permitted.

e   A kisser button or string peepsight will be permitted but not both. No form of magnifying device may be incorporated in, or attached to, the peepsight.

f   All other rules for the Bowhunter style will apply.

6 *Bowhunter Limited (BL)*

a   The same rules apply as for Bowhunter Unlimited except that release aids are not permitted.

7 *Longbow (LB)*

a   A one-piece straight-ended bow of any material, which when strung displays one continued unidirectional curve, which is measured as follows:

When the strung bow is placed with the bowstring in a vertical position, the angle as measured between the tangent of any point on the limb and an imaginary horizontal line must always decrease as this point is moved further away from the bow grip.

Tip reinforcing not exceeding ½ inch in height, as measured from the surface of the bow limb and not exceeding 1½ inches in length as measured from the limb tip will be permitted.

b   The belly must be free of any marks and blemishes that can be used as sighting aids.

c   The bow may contain a window and an arrow shelf.

d   Only one nocking point is allowed on the string, which may be marked by one or two nocking point locators.

e   Arrows must be of wood, fletched with natural feather, and must be of the same length, fletch and pile, without regard for colour.

f   Nocks may be of any material, any weight of pile may be used.

g   The bow must be shot with the Mediterranean loose.

h   One consistent anchor point must be used.

F *Divisions of Competition*

1 *Professional Adults Only – Professional Status*

Those who claim themselves as Professionals, or who register themselves as Professionals at any shoot, or who compete for Professional cash prizes or Professional awards at a tournament.

Two styles of competition:

> Unlimited – no restriction. Men and women will compete in separate divisions.
> Limited – no release aids.

A Professional may retire from the Professional Division after no less than one year as a Professional shooter. After retiring, this archer may not compete for championship awards for one full year. Notice of retiring will be posted with the IFAA Secretary, who will notify each member nation through its IFAA Committee member.

The action of retiring from the Professional Division shall be afforded once only during the archer's competition life.

2 *Amateur – Adults, Veterans, Juniors and Cubs.*

Every archer registered as a member of an IFAA affiliated Association will be recognised as an Amateur until such time as they become Professionals under IFAA rules.

Adult Men and Women:

Barebow recurve and compound	BB
Freestyle limited recurve and compound	FS
Freestyle unlimited	FU
Bowhunter recurve and compound	BH
Bowhunter unlimited	BU
Bowhunter limited	BL
Longbow	LB

Veterans Men and Women.

Those archers who are fifty-five years of age on or before the first day of a tournament will be given the choice to participate in the Veteran or Adult division (but not both). The decision to participate in the Veteran Division is not binding on subsequent tournaments. The choice is always optional. Proof of age will be compulsory. There will be no classes in the Veteran Division and shooting styles are as for Adult Men and Women above.

Junior, boys and girls (13–16 years of age).

Barebow recurve and compound	BB
Freestyle limited recurve and compound	FS
Freestyle unlimited	FL
Bowhunter recurve and compound	BH
Bowhunter unlimited	BU
Bowhunter limited	BL
Longbow	LB

Cubs, boys and girls (under 13 years of age).

Barebow recurve and compound	BB
Freestyle limited recurve and compound	FS

G Tournament Officials

1 At every tournament a Field Captain shall be appointed and it shall be his duty to:

   a Make up the groups.

   b Appoint a Target Captain and two scorers for each group.

   c Designate the targets from which each group will start.

   d Have the option in any tournament to set a time limit, either by target or round, when such a tournament must be completed.

2 The duty of a Target Captain shall be to order the shooting in a group and to settle all local questions. His decision on arrow values shall be final except on his own arrow values when the decision shall be made by the first scorer.

3 The scorers shall keep an accurate account of scores at each target, maintain a running total and compare these at each target.

H Tournament Rules

1 Archers shall shoot in groups of not less than three and not more than six. Normally the preferred number is four.

2 Juniors shall shoot in their own groups at IFAA sanctioned tournaments.

3 Cubs shall shoot in their own groups with a non-shooting responsible adult at IFAA sanctioned tournaments.

4 The shooting positions of the group shall be decided by mutual agreement. Each archer shall shoot from the same side for the first fourteen-target unit, for the remaining fourteen-target unit the archer shall shoot from the other side. An archer may opt, with the consent of the Target Captain, to shoot from the opposite side if he considers himself to be at a disadvantage from his own side at a particular target. At the conclusion of each fourteen-target unit the archers shall change their order of shooting. Those who shot first shall shoot last, and those who shot last shall shoot first.

5 Single-marker lay-out:

No archer shall shoot from in front of an imaginary line, parallel to the target, running through the appropriate marker. One foot shall not be more than 6 inches behind or a maximum of 3 feet to either side of such marker. For all animal rounds, marked or unmarked, one foot shall touch or not be more than 6 inches behind or to either side of such marker.

Double-marker lay-out:

No archer shall shoot from in front of the appropriate marker. One foot shall touch or be not more than 6 inches behind or to the side of such marker.

6 One group shall not hold up the following group by looking for lost arrows. Enough arrows shall be carried so that each archer may continue shooting and return to find missing arrows when shooting has ceased.

7 No archer may practise on any target of a course that is currently being used for purposes of a tournament. Special practice targets must be provided. In the event of an indoor range 'sighters' are permitted if the organizers of the event so allow.

8 If for any reason a group is holding up another group mutual arrangement may be made between the Target Captains to allow the following group to pass through.

9 An archer obtaining the Target Captain's permission to leave the range for any reason may be privileged to return to his group and

complete the unfinished round. His group may wait for his return but must allow the other groups to pass through. The Target Captain shall set a reasonable time limit for his return, upon the expiry of which the group will continue. He may make up any targets missed in the interim at the discretion of the Field Captain.

10   No archer may shoot (or compete) in any one tournament more than once unless advertised as a multiple-registration tournament.

11   Competitors may not shoot at practice targets during the course of a round except at an official break. In the event of an equipment failure, after repairs, an archer may shoot four arrows at a practice target under a Field or Range Captain's supervision.

12   Archers must shoot for the full duration of a tournament as laid down in the tournament specifications. Any scores made by an archer who does not complete the tournament will not be taken into consideration for any awards. In the event of inclement weather the tournament shall continue unless a prearranged signal is given by the Field Captain. Archers leaving the range before such a signal shall be withdrawn from the competition.

13   Targets shall be shot in the sequence intended. Any targets omitted shall be forfeited at the discretion of the Field Captain.

14   Groups shall not approach or interfere with other groups whilst either is shooting a target but shall remain separate until all members of the group have finished shooting.

15   A Technical Control is to be appointed before the tournament. Each competitor must present their equipment to the Technical Control for equipment check at the designated time and place. It is the responsibility of the archer to maintain his/her equipment within the rules. Failure to do so may result in a protest by another archer resulting in disqualification.

16   No archer shall draw a bow with the bow hand above the top of the head, when drawing on a horizontal plane.

1 *Scoring*

1   No arrows in the target or butt may be touched until the arrows have been scored.

2   On all targets less than 55 yards, arrows may be scored and drawn in the prescribed manner after each pair of archers has shot, to

minimize arrow damage. The Target Captain and both scorers must go to the target to record the score.

3   Arrows passing through the target face but still in the butt may be pushed back by the Target Captain or deputy who did not shoot the arrow, and scored accordingly.

4   Skids or glances off the ground into the target shall not be counted.

5   'Bounce-outs' believed to have hit the scoring area shall be reshot. Arrows believed to have passed through the scoring area but not retained in the butt shall be reshot with a marked arrow.

6   In the event of a tie for any award in any tournament, the archers concerned will break the tie by shooting off over three targets. If the tie is not then broken they will continue until one wins a target. If the archers agree they may shoot 'sudden death' from the first target.

7   An archer who shoots an arrow in excess of the prescribed number shall lose the score of the arrow or arrows of a higher value.

8   An archer who shoots from the wrong marker or at the wrong face will lose the score of that arrow. It may not be reshot.

9   In the event of a mis-shot arrow, an archer may shoot another arrow provided the mis-shot arrow can be reached with the bow from the archer's position at the marker.

10   An arrow hitting another within the target and remaining embedded in that arrow shall have the same scoring value as that arrow. Arrows being deflected by other arrows shall be scored by their position.

11   Where a line having a specific width separates one scoring zone from another on the face, the line is in the lower scoring area. Where there is no line the arrow must cut the higher scoring area to score the higher value.

12   The number of times an archer draws an arrow before releasing that arrow will be limited to four. If the arrow is not then shot, it will be scored as a miss. The only exception to this rule will be in a dangerous situation at the discretion of the Target Captain (or the first scorer if it is the Target Captain in question).

ARTICLE VII – OFFICIAL ROUNDS

A Field Round

1 The standard unit shall consist of the following shots:

Size of face	Number of Positions	Distance of Positions Adult	Junior
65 cm	4	80-70-60-50yd	50yd
65 cm	1	65yd	50yd
65 cm	1	60yd	45yd
65 cm	1	55yd	40yd
50 cm	4	45-40-35-30yd	as adult
50 cm	4	35-35-35-35yd	as adult
50 cm	1	50yd	as adult
50 cm	1	45yd	as adult
50 cm	1	40yd	as adult
35 cm	1	30yd	as adult
35 cm	1	25yd	as adult
35 cm	1	20yd	as adult
35 cm	1	15yd	as adult
20 cm	4	35-30-25-20 ft	as adult

2 The field face shall have a black spot with a white inner ring and black outer ring, four face sizes shall be used:

20 cm face	12 cm inner ring	4 cm spot
35 cm face	21 cm inner ring	7 cm spot.
50 cm face	30 cm inner ring	10 cm spot
65 cm face	39 cm inner ring	13 cm spot.

The scoring is five for the spot, four for the inner ring, three for the outer ring. All markers to be coloured white.

B Hunter Round

The standard unit shall consist of the following shots:-

Size of face	Number of Positions	Distance of Positions Adult	Junior
65 cm	4	70-65-61-58 yd	50yd
65 cm	4	64-59-55-52yd	50yd
65 cm	4	58-53-48-45yd	45yd
50 cm	4	53-48-44-41yd	41yd
50 cm	1	48yd	as adult
50 cm	1	44yd	as adult

50 cm	1	40yd	as adult
50 cm	4	36-36-36-36yd	as adult
35 cm	4	32-32-32-32yd	as adult
35 cm	4	28-28-28-28yd	as adult
35 cm	2	23-20yd	as adult
35 cm	2	19-17yd	as adult
35 cm	2	15-14yd	as adult
20 cm	1	11yd	as adult

2   The Hunter face shall be all black with white spot. Four face sizes shall be used with dimensions the same as the Field faces. The scoring is the same as for the Field round. All markers to be coloured red.

C *Animal Round Marked Distances*

   1   The standard unit shall consist of the following shots:

     Group 1 face.   Three 5-yard walk-up shots with first marker set between 60 and 40 yards (three markers)

     Group 2 face.   Three 3-yard walk-up shots with first marker set between 45 and 30 yards (three markers)

     Group 3 face.   Four one-position shots (one marker) with marker set between 35 and 20 yards.

     Group 4 face.   Four one-position shots (one marker) with marker set between 20 and 10 yards.

3 *Targets*

   a   The targets for this round are Animal faces with the scoring area divided into two parts. The high-scoring area is oblong while the low-scoring area is between the high-scoring area and the 'hide and hair' line or 'feathers' as the case may be. The area between the 'hide and hair' line (including the line) to the outside of the carcass is considered a non-scoring area.

   b   The high-scoring area of Group 1 faces is 9 inches wide by 14½ inches long with rounded ends.

   c   The high-scoring area of Group 2 faces is 7 inches wide by 10½ inches long with rounded ends.

   d   The high-scoring area of Group 3 faces is 4½ inches wide by 7 inches long with rounded ends.

   e   The high-scoring area of Group 4 faces is 2½ inches wide by 3⅝ inches long with rounded ends.

2 *Shooting Positions*

   a   A maximum of three shots is allowed, but an archer shoots only until a hit is made. If the first arrow hits the scoring area no more arrows need be shot.

   b   An archer may not return to shoot the other arrows if he has moved towards the target.

   c   An archer's arrows must be clearly defined by rings, arrows to be shot in ascending order. If an archer accidentally shoots the wrong arrow first, he must immediately declare the fact to the Target Captain.

   d   Juniors shall shoot Group 1 targets from the closest marker on these walk-ups.

   e   The first archer shall shoot at the first target face and the sequence of first, second, third and fourth archer (etc.) thereafter shall be in rotation according to the score-card order.

4 *Scoring*

	KILL	WOUND
1st arrow	20 points	18 points
2nd arrow	16 points	14 points
3rd arrow	12 points	10 points

All markers to be coloured yellow.

D *Animal Round Unmarked Distances*

1 *Standard Unit*

Shall be as the Animal round marked distances except that the markers shall have no distances indicated on them.

2 *Targets*

Shall be as the Animal round marked distances.

3 *Shooting Positions*

Shall be as the Animal round marked distances.

4 *Scoring*

Shall be as the Animal round marked distance.

5 The use of range finders shall not be allowed.

E *International Round*

The International round is a twenty-target round (ten targets per unit) and shall consist of the following shots:

Size of face	Number of positions	Distance of Positions Adult	Junior
65 cm	1	65 yd	50yd
65 cm	1	60 yd	45yd
65 cm	1	55 yd	40yd
50 cm	1	50 yd	as adult
50 cm	1	45 yd	as adult
50 cm	1	40 yd	as adult
50 cm	1	35 yd	as adult
35 cm	1	30 yd	as adult
35 cm	1	25 yd	as adult
35 cm	1	20 yd	as adult

2 Targets shall conform to the specification of the IFAA Hunter round. Three face sizes shall be used – 35 cm, 50 cm, 65 cm.

Three arrows to be shot at each distance. The scoring is five for the spot, four for the inner ring, three for the outer ring . On the 35-yard field fan the two centre markers shall be used for the shooting positions in the International round. All other rules of the Field round shall apply to the International round.

F *Expert Field Round*

1 All distances and target faces as for the IFAA Field round shall apply, except that the subdividing lines shall be used, these lines being midway in each of the spot (for tie breakers only), inner and outer.

2 The scoring is as follows:

Five points for the spot, four points for the second circle, three points for the third circle, two points for the fourth circle and one point for the fifth circle. The white x in the centre spot is used for tie breakers only. All other rules of the IFAA Field round shall apply to the Expert round.

[There follow rules for the Flint Indoor round, which have not been included]

ARTICLE VIII – COURSE LAY-OUT REQUIREMENTS

A *In setting out a field course, the following points are to be adhered to:*

1 Distances used shall be those designated for the round to be shot.

2 All distances shall be correct to within 6 inches, the distance of the

target is the distance from the archer's side of the marker to the centre of the butt.

3   All butts must be stable so there is no danger of tipping.

4   Shooting lanes must be cleared so that arrows will not strike foliage or branches.

5   Any person, regardless of height, must have a clear view of the full face of the target.

6   Paths must never pass directly behind a target butt; it is preferred that paths should leave the butt at such an angle that archers leave the line of shooting quickly. Paths and target lanes must be clearly marked and adequate direction signs placed.

7   Target butts must be placed so that misses do not constitute a hazard to other groups of archers. Bales or butts must not leak arrows or be reinforced with any material which will damage arrows or be likely to cause bounce-outs.

B   *Safety Requirements*

1   No course shall receive approval until all hazards to safety, in the opinion of the Range Inspector, have been removed.

2   If a target butt is situated so that any path, target, road or building is behind at an unreasonable distance, then the target must be provided with an adequate backstop.

3   The practice area must be placed so that no paths or roads pass behind the practice butts.

4   A minimum of 25 feet is necessary between any paths or shooting lanes parallel to another shooting lane. This minimum permits a tolerance depending on terrain and length of shot, but the distance used must preserve absolute safety.

C   *Approvals and Procedures*

1   Courses shall be inspected and approved annually. No alterations are permitted without prior consent of the Range Inspector.

2   At an IFAA world and regional tournament or any special tournament sponsored by the IFAA, course approval by the IFAA is required. Official approval will be through the Vice-President of the IFAA or his designated representative.

3   For sanctioned IFAA tournaments, course approval shall be by the Committee member for that particular nation and approval shall be for that particular tournament only.

ARTICLE IX – CLASSIFICATION

A *Records*

1   Each member nation shall adopt and maintain a system which accurately records scores shot by archers on each twenty-eight targets, whether shot in Field or Hunter rounds or a combination thereof. Only scores shot in sanctioned tournaments shall be recorded.

2   In tournaments sponsored or sanctioned by the IFAA each member nation and the archer shall make available to the Tournament Chairman such records as he deems necessary to ensure proper classification of all participants.

3   The IFAA World Field Archery Championships shall be used to establish world ranking.

B *Classification Classes*

1   In the Barebow, Freestyle Limited and Freestyle Unlimited divisions for Men, Women and Junior Boys and Girls, there shall be the following classes based on a twenty-eight-target round.

Class	Freestyle Limited	Freestyle Unlimited	Barebow
A	450-plus	500-plus	400-plus
B	350–449	400–499	300–399
C	0–349	0–399	0–299

2   In the Bowhunter, Bowhunter Limited and Bowhunter Unlimited divisions for Men, Women and Junior Boys and Girls there shall be the following classes based on a twenty-eight target round:

Class	Bowhunter Limited	Bowhunter Unlimited	Bowhunter
A	450-plus	475-plus	375-plus
B	300–449	325–474	225–374
C	0–299	0–324	0–224

3   In the Longbow Division for Men, Women and Junior Boys and Girls there shall be the following classes based on a twenty-eight target round:

Class	Longbow
A	250-plus
B	150–249
C	0–149

4 For the world and regional championship tournaments and other tournaments sponsored by the IFAA classes shall be in accordance with this Article.

5 For sanctioned IFAA tournaments and/or tournaments sanctioned by a member association within that nation, classes shall be in accordance with the system adopted by that member nation.

C *Classification Procedures*

1 For the world and regional tournaments and other tournaments sponsored by the IFAA the Tournament Chairman shall follow the procedure as follows to determine an archer's class:

   a No score recorded two years prior to the tournament shall be considered.

   b An archer who is not classified shall compete in the highest contested class in his style in that tournament.

   c Classification of an archer shall be determined by the archer's two highest scores in a twelve-month period.

   d Reclassification shall occur on an archer attaining two higher classification-level scores in a twelve-month period where the higher classification shall apply for the balance of that twelve-month period and for the following twelve-month period unless a higher class is attained in that period.

[There follows Article X, Junior Division Rules, and Article XI, Cub Division Rules. These are followed by several pages of rules for the IFAA World Bowhunter Championships. These can be seen, by anyone interested, in the IFAA Book of Rules Incorporating the Constitution, the Bye-Laws, the WBHC Rules and the Policies, copies of which are available from the General Secretary of the EFAA.]

GNAS

200 General Field Archery Rules

(a) GNAS Rules of shooting 102, 103, and 200 to 205 shall apply to

GNAS recognised rounds and other traditional or local rounds run under the GNAS rules of shooting.

(b) There shall be separate styles and classes and for Ladies, Gentlemen and Juniors (see 202, 203).

(c) Before shooting commences at any venue, the Organizer, Judge in Charge, Field Captain, Club Captain or responsible archer shall satisfy by inspection that all the archers' equipment conforms to GNAS, FITA rules and the archer's given style. If applicable a judge, being satisfied that the archers' equipment conforms to the style written on the score cards, will sign to that effect on the front of the score cards.

(d) Suitable barriers shall be placed around the course, wherever necessary, to keep spectators at a safe distance. Only those persons having obtained permission shall be allowed on the course inside the barriers.

(e) Although there are no specific dress regulations in field archery, all competitors field party and officials shall wear bright visible colours.

(f) Where judges are appointed, one shall be Chairman in charge of the event.

(g) The duties of the Chairman and other judges shall be:

(i) To ensure that adequate safety precautions have been observed in the layout of the course and warm-up area. During warm-up, the warm-up area shall be under the control of a judge or competent archer. It is recommended that shooting periods of five minutes be allowed and a sound signal given for the archers to approach and clear the targets.

(ii) To address the assembled competitors, before the shoot commences about safety precautions and any other appropriate matter, including the method of starting the event, the starting point of each group, etc.

(iii) To ensure that all competitors are conversant with the rules of the competition and the method of scoring.

(iv) To resolve disputes or queries that may arise in interpretation of the rules or other matters.

(v) When drawing back the string of his/her bow a competitor shall not use any technique which, in the opinion of the judges, could allow the arrow, if accidently released, to fly beyond a safety zone or safety arrangement (overshoot net, area, wall, etc.). If a competitor persists in using such a technique, he/she will, in the interest of safety, be immediately asked by the Chairman of judges to stop shooting and leave the field.

(h) In competition, each shooting group shall consist of not more than six and not fewer than three archers. Number 1 of each shooting group on the target list will be the Target Captain.

(i) The Target Captain shall be responsible for the orderly conduct of shooting within the group, and have general responsibility for scoring the arrows. In the case of a dispute, a judge shall make the final decision.

(j) Two of each shooting group shall be scorers. Each shall be supplied with and complete a separate set of score-cards for the group and the duties of the scorers shall be as follows:

(i) To write down the scores of each competitor in the group.

(ii) To complete the score-card at the end of shooting.

(iii) To ensure that the score-cards are returned without delay to the Scores Commission.

(k) A mistake on a score-card may be corrected before the arrows are drawn provided all the archers in the group agree to the correction. The correction shall be witnessed and initialled by all archers and shown to a judge at the first opportunity. The judge shall initial the archers' action.

(l) The score-cards shall be signed by the Scorer at the end of shooting, and by the archer as an acceptance of the final score.

(m) Should the two cards not agree, then the lower score shall be taken as the result.

(n) The use of binoculars and other visual aids ARE permitted in all GNAS and Arrowhead/FITA rounds, provided they give no aid to measuring distance.

(o) At all targets for Arrowhead/FITA and Stamp rounds there shall be sufficient area for two competitors to stand side by side and able to shoot at the same time.

(p) The archer's more forward foot must be in contact with and behind the shooting post while shooting, except in the Stamp unmarked, the Stamp marked, the Stamp combination, the new

FITA and Arrowhead rounds when the archer shall stand with both feet behind the relevant shooting line, which is an imaginary line through the shooting posts parallel to the target.

(q) If, in competitions where the arrow holes have not been marked an arrow is observed to rebound from, or is believed to have passed through the target face, a judge shall check it, and if it appears that the arrow has rebounded or passed through the target face, then another arrow may be shot at that face from the same position from which the bouncing or passing-through arrow was shot. But in Arrowhead rounds the current FITA rules apply.

(r) An arrow shall be deemed not to have been shot if the archer can touch it without moving his feet from his shooting position, in which case another may be shot in its place.

(s) All targets shall be numbered in succession and the number board, which can be used as a stop peg, placed within the approach to the shooting post for that target.

(t) Archers waiting their turn to shoot shall stand well back behind the archers who are shooting, preferably at the number board.

(u) Faces shall not be placed over any larger face, nor shall there be any marks on the butts or foreground that could be used as points of aim.

(v) The butts shall provide for a margin of at least 5 cm outside the lowest scoring zone(s) of the face(s) placed upon them. At no point may any target face be less than 15 cm from the ground. In all instances, regardless of the terrain, the butt should be placed reasonably perpendicular to the competitors' line of sight from the shooting post in order to present to the competitor the full target face(s) full size as is practically possible.

(w) *Timing.* Whether marked or unmarked distance, an archer is allowed five minutes overall where four shots are taken from one post, and four minutes overall where three shots are taken from one post. On walk-ups, the archer is allowed one and a half minutes per arrow. The timing begins when the archer takes his shooting position, which he shall do as soon as it becomes available.

(x) A judge, having observed an archer exceed the time limit, shall caution him by a signed note on the score card, indicating the time of the warning. At the second and subsequent warnings, during that tournament, the archer's highest scoring arrow at the target where the warning is given, shall be annulled.

(y) No person shall relate to competing archers the target distance on unmarked courses during the tournament.

(z) In the event of a tie, the result will be resolved as follows:

(i) The archer, of those tying, with the greatest number of scoring arrows (hits) will win.

(ii) If still tied, the archer with the greatest number of highest scoring zone hits will win.

(iii) If still tied, they shall be declared equal.

201 FITA Field Rules

(a) FITA ARROWHEAD ROUNDS: Arrowhead rounds are only shot when formally applied for as FITA award events, in which case current FITA field rules apply in their entirety (except as provided for under (ii) below) under the control of an international or national field Judge.

(i) FITA ARROWHEAD AWARDS – The award is open to Members of the society according to qualifications and applications as laid down in FITA rules. Claims for the award must be submitted to the GNAS office on the appropriate form. See Table D in 804 for Arrowhead awards.

(ii) When an official Arrowhead round is shot (b) (iv) &(v) of the following relaxations apply, but only those archers conforming to FITA regulations can claim FITA Arrowhead awards.

(b) NEW FITA ROUNDS shot according to current FITA Field Rules with the following exceptions:

(i) Control may be in the hands of an international, national or regional field judge (if record status).

(ii) Arrow holes need not be marked, for the GNAS bouncer/pass-through rules will apply (see 200 (q)).

(iii) Target numbers may be in any readily visible colours.

(iv) Compound Limited class and U/15 Unlimited class shoot from red posts. Full 5 scoring.

(v) Compound Barebow, Traditional Longbow and all juniors under fifteen (in any other class other than U/L Under fifteen) shoot from the blue posts. Full 5 scoring.

(vi) Special posts maybe set for Under 12s, in which case no records shall be available to them.

202 Shooting Styles

(a) OLYMPIC (Freestyle) – Archers using equipment that conforms to 102 (a)

(b) BAREBOW – A bow of any type, provided it subscribes to the accepted principle and meaning of the word bow as used in target archery: i.e. an instrument consisting of a handle (grip), riser and two flexible limbs each ending in a tip with a string nock. The bow is braced for use by a single bowstring attached directly between the two string nocks only, and in operation is held in one hand by its handle(grip) while the fingers of the other hand draw, hold back and release the string. The bow must be bare, except for the arrow rest as mentioned below, and free from protrusions, marks, blemishes or laminated pieces which could be used in aiming. The inside of the upper limb shall be without trademarks. Integrally fitted torque flight compensators are permitted provided that they are not fitted with stabilizers. Weights may be added to the lower part of the riser; however, the unbraced bow complete with accessories, must be capable of being passed through a hole or ring of 12.2 cm inside diameter +/- 0.5 cm. The bowstring can be of any number of strands of the material chosen for the purpose with a centre serving to accommodate the drawing fingers, a nocking point to which may be added serving(s) to fit the arrow nock and, to locate this point, one or two nock locators, as well as at each end of the bow string a loop to be placed in the string nocks of the bow when braced. The serving on the bowstring must not end within the archer's field of vision at full draw. The bowstring must in no way offer aid in aiming through a peephole, markings, or any other means. The arrowrest, which can be adjustable, a movable pressure button, pressure point or arrow plate on the bow provided they are not electric or electronic and do not offer any additional aid in aiming. Arrows of any type which subscribe to the generally accepted principle and meaning of the word arrow as used in target archery, and which do not cause undue damage to target faces or buttresses. An arrow consists of a shaft with head (point), nock, fletching, and, if desired, cresting. All arrows used at any one target (i.e. numbered target) shall carry the same pattern and colour(s) of fletching and cresting, if any. The arrows of each competitor shall be of the same length and marked on the shaft with the competitor's name or initials.

(c) **TRADITIONAL** – Archers using equipment as for Barebow above, but the arrow shafts shall be made of wood and may comprise a metallic pile and a plastic nock. Fletchings must be of natural feather. Furthermore, archers must adhere to one anchor-point and to one finger position on the string throughout a tournament. An arrow rest is permitted but may not be adjustable; a pressure button is not permitted.

(d) **LONGBOW** – Archers using equipment as defined in 601(a), (b), (c) except that the bow must be bare, therefore marks on bow limbs or rubber bands are not allowed neither is a 'kisser' allowed on the string. Archers must adhere to one anchor point and to one finger position on the string throughout a tournament.

(e) **CROSSBOW** – Archers using equipment as defined in 501.

(f) **COMPOUND UNLIMITED** – Archers using equipment as defined in 103(C)(i).

(g) **COMPOUND LIMITED** – Archers using equipment as defined in 103(C)(ii). Multipin sights are permitted.

(h) **COMPOUND BAREBOW** – Archers using equipment generally as above. No markings or attachments may, as in 202 (b) and 202(g) appear on the bow or the string which might be used as an aid to aiming. A cable guard, pressure button and an adjustable arrowrest and plate are permitted. Only one stabilizer no longer than 30.5 cm (12 inches) overall may be fitted. No release aid or draw check indicator or overdraw may be used.

NOTE – In all compound styles, peak weight must not exceed 60 pounds.

NOTE – In all the above styles(a) to (h) inclusive, the following exceptions to target archery practices apply:

(i)   No artificial points of aim are permitted.

(ii) For Stamp and Animal Face rounds arrows must be numbered by means of distinctive bands at least 3 mm in width and approximately 3 mm apart.

(iii) No notes or memoranda, other than the Rules of Shooting or extracts thereof, may be used which might assist in improving scores.

(iv) No aids for estimating distances are allowed.

203 Juniors (General)

(a) Junior archers are those under sixteen years of age. They are placed in three categories or age groups. The date of birth must fall before the (first) day of the tournament.

Juniors (15–17)
Juniors (12–14)
Juniors (under 12)

(b) There is nothing to prevent a junior choosing to shoot in a higher age group than his age would warrant provided that he complies with the regulations appertaining to that group.

204 Target Faces

(a) FITA five-zone face as described in current FITA rules scoring 5.4.3.2.1. FITA-licensed faces must be used for Arrowhead and all record status rounds.

(b) GNAS STAMP ROUND. The FITA five-zone face shall be used. FITA-licensed faces must be used for all record status rounds.

(c) FORESTER ROUND FACES. The target faces shall be of animal or bird design, and shall have inscribed on them an outer circle of fixed diameter, an inner circle of half that diameter and a spot of one sixth that diameter. Thus:

24 in face	12 in inner circle	4 in spot
18 in face	9 in inner circle	3 in spot
12 in face	6 in inner circle	2 in spot
6 in face	3 in inner circle	1 in spot

(d) BIG GAME ROUND FACES. The target faces shall be of animal or bird design, with the scoring areas divided into two parts. The higher-scoring area is the smaller area, situated in the heart/lung region of the animal, and is known as the 'kill' zone. The lower-scoring area is the remainder of the animal within the marked perimeter, and is known as the 'wound' zone. Targets are classed into groups of one, two, three and four according to size:

Group 1 – 40 in × 28 in. Bear, deer, moose, elk, caribou.
Group 2 – 28 in × 22 in. Antelope, small deer, wolf, mountain lion.
Group 3 – 22 in × 14 in. Coyote, javelina, turkey, fox, goose, wild cat, pheasant.
Group 4 – 14 in × 11 in. Turtle, duck, grouse, crow, skunk, jackrabbit, woodchuck.

Any animal or bird consistent in size with a particular group may be used.

(e) NATIONAL ANIMAL ROUND FACES. The target faces shall be of animal or bird design, and shall have described on them a circle of either 30, 22.5, 15, or 7.5 cm diameter according to the size of the animal picture and in the heart/lung region. The higher-scoring area (the 'kill' zone) shall be within the circle and the remainder of the animal shall be in the lower-scoring area (the 'wound' zone). Bengston Bowhunter faces fulfil the requirements set out above and shall be used at national record status events.

205 Field Rounds in GNAS

For target faces refer to 204.

Courses should be laid out in such a way as to provide safety, maximum interest and variety, and to make the best use of available terrain. Direction indicators should be placed as necessary to ensure safety.

(a) FITA ARROWHEAD ROUNDS shot over courses of 24-28-32-36 targets, comprising two units of 12, 16, 20 or 24 targets (i.e. 12+16 = 28) in multiples of four, Unmarked or Marked, combined (1 round unmarked + 1 round marked) or combinations (50 per cent unmarked + 50 per cent marked). Units can include walk-ups and/or fans (not recommended). Current FITA rules apply.

(b) NEW FITA ROUNDS, as (a) above with GNAS relaxations 201 (b).

(c) STAMP Unmarked, Stamp marked and Stamp Combination. GNAS Stamp Unmarked round shot on FITA (1994) faces. The round consists of twenty-eight targets with one arrow from each of four different positions for each target. Four targets with 20 cm faces placed between 5 and 15 metres, eight targets with 40 cm faces placed between 10 and 30 metres, ten targets with a 60 cm face placed between 20 and 40 metres, six targets with an 80 cm face is placed between 30 and 50 metres. Tolerance on distance from post to target shall not exceed +/- 25 cm on distances of 15 metres or less, and shall not exceed +/- 50 cm on distances longer than 15 metres. Total number of arrows, 112. Scoring 5,4,3,2,1 (full 5 all styles). Maximum possible score 560.

Juniors

Juniors (15/17) shoot from the same position as adults in all cases.

Juniors (12/14) shoot two arrows from each of the two nearest shooting positions at single-faced targets, which will be either 60 cm or 80 cm faces.

Juniors (under 12) shoot all four arrows from the front shooting position on all targets.

Organizers may provide suitably placed extra forward positions for under 12s at their discretion. In this case no under 12 records can be claimed and a statement to this effect must appear on entry forms for record status tournaments.

GNAS S Marked Round shot on FITA (1994) faces. The round consists of twenty-eight targets with four arrows at each target. Distances are marked.

Twice at each of 15, 20, 25, and 30 metres at 40 cm faces. Total 32 arrows.
Twice at each of 35, 40 and 45 metres at a 60 cm face. Total 24 arrows.
Twice at each of 50, 55, and 60 metres at an 80 cm face. Total 24 arrows.
Twice 6, 8, 10 and 12 metres at 20 cm face. Total 8 arrows.
Twice 15, 20, 25 and 30 metres at 20 cm face. Total 8 arrows.
Twice 30, 35, 40 and 45 metres at 60 cm face. Total 8 arrows.
Twice 45, 50, 55 and 60 metres at 80 cm face. Total 8 arrows.

Tolerance on distance from post to target shall not exceed +/- 25 cm on distances of 15 metres or less, and shall not exceed +/- 50 cm on distances longer than 15 metres. Total number of arrows, 112. Scoring 5,4,3,2,1 (full 5 all styles). Maximum possible score 560.

Juniors

Juniors(15/17) shoot from the same positions as adults in all cases.

Juniors (12/14) shoot all four shots from the front position on 80 cm walk-up target, and have a forward position provided 15 metres in advance of the adult position on the fixed position targets at 60, 55, 50 and 45 metres (note this latter target is a 60 cm face).

Juniors (under 12) shoot the same privilege shots as Juniors (12/14) and in addition, shoot from the front position at all walk-up targets.

Organizers may provide suitably placed extra forward positions for under 12s at their discretion. In this case no under 12 records can be claimed and a statement to this effect must appear on entry forms for record status tournaments.

GNAS Stamp Combination Round. The Combination round shall consist of one unit (fourteen targets representing a correct half of those shot in the full round) of Stamp unmarked targets and one unit of Stamp marked targets laid out consecutively. Where both units are shot over the same course, the unmarked unit shall be shot first.

Juniors.

The rules regarding shooting positions for juniors in the Marked and Unmarked Stamp rounds apply to the appropriate unit in this round.

NOTE for Stamp rounds:

(i) Arrows shall be shot in ascending numerical order.

(ii) 80 cm and 60 cm faces. After the first two archers have shot they will be allowed to go forward to score and withdraw their arrows, either at the request of the next detail or of their own volition.

40 cm faces. Four faces shall be placed in the form of a square. Archers shooting from the left side shall shoot their first two arrows at the top left face and the remaining two at the bottom left face; archers shooting from the right side shall shoot similarly at the top and lower right faces. After the first two archers have shot they will be allowed to go forward to score and withdraw their arrows, either at the request of the next detail or on their own volition.

20 cm faces. Sixteen faces shall be placed in four vertical columns (1, 2, 3 and 4 from the left) of four faces (A, B, C and D from the top). Archers shooting from the left side in the first detail shall shoot one arrow at each of the faces in column 1 starting at face A and then B, C and D. Archers shooting from the right side in the first detail shall shoot their arrows in a similar manner at faces in column 3 . The archers in the second detail shall shoot their arrows in a similar manner from the left side at faces in column 2, and from the right side at faces in column 4. When more than four archers are in the shooting group then the fifth archer shall shoot from the left side and the sixth from the right, in a similar manner, after the first four archers have scored and drawn their arrows.

(e) Foresters Round

Shot on Foresters faces. Distances may be marked or unmarked.
The round consists of twenty-eight targets (or two units).
The standard unit shall consist of the following fourteen shots:

Three 24-inch faces at a distance of up to 70 yards (64 metres)
Four 18-inch faces at a distance of up to 50 yards (45.7metres)
Four 12-inch faces at a distance of up to 40 yards (36.6 metres)
Three 6-inch faces at a distance of up to 20 yards (18.3 metres)

Shooting rules: at a 24-inch target, four arrows are shot, one from each of four posts. At an 18-inch target, three arrows are shot, one from each of three posts. At a 12-inch target, two arrows are shot, one from each of two posts. At a 6-inch target, one arrow is shot from one post. Multi-post shots may be equidistant from the target or walk-away or walk-up.

Scoring:

Aiming spot:	15 points
Inner circle:	10 points
Outer circle:	5 points
Total number of arrows:	70
Maximum possible score:	1050 points

Juniors

Juniors (15/17) shoot from the same posts as adults in all cases.
Juniors (12/14) shoot from the same posts as adults at the 12-inch and 6-inch faces.
They shoot two arrows from the middle distance post and one arrow from the front post at 18-inch faces.
Juniors (under 12) shoot all arrows from the front post at all targets.

(f) Four-shot Foresters round

Shot on Foresters faces. Distances shall be marked.
The Round consists of twenty-eight targets (or two units) with four walk-up shots on each target. Distribution of faces as in Foresters round. Scoring as in Foresters round. Total number of arrows, 112. Maximum possible score, 1680 points.

Juniors

Juniors (15/17) shoot from the same posts as adults in all cases.
Juniors (12/14) shoot two arrows from each of the two nearest posts at targets showing 18-inch and 24-inch faces.
Juniors (under/12) shoot all arrows from the front post at all targets.

(g) Big Game round

Shot on Big Game faces. The Big Game round consists of twenty-eight targets (or two units) marked or unmarked. The standard unit is made up of the following fourteen targets at the suggested ranges:

Three Group 1 targets at a distance of 70 to 40 yards (64.0 to 36.6 metres)
Three Group 2 targets at a distance of 50 to 30 yards (45.7 to 27.5 metres)

Four Group 3 targets at a distance of 40 to 20 yards (36.6. to 18.3 metres)

Four Group 4 targets at a distance 30 to 10 yards (27.5 to 9.1 metres)

Shooting rules: three shots at each target, one from each of three posts, each successive post being closer to the target than the previous one.

Arrows shall be identifiable as to the order of shooting. The archer shall stop shooting as soon as a hit is considered to have been made.

Scoring: the score is decided by the position of the arrow in the target (i.e. in the 'kill' or ' wound' zone) and the number of arrows shot.

	Kill	Wound
1st Arrow score	20	16
2nd arrow score	14	10
3rd arrow score	8	4

Only the score of the first arrow counts.

Maximum possible score, 560.

Juniors

Juniors (15/17) shoot from the same posts as adults.

Juniors (12/14) shoot two arrows from the middle distance post and one from the front post until a hit is scored.

Juniors (under 12) shoot up to three arrows from the front post until a hit is scored.

(h) The National Animal Round

Shot on animal faces conforming to the specification given in 204. The National Animal round is shot over thirty-two targets (or two units) not marked. When two units are shot, the targets shall be mixed so that the units are not consecutive.

The course shall be laid out so that each unit shall consist of the following targets set within the prescribed range. Organizers are required to provide a good variety of shots.

Number of faces	'Kill' zone diameter	Distance range
4	30 cm	55-30 metres
4	22.5 cm	42-20 metres
4	15 cm	35-10 metres
4	7.5 cm	20-5 metres

At targets using the smallest 'kill' zone diameter face, organizers can place two faces side by side, reducing the need of archers having shot to clear their arrows to reduce the possibility of damage.

Shooting: two arrows shall be shot at each target, one from each of two posts set within the prescribed range.

Scoring:

> Kill zone: 10 points
> Wound zone: 5 points.
> Total number of arrows in round, 64. Maximum possible score, 640.

Juniors

> Juniors (15/17) shoot from the same posts as adults in all cases.
> Juniors (12/14) shoot both arrows from the nearest shooting post at the 30 cm 'kill' zone faces.
> Juniors (under 12) shoot both arrows at the 30 cm 'kill' zone and the 22 cm 'kill' zone diameter faces from a single privilege post set at an appropriate distance.

(i) FITA Forester Round. Current FITA rules apply with GNAS relaxations 201(b).

(j) Local/Club Rounds. All current GNAS rules apply.

NFAS

Shooting

1 *General: Applying to All Classes*

All shoots held under the auspices of the NFAS will be over unmarked distances.

2 *Shooting Classes*

Longbow, American Flat Bow, Hunting Tackle, Bowhunter, Barebow, Freestyle, Crossbow, Compound Limited and Unlimited.

3 *Bows and Arrows*

The bow may be changed at lunch break. A broken bow may be replaced by a borrowed bow. If an archer retires due to bow or string breakage, he or she may only complete the round being shot with the Field Captain's permission and accompanied by chosen witnesses. Arrows which will unduly damage targets such as broadheads and blunts are not permitted, and no such hunting arrows, neither broadhead nor blunt, will be carried during a tournament. Every arrow shot must be clearly marked with the contestant's name, insignia or intitials.

4 *Accessories, etc.*

A No archer will make use of any mechanism for calibrating the distance to be shot. The use of a range finder or binoculars is prohibited. Neither shall a contestant receive such information from another person using such equipment nor from an archer waiting to shoot or having shot. Peg-to-peg and peg-to-target distances may not be paced.

B No contestant may record information relative to distances or condition of a target stand.

C Archers suffering from a prolonged physical disability may be allowed to use appropriate shooting aids and/or methods on production of adequate medical evidence to the Executive.

D The use of any electrical or electrical solenoid-operated shooting release aid or trigger mechanism is banned.

E Cameras may be used subject to their not being an annoyance to any other archer.

5 *Scoring*

A Status and scoring value of all arrows shall be determined before any arrow is withdrawn from any position within the target face.

B An arrow altering the contour of the line separating two scoring zones is to receive the higher score.

C A witnessed bounce or complete penetration can be scored. Its scoring value shall be that of the lowest scoring zone unless positive evidence of a higher score exists.

D An arrow hitting another arrow and remaining embedded in that arrow shall have the same score as that arrow. If it ricochets off an arrow, then its score shall be determined by the position of its own shaft.

E No archer shall score his/her own card.

6 *Juniors*

A   Age limits 12/15 years inclusive. From sixteenth birthday all archers must shoot in the Senior class.

B   For the Game and Bushman targets having A, B, and C pegs (red, white and blue) 14- and 15- year-olds will shoot pegs B, C, C. Twelve- and 13-year-olds will shoot pegs C, U12 , U12. On Group 1 targets a special Junior peg shall be positioned for lighter-weight bows.

C   For the Forester round, Juniors will shoot from the adult pegs at 6-inch and 12-inch targets (this also applies to 2-shot bushman). At 18-inch targets they will shoot as in Rule B. At 24-inch targets they will shoot two arrows from each of the third and fourth pegs.

D   For other rounds, organizers must make it clear from which peg(s) juniors are to shoot.

7 *Under 12*

For all rounds a special U12 peg is to be suitably positioned at each target, bearing in mind the small stature and low bow weight of most U12 archers.

8 *Shooting*

A   The archer's leading foot, even when kneeling, i.e. bow held in left hand, left foot, bow held in right hand, right foot, must touch and not be forward of the shooting peg.

B   At no time in a championship competition shall any contestant be allowed to shoot who has prior knowledge of the course to be shot over. [At times, people have been allowed to shoot after they have laid the course or part of it, but in the event of a winning score, they would be disallowed.]

EQUIPMENT

Rules For Each Class

A *Crossbows*

The crossbow and parts (except the prod) may be made of any materials; prods can be made of any material other than aluminium alloy. Pistol crossbows must have a pistol grip and prods less than 18 inches.

Bows shall be drawn by hand. No mechanical device for drawing is permitted. In the case of pistols, foot stirrups are not permitted. Telescopic or magnifying sights are not permitted.

Maximum draw weights/lengths:

Composite prods	1280 in lb @	16 in draw length.
Pistols	750 in lb @	10 in draw length.

The inch-pound draw-weight/length is obtained by multiplying the draw-length in inches by the draw weight in pounds. The draw length is measured from the string groove in the trigger to the further side of the prod. For pistols the minimum draw length allowed is 5 inches. Bolts may be made of any material but shall not be of such design as to cause unreasonable damage to targets. Bolts shall be not less than 12 inches.

Crossbowmen shall shoot off the hand, no rests of any description being permitted. Crossbowmen will only draw their weapons at the shooting position and then keep them pointed in the direction of the target, whether loaded or not. Shoot organizers may bar from further participation a crossbowman who exhibits carelessness in handling his weapon or whose weapon is considered to be dangerous to others. Junior crossbowmen may shoot but only under the care of an adult.

B *Unlimited*

1 A handbow, which can be a compound bow, of any draw weight, may be used.

2 Subject to the General Rules, archers shooting in this class have complete freedom of choice of equipment. Any release aid used must be safe and not prone to premature release from any cause.

C *Freestyle*

1 A handbow of any draw weight, but not a compound bow, may be used.

2 Subject to the General Rules, archers shooting in this class have complete freedom of choice of equipment. The sight may be moved at will during shooting. A sight calibrated for the course to be shot is not permitted. Attachments, knots or bands of any size or design may be used on the string irrespective of whether the use is for aiding the sighting or shooting technique. Any device or mechanism to aid in the establishment of the draw length may be used. Stabilizers are allowed. Bowslings are permitted. No form of release aid is permitted but finger protection, such as a shooting glove or tab, may be used.

D *Barebow*

1 A bow of any draw weight, but not a compound bow, may be used.

2 Bows must be free from any sight, mark or blemish which could be used for aiming. The belly or face of the upper limb shall be free from any protuberance mark (including trademark), dent, blemish, bulge, chipping or wood grain or ends of laminated pieces of distinctive appearance. Where means are used to cover up such an aid, the covering must obliterate completely and not be put on in such a way as to create an aid in itself. Nor shall there be any such aid visible at either side of the belly face. The bowstring shall be of one colour, as also shall the serving. One nocking point is permitted. Brush buttons and string silencers are permitted but no other knots or attachments in addition to the serving which could be used for sighting or location purposes. One anchor point must be maintained throughout the shoot and the index finger must touch the nock, i.e no face/string walking. No draw checks of any kind are permitted. Stabilizers not exceeding the archer's draw length are permitted but must be incapable of being used as a sight. The arrow support point shall not be positioned more than 2 inches (5 cm) behind the throat of the hand-grip measured in a direction perpendicular to the bowstring. No archer may refer to any memoranda which could in any manner be a means of improving his or her score. No form of release aid is permitted. Finger protection such as a shooting glove or tab may be used. Bowslings are permitted.

E *Hunting Tackle*

1 A bow of any draw weight, but not a compound bow, may be used.

2 Bows must be free of any sight, mark or blemish which could be used for aiming. The belly or face of the upper bow limb shall be free from any protuberance, mark (including trademark), dent, blemish, bulge, chipping or wood grain or ends of laminated pieces of distinctive appearance. Where means are used to cover up such an aid, the covering must obliterate completely and not be put on in such a way as to create an aid in itself. Nor shall there be any such aid visible at either side of the belly face. The bowstring shall be of one colour, as also shall the serving. One nocking point is permitted. Brush buttons and string silencers are permitted but no other knots or attachments in addition to the serving which could be of use for sighting or location purposes. One anchor point must be maintained throughout the shoot. The index finger

must touch the nock, the Mediterranean loose only is permitted. No draw checks of any kind are permitted. No external stabilizers are allowed. The arrow support point shall not be positioned more than 2 inches (5 cm) behind the throat of the hand-grip measured in a direction perpendicular to the bowstring. No archer may refer to any memoranda which could in any manner be a means of improving his or her scores. No form of release aid is permitted. Finger protection such as a shooting glove or tab may be used. Bowslings are permitted. Arrows must be of wood, fletched with natural feather. (Mediterranean loose means one finger above and the middle and ring fingers below the arrow nock.)

F. Bow Hunter

1 A handbow of any weight, including a compound bow, may be used.

2 Bows must be free of any sight, mark or blemish which could be used for aiming. The belly or face of the upper bow limb shall be free from any protruberance, mark (including trademark), dent, blemish, bulge, chipping or wood grain or ends of laminated pieces of distinctive appearance. Where means are used to cover up such an aid, the covering must obliterate completely and not be put on in such a way as to create an aid in itself. Nor shall there be any such aid visible at either side of the belly face. The bowstring shall be of one colour, as also shall the serving. One nocking point is permitted. Brush buttons and string silencers are permitted but no other knots or attachments in addition to the serving which could be of use for sighting or location purposes. One anchor point must be maintained throughout the shoot. The Mediterranean loose only is permitted. No draw checks of any kind are permitted. Stabilizers not exceeding the archer's draw length are permitted but must be incapable of being used as a sight. The arrow support point shall not be positioned more than 2 inches (5 cm) behind the throat of the hand-grip measured in a direction perpendicular to the bowstring. No archer may refer to any memoranda which could in any manner be a means of improving his or her score. No form of release aid is permitted. Finger protection such as a shooting glove or tab may be used. Bowslings are permitted. (Mediterranean loose means one finger above and the middle and ring fingers below the arrow nock.)

G American Flat Bow

The limb cross-section may vary from oval to rectangular. The braced limbs are to curve in one direction only from the handle riser to the string nock. The hand-grip may incorporate a cut-away of less than centre-cut to provide an arrow shelf and the shelf may have a protective cover. Arrows must be of wood fletched with natural feather. Only the Mediterranean loose is permitted. No form of arrow rest may be attached to the side of the bow.

[The remainder of the class specification is identical to the previous class.]

H *Longbow*

1   The bow must be of wood only, straight-limbed and of 'D' section with nocks of self nature or made of horn, wood or plastic and must be free of stabilizers, sights, arrow rests or cut-aways for the arrow to rest on. Arrows must be of wood fletched with natural feather but plastic nocks and metal piles may be used. Only the Mediterranean loose is permitted.

[All the remainder of the class specification is identical to that of the Bowhunter class.]

I *Compound Limited*

1   In this class a bow including a compound bow with a fixed up to five-pin hunting sight may be used. A peepsight or kisser button is permitted but not both. The arrow support point shall not be positioned more than 2 inches(5 cm) behind the throat of the hand-grip, measured in a direction perpendicular to the bowstring. One anchor point must be maintained throughout the shoot. No release aids, draw checks or spirit levels of any kind are permitted. Only the Mediterranean loose is permitted.

ROUNDS

The following are the most commonly shot rounds at NFAS shoots:

Game Round (also called Animal or Big Game)

The faces are pictures of animals, having an inner 'kill' zone and an outer 'wound' zone. Each target has three pegs, one arrow being shot from each but only until a score is made. The arrow from the first peg can score twenty (kill) or sixteen (wound), the arrow from the second peg fourteen or ten, and from the third peg eight or four. On the score-card put which arrow has scored and the score, e.g.. 2 for 10 for second arrow wound. On American faces, the 'kill' zone approximates the heart/lungs area and is rectangular with semicircular ends, the overall widths and lengths being, on the four target sizes:

Group 1   9 in × 14.5 in
Group 2   7 in × 10.5 in
Group 3   4.5 in × 7 in
Group 4   2.5 in × 3.75 in

The colourful Swedish faces have circular 'kills' – 12, 9, 6 and 3 inches in diameter, not necessarily over the heart/lungs area. A basic unit of fourteen targets should contain three Group 1, three Group 2, four Group 3, and four Group 4. Group 1s are usually shot at about 35–60 yards, Group 2s at 24–40 yards, Group 3s at 15–30 yards, and Group 4s at 10–20 yards. Juniors see Rule 6B.

Woodsman Round

This only differs from the Game round in that you stop shooting only when you 'kill' and scores are five for any 'wound' and thirty, twenty or ten for a 'kill' from the first, second and third peg respectively. On the score-card put number of hits and total score, e.g. for a first arrow 'wound', second arrow 'kill' put '2 for 25'. Juniors see Rule 6B.

Swedish Foresters, Bushman, Poacher Rounds

These versions use the Swedish Game faces to which a central spot has been added. The 'kill' rings become the inner 'ten' rings, the 'wound' line defines the 'five', the spots (one-third the diameter of the 'kill') score fifteen.

East Midland Round

Game round faces, three pegs per target and one arrow from each peg. Score ten for a 'kill', five for a 'wound'. It is like Poachers but on Game faces. It is a good idea to provide three faces for Group 4 shots. Juniors see Rule 6B.

Spotting

The Game and Woodsman rounds require spotters to tell the archer when he has scored. Spotters should indicate only whether or not the archer has scored successfully. Spotters should select their position with three points in mind:

1 personal safety
2 ability to see where 'shorts' and 'overshoots' land
3 ability to see target face

in that order of importance.

Order of Shooting

There is no rule but a good idea is to let the highest scorer on one target shoot first on the next target.

Appendix II

USEFUL ADDRESSES

Archery Dealers and Manufacturers

UK

Alternative Services
Cartref
Laurels Road
Offenham
Evesham
Worcestershire
WR11 8RE
Tel: 01386 443795
Website: *www.altservices.co.uk*
(compound bow makers)

Archery World
1 Kenyon's Farm
Gough Lane
Bamber Bridge
Preston
Lancashire
PR5 6AQ
Tel/Fax: 01772 698600
E-mail: *enquiries@archeryworld.co.uk*
Website: *www.archeryworld.co.uk*

Border Archery Ltd
Mellerstain
Gordon
Berwickshire
TD3 6LG
Tel: 01573 410295
Fax: 01573 224899
(bow makers)

Bow Plus
Oaktree Stores
Mill Lane
Higher Heath
Whitchurch
Shropshire
SY13 2HR
Tel/Fax: 01948 840240
(branch of Wales Archery)

Bowsports
Kings Pool
Cannock Road
Shareshill
Wolverhampton
WV10 7JP
Tel: 01922 412121
Website: *www.bowsports.com*

Chiltern Archery
Buckland
Aylesbury
Buckinghamshire
HP22 5HZ
Tel: 01296 630919
Website: *www.chiltern-archery.co.uk*
(main agents for Browning bows)

Clickers Archery
29a Belsize Road
Norwich
Norfolk
NR1 4HU
Tel: 01603 300490 (shop)
E-mail: *graham@clickersarchery.co.uk*
Website: *www.clickersarchery.co.uk*

Cluny Clays
Cluny Mains Farm
Cluny
Kirkcaldy
Fife
KY2 6QU
Tel: 01592 720374

Custom Built Archery
The Old Telephone Exchange
Eakring Road
Bilsthorpe
Nr Newark
Nottinghamshire
NG22 8PY
Tel: 01623 871560
E-mail: *tony@custombuilt.co.uk*
(new and secondhand bows)

Eagle Classic Archery
41 Spring Walk
Worksop
Nottinghamshire
S80 1XQ
Tel: 01909 478935
Fax: 01909 488115
(Asian and Turkish bow importers, English longbows)
E-mail: *eaglearc@globalnet.co.uk*
Website: *www.bownet.com/instore/eaglearc.html*

Carol Edwards
Craft Cottage
Bookham Lodge Stud
Cobham Road
Stoke D'Abernon
Surrey
KT11 3QG
Tel: 01932 865181

Richard Head
405 The Spa
Melksham
Wiltshire
SN12 6QL
Tel/Fax: 01225 790452
E-mail: *headbow@hotmail.com*
(longbow maker)

KG Archery
Kingstand Farm Archery Centre
Mansfield Road
Rufford
Nr Newark
Nottinghamshire
NG22 9DU
Tel: 01623 824877
Fax: 01623 824878
Website: *www.kgarchery.com*

Lyons Longbows
113 North Barcombe Road
Childwall
Liverpool
L16 7PX
Tel: 0151 722 8287

Merlin Bows
Bull-in-the-Hollow
Leicester Road
Loughborough
Leicestershire
LE12 8UE
Tel: 01509 233555
Fax: 01509 235252
E-mail: *info@merlin-bows.co.uk*
Website: *www.merlin-bows.co.uk*
(compound bow makers and shop)

Opechee Archery or Celtic Archery
Higher Dowha Farm
Troon
Nr Camborne
Cornwall
TR14 9JG
Tel: 01209 831620
Fax: 01209 831038
E-mail: *david.horder@virgin.net*

Perris Archery
Fennes Estate
Fennes Road
Bocking
Braintree
Essex
CM7 5PL
Tel: 01376 331017

Quicks Archery Centre
Apps Court Farm
Hurst Road
Walton-on-Thames
Surrey
KT12 2EG
Tel/Fax: 01932 232211

Quicks at Waterlooville
(mail order office)
18-22 Stakes Hill Road
Waterlooville
Hampshire
PO7 7JF
Tel: 01705 254114
Fax: 01705 251519

Quicks at Sapcote
11 Stanton Road
Sapcote
Leicestershire
LE9 4FR
Tel/Fax: 01455 272387

Quicks at Honiton
Unit B1
Reme Drive
Heathpark Trading Estate
Honiton
Devon
EX14 1SE
Tel: 01404 44400

Targetcraft Archery Centre
28b Duke Street
Burton Latimer
Northamptonshire
NN15 5SG
Tel: 01536 726677

Ten-Ring Archery
69a Ashburnham Road
Ramsgate
Kent
CT11 0BH
Tel/Fax: 01843 851819
E-mail: *tenring@adept.co.uk*
Website: *www.archery-ten-ring.co.uk*

Top Tox
Wyre Hall Farm
135a Wakefield Road
Drighlington
Bradford
Yorkshire
BD11 1EB
Tel: 01132 852439
(branch of Wales archery)

Wales Archery
Crick Manor
Crick
Caldicot
Monmouthshire
NP26 5XU
Tel: 01291 420321
Fax: 01291 430608

Westcliff Archery
859 London Road
Westcliff-on-Sea
Southend
Essex
SS0 9SZ
Tel: 01702 471718
Fax: 01702 471719
E-mail: *info@archery2000.co.uk*
Website: *www.archery2000.co.uk*

USA

Easton Archery
5040 W. Harold Getty Drive
Salt Lake City
Utah 84116
USA
Website: *www.eastonarchery.com*

Hoyt USA
475 North Neil Armstrong Road
Salt Lake City
Utah 84116-2887
USA
Tel: (801) 363 2990
Fax: (801) 537 1470
Website: *www.hoytusa.com*
(bow makers)

Archery Organizations

The Archery Association
PO Box 119
Evesham
Worcestershire
WR11 5ZU
Tel: 0410 019160
E-mail: *info@archery-assocation.org*
Website: *www.archery-association.org*

The British Crossbow Society
Mr Keith Reynolds, Secretary
2 Vicarage Road
Chellaston
Derbyshire
DE73 1SD
Tel: 01332 700180

The British Longbow Society
Mr M. Fairfield, Secretary and Treasurer
73 Fairfax Avenue
Hull
East Yorkshire
HU5 4QN
Tel: 01482 348082

The English Field Archery Association
Mr Richard Narey, General Secretary
'Greenacres'
Saxham Street
Stowupland
Stowmarket
Suffolk
IP14 5DF
Tel/Fax: 01449 677176

Grand National Archery Society
Mr D. Sherratt, Chief Executive
National Sports Centre
Lilleshall
Nr Newport
Shropshire
TF10 9AT
Tel: 01952 677888
Fax: 01952 606019
E-mail: *David@GNAS.org*
Website: *www.gnas.org*

The International Field Archery Association
Mr Kenneth A. Rodgers, President
283 Carlson Drive
Midway Park
NC 28544
USA
Fax: (603) 368 8582
E-mail: *Krogers-IFAA@worldnet.att.net*

The National Field Archery Society
Mr Mark Philips, Honorary Secretary
Ellendene
Nethertown
Rugeley
Staffordshire
WS15 3QH
Tel: 01889 504228

The Scottish Field Archery Association
Veronica Catignani
125 Dewar Street
Dunfermline
KY12 8AB
Tel: 01383 738561

The Welsh Field Archery Association
Mr V. Morgan, Secretary
27 Manor Park
Llantwit Major
South Glamorgan
CF61 1RS
Tel: 01446 792826

Addresses of NFAS club secretaries can be found in the NFAS
newsletter or obtained from the secretary. Addresses of GNAS
clubs can be obtained from the secretary. Addresses of EFAA clubs
can be obtained from the general secretary.

Appendix III

GLOSSARY

Anchoring. Placing the string hand in a specific place for each shot.

Anchor point. The place on the face or head which the archer has chosen for anchoring.

Anchor tab. A finger tab, sometimes known as a shelf tab, with a hard fitting attached that fits under the chin, to assist firm anchoring of the hand. Usually used only by freestyle class.

Arrow plate. An adjustable plate with the arrow rest mounted on it, capable of being adjusted horizontally to move the arrow position relative to the bow handle.

Arrow rest. A device upon which the arrow shaft rests in order to be shot.

Back (of bow). The side facing away from the archer.

Belly (of bow). The side facing the archer. Sometimes known as the face.

Big Game. Extensive series of animal target faces, some of them quite small, or set of rules for shooting such faces.

Blunt. Usually a thick rubber device fitted over the point of an arrow that has been designed for killing small game and birds. Sometimes used in situations where people might be in danger of being shot.

Bolt. A crossbow arrow. Much shorter than normal arrows. Has no nock, merely a flat blank end.

Boss. A round target, usually made of coiled straw rope, for target archery.

Bouncer. An arrow that has fallen short and bounced off the ground into the target, or one that has hit the target, failed to penetrate and fallen to the ground.

Bow quiver. A device attaching to the bow to hold arrows in an upright position, used for hunting but also sometimes seen in field archery.

Bracing the bow. Stringing the bow.

Bracer. An armguard to prevent bruising of the arm by the bowstring and also to hold loose clothing out of the way.

Bracing height. The distance between the nocking point of the arrow on the string and the arrow rest, although there are sometimes other points on the bow to measure from. Sometimes known in the USA by the Old English term 'fistmele'.

Broadhead. A sharp, wide arrow point, designed to kill, not allowed by any field archery organizations.

Brush buttons. Devices fitted to bowstring to prevent twigs and foliage from fouling in it.

Bullet piles. Arrow piles with bullet-shaped profiles. The most common type.

Bushes. Metal threaded inserts in bow handles for holding various fittings such as sights and stabilizers.

Butt. A rectangular block of material for stopping arrows with the target face attached to one side. Various sizes.

Cable guard. A metal rod fitted to compound bows to prevent cables fouling arrows.

Cam. A type of wheel on compound bows, which usually makes the bow shoot faster.

Cant. Bow held at angle other than vertical, usually by longbow archers.

Cast. The speed at which a bow shoots.

Centre serving. Reinforced binding on string to prevent wear of string against arm and fingers.

Clicker. An audible draw check device, normally used only in Freestyle class.

Cock feather. The feather on an arrow shaft that stands at right angles to the string slot of the nock. Shot at right angles to the bow.

Composite. A bow whose limbs are made from more than one material.

Compound. A bow with a mechanical advantage created by pulleys set at the ends of the limbs. Other compounds with different arrangements are possible.

Creep. Gradual, unconscious forward movement of the hand when holding the bow at full draw and on the aim.

Cresting. Bands of colour painted round an arrow shaft, just below the fletching, to identify it.

Dacron. A type of man-made fibre used for bowstrings.

Dead loose. Releasing the bowstring with no tension and recoil of the drawing hand. Usually causes arrow to drop low.

Draw. The action of pulling the string back.

Draw check. A device fitted to bow to indicate when it is at full draw. Usually a clicker.

Draw length. The critical distance each archer draws the string to his normal extent, also the distance a bow can be drawn to, usually determined by the manufacturer.

Draw weight. The weight required to draw the bow the required distance. Usually measured at 28 inches for adults' bows.

Face. The side of the bow facing the archer. Also the target face – the actual printed or painted target to be shot at.

Face walking. A technique for aiming, using reference points on the face for different distances.

Fast. The traditional cry to stop an archer from loosing if a sudden danger appears.

Finger tab. A shaped piece of leather or artificial leather worn on the fingers of the drawing hand for protection.

Field pile. A type of arrow pile formed with a step to reduce penetration of targets, normally used only on wooden arrows.

Fletching. Gluing feathers or vanes to shaft.

Fletching jig. A device for assisting in the process of fixing fletchings to the shaft.

Fletchings. Feathers or plastic for giving an arrow stability and accuracy. Usually in threes but can be more.

Flipper rest. A type of arrow rest, spring loaded to hold in position, moving in when the arrow is shot.

Flu-flu. A type of fletching, usually feather, wound round a shaft to slow it down rapidly in flight, intended only for very short-range use.

Follow-through. The final part of a shot, holding on the target until the arrow strikes.

Footed arrow. An old type of arrow made by splicing a softwood shaft into a hardwood forward end to take shock. Still made, but expensive.

Foresters. A type of target face or a round using such faces. An

345

animal face with scoring rings surmounted, with a black or yellow spot. These faces are no longer made.

Full draw. The position in which the archer is at full extension of body in the bow, at the most comfortable and efficient position.

Fur fletch. A brightly coloured strip of fur or feather glued round the arrow shaft behind the fletchings to assist visibility in target. Flares out when the arrow hits target but can also tend to slow arrows over longer distances.

Gap shooting. A method of aiming by judging the gap between the pile of the arrow and the target centre at full draw. The gap decreases as the distance increases.

Group. A pattern of arrows close together in the target. Also a group of archers detailed to shoot together.

Handle riser. The rigid metal or wooden part of a bow to which the limbs are attached.

Helical fletch. A method of fletching the shafts with the fletchings slightly turned round the shaft to cause the arrows to spin-stabilize in flight.

Hot melt cement. Glue heated to melting point, used to apply arrow piles.

Idler wheel. A recent introduction to compound bow technology, where the lower limb wheel or cam does the work, and the upper wheel merely balances the cables and string.

Instinctive. A class of archers not using sights. A misnomer, since most have learned how to shoot without sights.

'Kill' area. The centre area of an animal target, with a higher score. Not always clearly defined or seen.

Kisser. An attachment on a bowstring enabling the string position to be felt by the lips to indicate the correct draw length and other factors.

Laminations. Layers of material, carbon fibre, wood and fibreglass used in bow construction.

Level. A spirit level built into some compound sights to show the archer when the bow is vertical.

Limb. The bending part of the bow, which does the work.

Longbow. A traditional English bow. Long, D-section, with no built-in recurve.

Mackenzie. A make of American 3D animal target.

Monofilament. Single-strand nylon thread used for serving the centre sections of bowstrings. Similar to fishing line, very hard wearing.

Nock. Usually plastic fitting glued to the end of an arrow to hold the string in place.

Nocking point. The part of the bowstring marked to take the arrow nock.

Nock-sets. Brass clips with soft plastic lining to fit round the string to indicate nocking point.

Offset fletchings. Fletchings glued on the shaft at a slight angle to centre line, to make the arrow spin in flight and thus aid accuracy. Similar to helical fletch.

Peepsight. A device fitted into the bowstring to aid aiming through sights. Acts as a rear sight.

Pile. The arrow point. Several different profiles are available, and different weights.

Plunger. A spring loaded device fitted into the bow handle to bear sideways on the arrow shaft while it is on its rest. Its purpose is to absorb side movement from the fingers.

Point of aim. A mark selected to aim at with the arrow point, sometimes below the target, sometimes above.

Pressure point. The part of an arrow rest or bow handle on which the side pressure from the arrow bears. There should not be a pressure point.

Quiver. A holder for arrows, carried on the person or on the bow.

Recurve. A bow limb with a reverse curve from the major curve. Properly known as the reflex. It has now developed into a term for this type of bow.

Release or release aid. A device used only on compound bows to give a more accurate loose, useful for relieving the strain on fingers.

Robin Hood shot. A shot in which an arrow is embedded in the end of another already in the target. Only counts if both belong to the same archer.

Riser. See 'Handle riser'.

Round. A fixed number of targets set out for a shoot.

Scope. A magnifying lens fitted to a sight, usually for compounds only.

Screw-in pile. A type of pile that screws into a threaded sleeve glued into a shaft. Enables pile to be changed.

Serving. Reinforcement thread bound round a bowstring to prevent wear from the arm and fingers.

Shaft. The main part of the arrow, the long straight part.

Sight. A device fixed to a bow for aiming. It can be a pin on a strip of tape, or an expensive bit of equipment fitted with a magnifying lens, etc.

Sight bar. An extension arm which moves the sight further from the bow to make aiming more accurate.

Sight block. A block screwed to the handle riser to take a sight bar.

Sight track. A vertical bar on which sight is moved to change distances.

Sling. A cord or strap, usually round wrist, attached to the bow to prevent it falling forward on loose when shooting with an open bow hand.

Spine. The degree of stiffness of an arrow shaft.

Spot. The aiming spot on some types of target faces.

Stabilizer. A weighted rod attached to a bow to aid balance, stability and shock absorption.

Stacking draw. Describes a bow whose draw weight rises too rapidly when nearly at full draw.

String keeper. A cord on a bowstring to hold it on the bow when it is unstrung.

String walking. A method of aiming by moving the fingers up or down the bowstring, sometimes counting rings of serving for different distances. Not permitted in any class by any field archery organization.

Take-down bow. A bow with removable limbs for easy carriage when not in use.

Tiller. The balance of the bend of the limbs.

Torque. The movement of the bow in the hand on loosing, usually forward if well balanced, but can be sideways.

Tuning. Setting up a bow for personal fit and performance.

Vane. A plastic fletching, available in a wide range of colours and sizes.

V-Bars. Twin rearward stabilizers, useful for balancing the bow in two planes and for use as a bow stand.

Window. A piece cut out in the handle riser to allow the arrow to be shot near or on the bow's vertical centre line.

'Wound'. The outer scoring area on animal target faces.

Bibliography

Books

Bickerstaffe, Pip, *The Heritage of the Longbow* (self-published, 1999)

Featherstone, Donald, *Bowmen of England* (New English Library, 1967)

Hardy, Robert, *The Longbow* (Patrick Stevens, Revised Edition, 1996)

Heath, E.G., *Archery, A Military History* (Osprey Publishing, 1980)

Henderson, Al, *Understanding Winning Archery* (Target Communication Corp., 1983)

Holden, John, *Shooting Stars* (Crowood Press, 1987)

Matthews, Roy and Holden, J., *Archery in Earnest* (Crowood Press, 1985)

Smith, Mike, *Archery* (Ward Lock, 1978)

Stamp, Don, *Field Archery* (Adam & Charles Black, 1979)

The range of books on archery is not great, and many are only available at archery shops, where archery videos are also available. The archery dealers' catalogues will give an idea of what is available; many of the books and videos are American. It should be said that some of the instructional videos are very good and are good value for money, but a few are very poor. It is probably wise to get advice on which to purchase.

Magazines

Archery Focus. (USA.) Mainly target archery, but quite a lot of useful technical information. Available from archery shops or direct from AFM, PO Box 520851, Salt Lake City, UT. 84152-0851, USA. *www.archeryfocus.com*

Bow International. Editorial: Bow House, The Dale, Wootten Wawen, Solihull, West Midlands B95 6AZ. Tel: 01564 794094; fax 01564 795319; e-mail *editor@bownet.com*
www.bownet.com

The Glade, 62 Hook Rise North, Tolworth, Surrey KT6 7JY. Tel: 020 8397 2603; fax: 020 8397 5193; e-mail *ted@theglade.co.uk*;
www.theglade.co.uk

The archery organizations have their own publications, distributed to members only.

Archery UK (GNAS)

The Field Archer (EFAA)

Newsletter (NFAS)

The US and International Archer is the official publication of the IFAA. Other magazines, mainly from the USA, can be found at archery shops.